FODO]
AND (

The Southwest's Best
Bed & Breakfasts
3rd Edition

Delightful Places to Stay
Wonderful Things to Do
When You Get There

Fodor's Travel Publications, Inc.
New York • Toronto • London • Sydney • Auckland
www.fodors.com/

Copyright © 1998 by Fodor's Travel Publications, Inc.

Third Edition

ISBN 0–679–03436–6

The Southwest's Best Bed and Breakfasts

Editor: Rebecca Miller Ffrench
Editorial Contributors: John Bigley, Shane Christensen, Stacey Clark, Edie Jarolim, Paris Permenter
Editorial Production: Stacey Kulig
Maps: David Lindroth, Mapping Specialists, cartographers; Robert Blake, map editor
Design: Fabrizio La Rocca, creative director; Guido Caroti, cover design; Jolie Novak, photo editor
Illustrators: Alida Beck, Karl Tanner
Production/Manufacturing: Mike Costa
Cover Photograph: Michael Goldman/FPG

Special Sales

Fodor's Travel Publications are available at special discounts for bulk purchases for sales promotions or premiums. Special editions, including personalized covers, excerpts of existing guides, and corporate imprints, can be created in large quantities for special needs. For more information, contact your local bookseller or write to Special Markets, Fodor's Travel Publications, 201 East 50th Street, New York, NY 10022. Inquiries from Canada should be directed to your local Canadian bookseller or sent to Random House of Canada, Ltd., Marketing Department, 2775 Matheson Blvd. E., Mississauga, Ontario L4W 4P7. Inquiries from the United Kingdom should be sent to Fodor's Travel Publications, 20 Vauxhall Bridge Road, London, England SW1V 2SA.

Contributors

John Bigley and **Paris Permenter** updated the Texas chapter and wrote the new section on West Texas. Longtime residents of the Lone Star State, they work as travel writers and specialize in southwestern and Caribbean destinations. They have written for such newspapers and magazines as Texas Highways, Flower and Garden, and the San-Antonio Express-News. For their recent book Texas Barbecue, they spent six months eating almost nothing but meat and potatoes.

Shane Christensen updated the New Mexico chapter and the Central and Northern Arizona sections of this guide. An alum of UC Berkeley and former Fulbright Scholar to the United Kingdom, Shane studied foreign affairs and subsequently decided that, for the meantime, travel writing offers far greater exposure to international relations than does sitting behind a Washington, D.C., desk. He has updated a business traveler's guide to the nation's capital and has also worked on various other Fodor's guides, including South America and Los Angeles.

Stacey Clark, who wrote and updated the Utah chapter, is a Utah native who writes frequently about the state's people and places for a variety of local and statewide publications. She is a regular Fodor's writer and updater, with chapters of Fodor's USA, Rockies, and America's Best Bed and Breakfasts to her credit.

Edie Jarolim edited the first edition of this guide, wrote its Albuquerque and Southern New Mexico sections, and contributed to the Arizona sections. She is a regular contributor to Fodor's guides and has also been published in the Wall Street Journal, the New York Times, and the London Guardian. She lives in Tucson.

Contents

Foreword

While every care has been taken to ensure the accuracy of the information in this guide, the passage of time will always bring change and, consequently, the publisher cannot accept responsibility for errors that may occur.

All prices and listings are based on information supplied to us at press time. Details may change, however, and the prudent traveler will avoid inconvenience by calling ahead.

Fodor's wants to hear about your travel experiences, both pleasant and unpleasant. When an inn or B&B fails to live up to its billing, let us know and we will investigate the complaint and revise our entries where the facts warrant it.

Send your letters to the editors of Fodor's Travel Publications, 201 East 50th Street, New York, NY 10022.

Introduction

You'll find bed-and-breakfasts in big houses with turrets and little houses with decks, in mansions by the water and cabins in the forest, not to mention structures of many sizes and shapes in between. B&Bs are run by people who were once lawyers and writers, homemakers and artists, nurses and architects, singers and businesspeople. Some B&Bs are just a room or two in a hospitable local's home; others are more like small inns. So there's an element of serendipity to every B&B stay.

But while that's part of the pleasure of the experience, it's also an excellent reason to plan your travels with a good B&B guide. The one you hold in your hands serves the purpose neatly.

To create it, we've handpicked a team of professional writers who are also confirmed B&B lovers: people who adore the many manifestations of the Victorian era; who go wild over wicker and brass beds, four-posters and fireplaces; and who know a well-run operation when they see it and are only too eager to communicate their knowledge to you. We've instructed them to inspect the premises and check out every corner of the premier inns and B&Bs in the areas they cover, and to report critically on only the best in every price range.

They've returned from their travels with comprehensive reports on the pleasure of B&B travel, which may well become your pleasure as you read their reports in the pages that follow. These are establishments that promise a unique experience, a distinctive sense of time and place. All are destinations in themselves, not just spots to rest your head at night, but an integral part of a weekend escape. You'll learn what's good, what's bad, and what could be better; what our writers liked and what you might not like.

At the same time, Fodor's reviewers tell you what's up in the area and what you should and shouldn't miss—everything from historic sites and parks to antiques shops, boutiques, and the area's niftiest restaurants and nightspots. We also include names and addresses of B&B reservation services, just in case you're inspired to seek out additional properties on your own. Reviews are organized by state, and, within each state, by region.

In the italicized service information that ends every review, a second address in parentheses is a mailing address. A double room is for two people, regardless of the size or type of its beds. Unless otherwise noted, rooms don't have phones or TVs. Note that even the most stunning homes, farmhouses and mansions alike, may not provide a private bathroom for each individual. Rates are for two, excluding tax, in the high season and include breakfast unless otherwise noted; ask about special packages and midweek or off-season discounts.

What we call a restaurant serves meals other than breakfast and is usually open to the general public.

The following credit card abbreviations are used throughout this guide: AE, American Express; D, Discover; DC, Diners Club; MC, MasterCard; V, Visa.

Where applicable, we note seasonal and other restrictions. Although we abhor discrimination, we have conveyed information about innkeepers' restrictive practices so that you will be aware of the prevailing attitudes. Such discriminatory practices are most often applied to parents who are traveling with small children and who may not, in any case, feel comfortable having their offspring toddle amid breakable bric-a-brac and near precipitous stairways.

When traveling the B&B way, always call ahead; and if you have mobility problems or are traveling with children, if you prefer a private bath or a certain type of bed, or if you have specific dietary needs or any other concerns, discuss them with the innkeeper. At the same time, if you're traveling to an inn because of a specific feature, make sure that it will be available when you get there and not closed for renovation. The same goes if you're making a detour to take advantage of specific sights or attractions.

It's a sad commentary on other B&B guides today that we feel obliged to tell you that our writers did, in fact, visit every property in person, and that it is they, not the innkeepers, who wrote the reviews. No one paid a fee or promised to sell or promote the book in order to be included in it. (In fact, one of the most challenging parts of the work of a Fodor's writer is to persuade innkeepers and B&B owners that he or she wants nothing more than a tour of the premises and the answers to a few questions!) Fodor's has no stake in anything but the truth. If a room is dark, with peeling wallpaper, we don't call it quaint or atmospheric—we call it run-down, and then steer you to a more appealing section of the property.

So trust us, the way you'd trust a knowledgeable, well-traveled friend. Let us hear from you about your travels, whether you found that the B&Bs you visited surpassed their descriptions or the other way around. And have a wonderful trip!

Karen Cure
Editorial Director

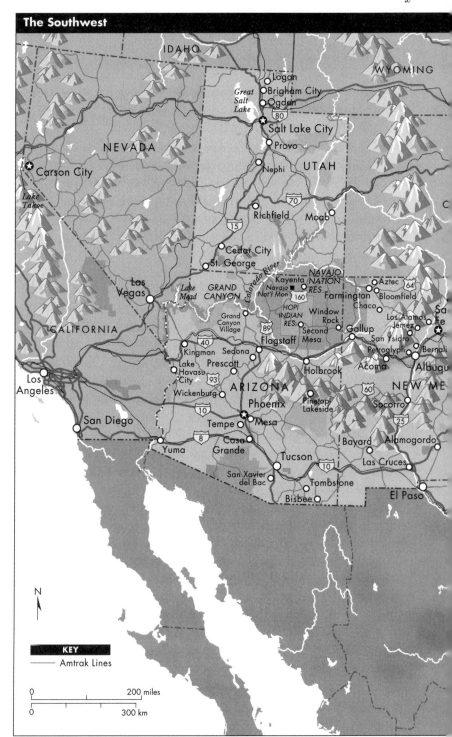

The Southwest

IDAHO

WYOMING

NEVADA

Logan
Great Salt Lake
Brigham City
Ogden
80
Salt Lake City
Provo
UTAH
Nephi

Carson City

Lake Tahoe

70

Richfield
Moab
15

Cedar City
St. George
Colorado River

NAVAJO NATION
Kayenta
Navajo Nat'l Mon.
RES.
160
Aztec
64
Bloomfield
Farmington
Chaco

Las Vegas

Lake Mead
GRAND CANYON

HOPI INDIAN RES.
Window Rock
Second Mesa

Los Alamos
Jemez
Sa Fe

Grand Canyon Village
89

Gallup
San Ysidro
Petroglyph
Bernali

CALIFORNIA

40
Kingman
Sedona
Flagstaff

Holbrook
Acoma
Albuqu

Lake Havasu City
93
Prescott

ARIZONA
Phoenix

NEW ME

Wickenburg

Pinetop Lakeside
Socorro
60

Los Angeles

10

Tempe
Mesa

25

San Diego

8
Yuma
Casa Grande
Tucson
10

Bayard
Alamogordo
Las Cruces

San Xavier del Bac
Tombstone
Bisbee
El Paso

N

0 — 200 miles
0 — 300 km

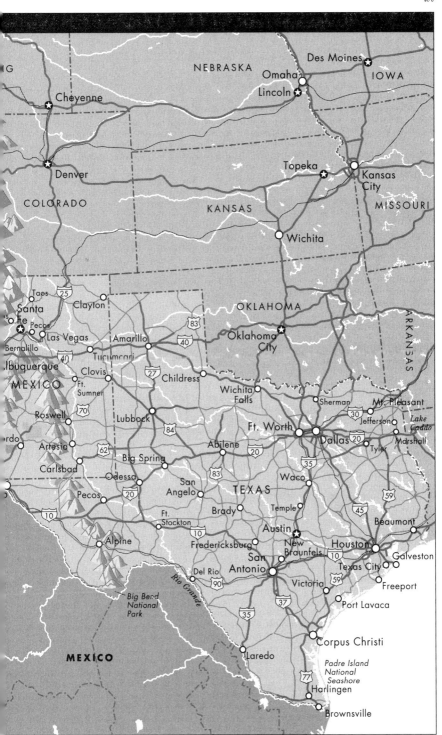

Special Features at a Glance

Name of Property	Antiques	On the Water	Good Value	Car Not Necessary	Full Meal Service	Historic Building	Romantic Hideaway		
ARIZONA									
Adobe Rose Inn						✓			
Amado Territory Inn					✓				
Apple Orchard Inn	✓				✓	✓			
Bartram's White Mountain Bed & Breakfast							✓		
Bienestar	✓						✓		
Birch Tree Inn			✓			✓			
The Bisbee Grand Hotel	✓					✓	✓		
Boots and Saddles			✓				✓		
Briar Patch Inn		✓				✓	✓		
The Cactus Quail							✓		
Canyon Villa Bed & Breakfast Inn							✓		
Casa Alegre Bed and Breakfast Inn	✓					✓	✓		
Casa de San Pedro									
Casa Sedona	✓						✓		
Casa Tierra Adobe Bed & Breakfast			✓				✓		
Catalina Park Inn	✓					✓	✓		
Cathedral Rock Lodge	✓		✓				✓		
The Clawson House	✓					✓	✓		
The Coldstream Bed & Breakfast						✓			
Copper Queen Hotel					✓	✓	✓		
The Cottages at Prescott Country Inn			✓						
Coyote Pass Hospitality					✓				
Cozy Cactus Bed & Breakfast	✓						✓		
The Duquesne House Bed and Breakfast						✓			
El Presidio Bed & Breakfast Inn	✓					✓	✓		

Luxurious	Pets Allowed	No Smoking Indoors	Good Place for Families	Near Arts Festival	Beach Nearby	Cross-Country Ski Trail	Golf within 5 miles	Fitness Facilities	Good Biking Terrain	Skiing	Horseback Riding	Tennis	Swimming on Premises	Conference Facilities
		✓	✓	✓			✓						✓	
		✓					✓							
		✓		✓		✓	✓		✓	✓				
		✓	✓				✓			✓	✓			
✓		✓		✓			✓				✓		✓	
		✓		✓						✓				
		✓		✓										
		✓		✓					✓	✓				
		✓	✓	✓										
✓		✓		✓							✓			
✓		✓		✓			✓						✓	
		✓		✓			✓				✓		✓	
		✓					✓							
✓		✓		✓			✓				✓			
		✓					✓					✓		
✓		✓		✓										
		✓	✓	✓							✓			
		✓		✓			✓							
						✓								✓
				✓			✓						✓	✓
		✓	✓	✓					✓					
	✓	✓	✓								✓			
		✓	✓	✓			✓							
		✓	✓											
✓		✓		✓			✓							

xiv

Special Features at a Glance

Name of Property	Antiques	On the Water	Good Value	Car Not Necessary	Full Meal Service	Historic Building	Romantic Hideaway		
Elysian Grove Market			✓			✓	✓		
The Graham B&B Inn			✓				✓		
Grapevine Canyon Ranch					✓				
Greer Lodge		✓			✓	✓	✓		
The Guest House Inn	✓		✓			✓			
Hacienda del Desierto	✓						✓		
Hassayampa Inn	✓		✓		✓	✓			
High Desert Inn			✓			✓	✓		
Hillside Hideaway Bed and Breakfast	✓		✓				✓		
The Inn at Four Ten	✓					✓	✓		
The Inn on Oak Creek		✓					✓		
Jeanette's Bed-and-Breakfast	✓		✓				✓		
The Jeremiah Inn									
Juniper Well Ranch	✓		✓				✓		
La Posada del Valle	✓					✓	✓		
Lantern Light Inn Bed & Breakfast	✓						✓		
The Lodge at Sedona							✓		
Log Cabin Bed-and-Breakfast	✓		✓				✓		
Lynx Creek Farm	✓	✓					✓		
Main Street Inn			✓			✓			
Maricopa Manor Bed and Breakfast Inn	✓		✓			✓			
The Marks House	✓		✓			✓	✓		
The Meadows	✓		✓		✓		✓		
Mi Gatita	✓						✓		
The Mine Manager's House Inn						✓	✓		
Mount Vernon Inn	✓		✓			✓			

Luxurious	Pets Allowed	No Smoking Indoors	Good Place for Families	Near Arts Festival	Beach Nearby	Cross-Country Ski Trail	Golf within 5 miles	Fitness Facilities	Good Biking Terrain	Skiing	Horseback Riding	Tennis	Swimming on Premises	Conference Facilities
		✓		✓			✓							
✓		✓	✓	✓			✓		✓				✓	
			✓				✓				✓		✓	✓
✓			✓			✓				✓	✓			✓
		✓					✓							✓
		✓	✓	✓			✓				✓			
✓				✓					✓					✓
✓		✓		✓										
		✓				✓			✓					
✓		✓	✓	✓			✓	✓	✓					
✓		✓		✓					✓	✓				
		✓		✓			✓		✓					
		✓	✓	✓			✓			✓	✓		✓	
	✓	✓	✓						✓		✓			
		✓		✓			✓							
		✓	✓	✓			✓							
		✓		✓										✓
		✓		✓					✓					
	✓	✓	✓	✓					✓					
		✓	✓	✓			✓							
✓			✓	✓			✓							
✓		✓		✓					✓					
		✓				✓	✓		✓	✓				
		✓		✓			✓				✓			
		✓					✓							
	✓	✓	✓											

Special Features at a Glance

Name of Property	Antiques	On the Water	Good Value	Car Not Necessary	Full Meal Service	Historic Building	Romantic Hideaway		
Noftsger Hill Inn	✓		✓			✓			
The OK Street Jailhouse						✓	✓		
Olney House Bed & Breakfast	✓		✓			✓	✓		
Paisley Corner Bed & Breakfast	✓		✓			✓	✓		
The Peppertrees Bed and Breakfast Inn	✓					✓	✓		
The Pleasant Street Inn Bed & Breakfast						✓	✓		
Quail's Vista Bed and Breakfast	✓								
Ramsey Canyon Inn	✓	✓					✓		
Rancho Quieto							✓		
Red Setter Inn	✓	✓					✓		
Rimrock West Hacienda			✓				✓		
Saddle Rock Ranch	✓					✓	✓		
San Pedro River Inn		✓	✓			✓			
School House Inn Bed & Breakfast			✓			✓			
Skywatcher's Inn			✓						
Territorial House	✓						✓		
Tombstone Boarding House	✓					✓			
The Triangle L Ranch Bed & Breakfast	✓					✓	✓		
Valle Verde Ranch Bed and Breakfast	✓					✓	✓		
Victoria's	✓		✓			✓			
The Vineyard Bed-and-Breakfast	✓		✓			✓			
White Mountain Lodge		✓	✓			✓	✓		
Yee Ha Ranch							✓		

Luxurious	Pets Allowed	No Smoking Indoors	Good Place for Families	Near Arts Festival	Beach Nearby	Cross-Country Ski Trail	Golf within 5 miles	Fitness Facilities	Good Biking Terrain	Skiing	Horseback Riding	Tennis	Swimming on Premises	Conference Facilities
		✓	✓	✓			✓							✓
	✓	✓	✓	✓			✓							
		✓	✓											
			✓			✓				✓				
		✓	✓	✓			✓							
✓		✓		✓					✓					
		✓	✓				✓	✓			✓		✓	
		✓												
✓			✓	✓			✓				✓		✓	✓
✓		✓				✓	✓		✓	✓				✓
		✓		✓			✓				✓		✓	
✓		✓											✓	
	✓		✓											✓
		✓		✓			✓							
	✓	✓	✓											
		✓	✓	✓					✓	✓				
		✓		✓										
		✓	✓								✓			
✓		✓		✓			✓							
		✓												
		✓									✓		✓	
	✓		✓							✓				
✓		✓									✓			

Special Features at a Glance

Name of Property	Antiques	On the Water	Good Value	Car Not Necessary	Full Meal Service	Historic Building	Romantic Hideaway		
NEW MEXICO									
Adobe Abode	✓			✓		✓	✓		
Adobe & Pines	✓					✓	✓		
Adobe and Roses			✓				✓		
Adobe Garden	✓		✓			✓	✓		
Alexander's Inn	✓			✓		✓	✓		
American Gallery Artists House	✓		✓				✓		
Bear Mountain Guest Ranch					✓	✓			
The Black Range Lodge			✓			✓			
The Blue Door	✓						✓		
Bottgër Mansion	✓			✓	✓	✓	✓		
Britannia and W.E. Mauger Estate	✓			✓		✓	✓		
Brooks Street Inn	✓			✓			✓		
The Carter House	✓		✓			✓			
Casa de Milagros	✓					✓	✓		
Casa de Patrón	✓		✓			✓	✓		
Casa de las Chimeneas	✓					✓	✓		
Casa del Granjero						✓	✓		
Casa del Rio	✓						✓		
Casa Escondida	✓					✓	✓		
Casa Europa	✓		✓			✓	✓		
Casas de Sueños	✓			✓		✓	✓		
Casita Chamisa	✓		✓			✓	✓		
Cottonwood Inn	✓		✓	✓			✓		
The Don Gaspar Compound Inn	✓		✓			✓	✓		
Dos Casas Viejas	✓						✓		

Luxurious	Pets Allowed	No Smoking Indoors	Good Place for Families	Near Arts Festival	Beach Nearby	Cross-Country Ski Trail	Golf within 5 miles	Fitness Facilities	Good Biking Terrain	Skiing	Horseback Riding	Tennis	Swimming on Premises	Conference Facilities
	✓	✓		✓		✓	✓		✓	✓	✓			
✓		✓		✓		✓	✓		✓	✓				
	✓	✓	✓	✓		✓	✓		✓	✓				
		✓	✓	✓		✓	✓		✓	✓			✓	
		✓	✓	✓		✓	✓		✓	✓				
✓		✓		✓		✓	✓		✓	✓				
	✓	✓				✓			✓					✓
	✓	✓	✓						✓					
		✓	✓	✓		✓	✓		✓	✓				
		✓	✓	✓			✓		✓	✓				
✓	✓	✓		✓			✓		✓	✓				
		✓	✓	✓		✓	✓	✓	✓	✓				
		✓	✓				✓		✓					
		✓	✓	✓		✓	✓		✓	✓				
		✓	✓	✓					✓	✓	✓			✓
✓		✓	✓	✓		✓	✓	✓	✓	✓				
		✓	✓	✓			✓		✓	✓				
		✓				✓			✓	✓				
		✓	✓	✓		✓			✓	✓				
✓		✓	✓	✓		✓	✓		✓	✓				
✓		✓		✓			✓		✓	✓				
	✓	✓	✓				✓		✓	✓			✓	
✓		✓		✓		✓			✓	✓				
✓		✓	✓	✓		✓	✓		✓	✓				✓
✓		✓		✓		✓	✓		✓	✓			✓	

Special Features at a Glance

Name of Property	Antiques	On the Water	Good Value	Car Not Necessary	Full Meal Service	Historic Building	Romantic Hideaway		
Dunshee's	✓		✓			✓			
Eaton House	✓					✓	✓		
Elaine's	✓		✓			✓			
The Ellis Store & Co. Country Inn	✓	✓			✓	✓	✓		
El Paradero				✓	✓	✓			
El Rincón	✓				✓	✓	✓		
The Enchanted Villa	✓				✓	✓			
Grant Corner Inn	✓				✓	✓	✓		
The Guadalupe Inn						✓	✓		
Hacienda del Sol	✓					✓	✓		
Hacienda Vargas	✓					✓	✓		
Inn of the Animal Tracks						✓	✓		
Inn on La Loma Plaza						✓	✓		
Inn on the Alameda				✓					
Inn on the Paseo				✓		✓	✓		
La Posada de Chimayo						✓			
La Posada de Taos	✓			✓		✓	✓		
La Tienda			✓			✓	✓		
Little Tree	✓						✓		
The Lodge	✓				✓	✓	✓		
Lundeen Inn of the Arts	✓			✓		✓	✓		
Mabel Dodge Luhan House	✓				✓	✓	✓		
Mesón de Mesilla				✓	✓				
Old Taos Guesthouse	✓		✓				✓		
Old Town Bed & Breakfast			✓	✓		✓	✓		
Orinda Bed and Breakfast	✓			✓			✓		

Luxurious	Pets Allowed	No Smoking Indoors	Good Place for Families	Near Arts Festival	Beach Nearby	Cross-Country Ski Trail	Golf within 5 miles	Fitness Facilities	Good Biking Terrain	Skiing	Horseback Riding	Tennis	Swimming on Premises	Conference Facilities
		✓	✓	✓		✓	✓		✓	✓				
✓		✓					✓		✓					
		✓		✓			✓		✓	✓				
		✓	✓						✓	✓	✓			✓
	✓	✓		✓		✓	✓		✓	✓				
✓	✓		✓	✓		✓	✓		✓	✓				
	✓			✓					✓		✓		✓	✓
✓	✓	✓		✓		✓	✓		✓	✓				
		✓		✓		✓	✓		✓	✓				
		✓		✓		✓	✓		✓	✓				
✓		✓	✓	✓		✓	✓		✓	✓				
✓	✓	✓		✓	✓	✓	✓	✓	✓	✓				✓
		✓		✓		✓	✓		✓	✓				
	✓	✓							✓	✓				
		✓		✓		✓	✓		✓	✓				
		✓		✓		✓	✓		✓	✓				
	✓	✓	✓	✓		✓	✓	✓	✓	✓				
			✓			✓	✓		✓	✓			✓	✓
✓	✓	✓	✓				✓	✓			✓			✓
	✓	✓	✓	✓			✓		✓	✓				
	✓						✓		✓				✓	✓
		✓	✓	✓		✓	✓		✓	✓	✓			
		✓		✓			✓		✓	✓				
		✓	✓	✓		✓	✓	✓	✓	✓				

Special Features at a Glance

Name of Property	Antiques	On the Water	Good Value	Car Not Necessary	Full Meal Service	Historic Building	Romantic Hideaway		
Preston House	✓			✓		✓	✓		
Pueblo Bonito				✓		✓			
Rancho de San Juan	✓	·			✓		✓		
The Ruby Slipper				✓			✓		
Salsa del Salto							✓		
Sarabande	✓		✓				✓		
Sierra Mesa Lodge	✓						✓		
Taos Country Inn at Rancho Rio Pueblo	✓					✓	✓		
Territorial Inn	✓			✓		✓	✓		
Water Street Inn	✓		✓	✓		✓	✓		
Yours Truly			✓				✓		
TEXAS									
Austin Street Retreat	✓			✓			✓		
The Beckmann Inn and Carriage House	✓			✓		✓	✓		
The Bonner Garden	✓					✓			
Broadway Manor	✓								
The Bullis House Inn	✓					✓			
Caddo Cottage		✓							
Carrington's Bluff	✓								
Charnwood Hill	✓					✓			
The Comfort Common	✓					✓			
Crystal River Inn	✓		✓						
Das Kleine Nest							✓		
Delforge Place	✓								
The Excelsior House	✓		✓			✓			

Luxurious	Pets Allowed	No Smoking Indoors	Good Place for Families	Near Arts Festival	Beach Nearby	Cross-Country Ski Trail	Golf within 5 miles	Fitness Facilities	Good Biking Terrain	Skiing	Horseback Riding	Tennis	Swimming on Premises	Conference Facilities
✓	✓	✓		✓		✓	✓		✓	✓				
		✓		✓		✓	✓		✓	✓				
✓		✓				✓			✓					✓
		✓		✓		✓	✓		✓	✓				
		✓	✓	✓		✓	✓		✓	✓	✓	✓		
✓		✓					✓		✓	✓			✓	
✓		✓		✓			✓		✓	✓	✓			
			✓			✓	✓		✓	✓				
✓		✓		✓		✓	✓		✓	✓				
✓	✓	✓	✓	✓		✓	✓		✓	✓				
	✓		✓	✓			✓		✓	✓				
✓		✓					✓		✓					
			✓			✓								
		✓		✓			✓						✓	
		✓		✓			✓							
		✓		✓			✓							
			✓						✓					
		✓		✓			✓							
✓		✓					✓							✓
		✓					✓		✓					
		✓					✓		✓					
							✓		✓					
		✓					✓		✓					
		✓		✓					✓					

Special Features at a Glance

Name of Property	Antiques	On the Water	Good Value	Car Not Necessary	Full Meal Service	Historic Building	Romantic Hideaway		
Fredericksburg Bed and Brew									
Harrison House	✓								
The Herb Haus									
Hotel Garza Historic Inn and Conference Center	✓		✓						
The Hotel St. Germain	✓			✓					
House of the Seasons	✓					✓	✓		
Inn on the Creek	✓	✓							
Inn on the River		✓				✓			
Maison-Bayou									
Mansion on Main	✓								
McKay House	✓			✓		✓	✓		
Miss Molly's Bed & Breakfast			✓	✓					
The Nagel House	✓								
1934 Bed and Breakfast	✓								
The Ogé House on the Riverwalk	✓	✓		✓		✓			
Oxford House	✓								
Page House	✓					✓			
Parkview House									
Pride House	✓								
Riverwalk Inn	✓	✓		✓		✓	✓		
Sanford House	✓								
Schmidt Barn							✓		
The Seasons									
Settlers Crossing	✓		✓			✓	✓		
Stage Stop Ranch									
Stillwater Inn	✓				✓				

Luxurious	Pets Allowed	No Smoking Indoors	Good Place for Families	Near Arts Festival	Beach Nearby	Cross-Country Ski Trail	Golf within 5 miles	Fitness Facilities	Good Biking Terrain	Skiing	Horseback Riding	Tennis	Swimming on Premises	Conference Facilities
		✓					✓							✓
	✓	✓		✓			✓		✓					
		✓					✓		✓					
		✓							✓					✓
✓		✓		✓			✓							✓
✓		✓		✓										
		✓		✓			✓		✓					✓
		✓					✓						✓	✓
		✓	✓	✓			✓		✓		✓			
		✓												
		✓		✓										
		✓		✓			✓							
		✓					✓							
		✓		✓										✓
✓		✓		✓			✓							
		✓												✓
		✓		✓			✓							
		✓		✓			✓		✓					
		✓		✓										
		✓		✓			✓							✓
✓		✓		✓										
		✓					✓							
✓		✓		✓			✓		✓					
		✓	✓						✓					
		✓	✓	✓					✓		✓			
		✓		✓										✓

Special Features at a Glance

Name of Property	Antiques	On the Water	Good Value	Car Not Necessary	Full Meal Service	Historic Building	Romantic Hideaway		
The Village Bed and Breakfast	✓		✓						
Woodburn House	✓								
A Yellow Rose									
Ziller House							✓		
UTAH									
An Olde Penny Farthing Inn	✓					✓			
Bankurz Hatt	✓				✓	✓	✓		
The Bard's Inn	✓		✓			✓	✓		
The Blue Heron Bed and Breakfast									
Boulder Mountain Lodge		✓			✓		✓		
Bryce Point Bed and Breakfast									
Castle Valley Inn	✓				✓		✓		
Desert Rose Inn	✓					✓	✓		
Dream Keeper Bed and Breakfast	✓								
Eagle's Nest Bed & Breakfast	✓			✓	✓		✓		
Entrada Ranch				✓	✓				
Fox's Bryce Trails Bed and Breakfast									
Francisco's									
Grayson Country Inn	✓					✓			
Greene Gate Village	✓				✓	✓	✓		
The Grist Mill Inn	✓		✓		✓	✓	✓		
Harvest House							✓		
La Sal Mountain Guest Ranch	✓								
The Lodge at Red River Ranch	✓	✓			✓		✓		
Mt. Peale Bed-and-Breakfast			✓		✓		✓		

Luxurious	Pets Allowed	No Smoking Indoors	Good Place for Families	Near Arts Festival	Beach Nearby	Cross-Country Ski Trail	Golf within 5 miles	Fitness Facilities	Good Biking Terrain	Skiing	Horseback Riding	Tennis	Swimming on Premises	Conference Facilities
		✓												
		✓		✓			✓							
		✓		✓			✓							
✓			✓				✓						✓	
		✓		✓			✓		✓					
✓		✓					✓		✓					
✓		✓	✓	✓			✓		✓	✓				
		✓		✓			✓		✓					
		✓				✓			✓		✓			✓
		✓	✓			✓			✓					
✓		✓		✓		✓			✓					✓
		✓		✓					✓		✓			
		✓		✓			✓		✓				✓	
		✓							✓					✓
		✓				✓			✓		✓			
		✓				✓			✓					
		✓	✓						✓					
		✓	✓						✓					
✓		✓	✓	✓			✓		✓				✓	✓
✓		✓	✓			✓	✓		✓					✓
		✓		✓			✓		✓					
		✓	✓											✓
✓		✓		✓		✓		✓	✓		✓			✓
		✓		✓		✓			✓					✓

Special Features at a Glance

Name of Property	Antiques	On the Water	Good Value	Car Not Necessary	Full Meal Service	Historic Building	Romantic Hideaway		
Nine Gables Inn	✓					✓	✓		
Nine Mile Ranch Bunk and Breakfast			✓		✓				
Novel House Inn	✓		✓				✓		
O'Toole's Under the Eaves Bed & Breakfast	✓					✓	✓		
Pack Creek Ranch				✓	✓		✓		
Paxman's Summer House	✓		✓			✓			
Quicksand and Cactus Bed & Breakfast	✓					✓			
Red Rock Inn			✓						
Rogers House Bed & Breakfast	✓		✓				✓		
Seven Wives Inn	✓					✓	✓		
SkyRidge Bed & Breakfast	✓						✓		
Snow Family Guest Ranch			✓				✓		
Sunflower Hill	✓		✓		✓	✓	✓		
Valley of the Gods Bed and Breakfast	✓		✓		✓	✓	✓		
William Prince Inn	✓		✓	.		✓			

Luxurious	Pets Allowed	No Smoking Indoors	Good Place for Families	Near Arts Festival	Beach Nearby	Cross-Country Ski Trail	Golf within 5 miles	Fitness Facilities	Good Biking Terrain	Skiing	Horseback Riding	Tennis	Swimming on Premises	Conference Facilities
		✓							✓					
	✓	✓	✓						✓					
✓		✓		✓					✓					✓
		✓	✓						✓					
		✓	✓	✓		✓	✓	✓	✓		✓			✓
		✓	✓				✓		✓					
		✓	✓				✓		✓					
✓		✓							✓					
✓		✓	✓	✓			✓		✓				✓	✓
✓		✓		✓		✓			✓		✓			
		✓	✓						✓		✓		✓	✓
✓		✓	✓	✓		✓	✓		✓		✓			✓
		✓	✓						✓					
		✓							✓					

Glossary of Southwestern Terms

Perhaps more than any other region in the United States, the Southwest has a unique architectural style, adapted to the desert landscape and heavily influenced by the area's Native American and Spanish settlers. Southwest interior furnishings are similarly distinctive, blending eclectic elements that might include Mission chests, Navajo blankets, Mexican tinwork mirrors, and bleached cow skulls à la Georgia O'Keeffe. The brief glossary that follows explains terms frequently used in this book's bed-and-breakfast reviews, particularly in the New Mexico and Arizona chapters.

Adobe. A brick of sun-dried earth and clay, usually stabilized with straw; a structure made of adobe.

Bulto. Folk-art figures of a saint (santo), usually carved out of wood.

Casita. Literally, "small house," the term is generally used to describe a separate guest house.

Equipale. Pigskin-and-cedar furniture from Jalisco, Mexico. The chairs have rounded backs and bases rather than legs.

Kachina. A figure representing a spirit or god of the Hopi or Pueblo Indians. Although commonly called dolls, kachinas are used as teaching aids, not as playthings.

Kiva fireplace. A corner fireplace whose round form resembles that of a kiva; a ceremonial room used by Native Americans of the Southwest.

Latilla. Small pole, often made of aspen, used as a lath in a ceiling.

Luminaria. The term used in Arizona for a small votive candle set in a paper-bag lantern, popular at Christmas; in northern New Mexico, it is called a farolito.

Portale. A porch or large, covered area adjacent to the house.

Pueblo style. Modeled after the traditional dwellings of the Southwest Pueblo Indians. Most homes in this style are cube-shaped. Other characteristics are flat roofs, small windows, rounded corners, and viga beams.

Ristra. String of dried red chili peppers, often used as decoration.

Saltillo tile. Large floor tile of baked, reddish-brown clay made in Saltillo, Mexico; often used as a generic term for this type of tile.

Talavera tile. Colorful ceramic bathroom or kitchen tile with elaborate, interlocking, Moorish designs, made in Puebla, Mexico. The name derives from the pottery town in Spain where the tile originated—Talavera de la Reina.

Territorial style. Modified Pueblo style that evolved in the late 19th century when New Mexico and Arizona were still U.S. territories. The territorial home incorporates a broad central hallway and entryway and adds wooden elements, like window frames, in neoclassic style; some structures have pitched rather than flat roofs, and brick copings.

Trastero. Cupboard, china closet, or other upright cabinet.

Viga. Horizontal roof beam made of logs, usually protruding from the side of the house.

Arizona

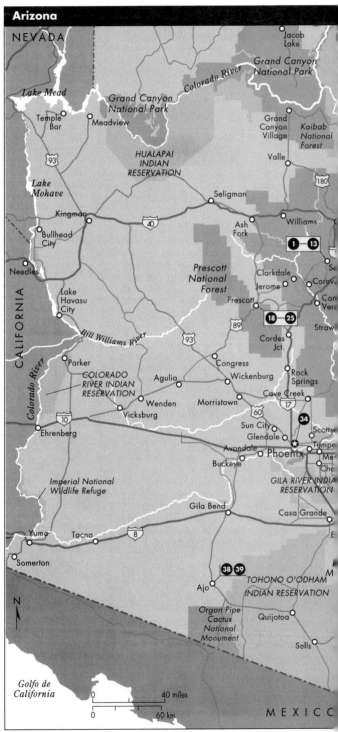

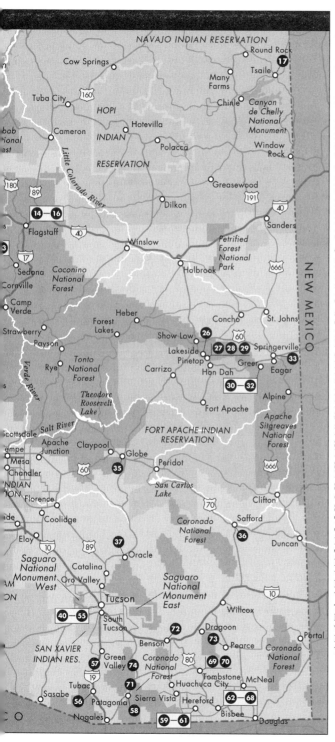

Northern Arizona

The Graham B&B Inn

Including the Grand Canyon, Sedona, Flagstaff, and Indian Country

More than 4 million people come to northern Arizona each year to gaze into the vast, multihued abyss of the Grand Canyon. Far fewer live in this part of the state year-round: The top third of Arizona, which is about the size of Pennsylvania, has only 207,000 inhabitants—fewer than six per square mile. Much of the area is true wilderness, devoid of water, frightening and fatal to early pioneers.

The Grand Canyon is the most astonishing of the natural attractions of the region, but the many other sights have a closer-to-human scale that renders them more fathomable— and less crowded. The black-and-rust lava cones of Sunset Crater-Volcano; the subtle pastel Painted Desert; and the old red monoliths of Monument Valley and Sedona show off the varied palette of nature, which together with manual labor created the surrealistic buff-and-blue Lake Powell. Long-abandoned ruins at Canyon de Chelly, Navajo, Wupatki, and Walnut Canyon national monuments bear testimony to the ways the original Native American inhabitants survived this often harsh, but strikingly beautiful, environment.

In the northeastern corner of the state, 25,000 square miles belong to the Navajo Nation, and in the center of that reservation is the smaller preserve of the Hopi tribe. Poor in material terms, these nations are rich in cultural traditions: At trading posts that were established in the 19th century, visitors can buy jewelry, pottery, and weavings created in the same way as they have been for hundreds of years.

A jumping-off point for visits to the Grand Canyon and Indian country, Flagstaff is rarely a destination in its own right. But this thriving university town set among the pine-covered, snowcapped San Francisco Mountains forms the cultural center of the region and retains a frontier flavor despite a proliferation of fast-food places and motels. In contrast, Sedona, less than 20 miles south and reached via lovely Oak Creek Canyon, has come to rival Santa Fe in its number of tony art galleries and chic visitors. New Agers believe that creative energy points, or vortices, are concentrated among the region's spectacular red rock spires.

The accommodations listed for this region are as varied as the landscape itself, ranging from the small Victorian bed-and-breakfasts of Prescott to the opulent inns of Sedona, as luxurious—and as expensive—as any you'll find in large urban centers. The B&Bs in Flagstaff are friendly, reasonably priced alternatives to the town's myriad faceless motels.

Places to Go, Sights to See

Canyon de Chelly National Monument (Box 588, Chinle 86503, tel. 520/674–5500). The sheer sandstone walls of the spectacular Canyon de Chelly (pronounced *d'SHAY*) on the Navajo Reservation stand 1,000 feet tall in some places; more than 100 prehistoric Anasazi cliff dwellings perch under precipitous overhangs. Two paved rim drives take visitors to scenic overlooks of the two main canyons—Canyon de Chelly and Canyon del Muerto. For most hikes and all

Jeep tours into the canyons, visitors must be accompanied by rangers or Navajo guides; call ahead or make arrangements at the visitor center.

Flagstaff. The largest city in northern Arizona, Flagstaff is the place to head for cultural attractions. The *Lowell Observatory* (1400 W. Mars Hill Rd., Flagstaff 86001, tel. 520/774–2096), built in 1894, is the oldest in Arizona; astronomers discovered the planet Pluto here in 1930. Filled with fascinating artifacts of Flagstaff's logging heyday, the 40-room log-and-stone Riordon House in the *Riordon Mansion State Historic Park* (1300 Riordon Ranch St., tel. 520/779–4395) was built in 1904 by two lumber-baron brothers who married two sisters. The *Museum of Northern Arizona* (3101 N. Valley Rd., tel. 520/774–5213) is respected worldwide for its research and its collections centering on the natural and cultural history of the Colorado Plateau; a large array of Navajo rugs and an authentic Hopi kiva are among its fine, permanent exhibitions. In winter, the *Arizona Snowbowl* (Snowbowl Rd., 12 mi north of Flagstaff, tel. 520/779–1951 or 800/828–7285) draws skiers of all levels of expertise to its 35 downhill trails; year-round, the skyride lifts visitors through the Coconino National Forest to a height of 11,500 feet, where they can view the North Rim of the Grand Canyon.

Grand Canyon National Park (Box 129, Grand Canyon 86023, tel. 520/638–7888). The most visited attraction in Arizona and one of the Seven Natural Wonders of the World, the vast erosion-carved canyon is 1 mile deep, 277 miles long, and just over 2 billion years old. The view into its ever-changing vastness is awe-inspiring—but if you go to the South Rim in summer, you'll have to share it with thousands of others. *Trip Planner,* available from the address above, is a useful guide to the national park. A fun way to visit is via the *Grand Canyon Railway* (233 W. Grand Canyon Blvd., Williams 86046, tel. 520/773–1976 or 800/THE–TRAIN), which recreates the steam train run from Williams to the South Rim of the canyon inaugurated in 1901 by a subsidiary of the Atchison, Topeka & Santa Fe Railway; the museum at the Williams depot displays many interesting artifacts of the era.

Hopi Reservation. In the center of the sprawling Navajo Reservation are 4,000 square miles of land belonging to the Hopi. About 10,000 members of the tribe live here in 12 villages on top of three mesas; to the west of Third Mesa, the town of Oraibi is widely believed to be the oldest continually inhabited community in the United States, dating from around AD 1150. Some of the Hopi dances and ceremonies are open to the public; contact the *Hopi Tribe Office of Public Relations* (*see* Tourist Information, *below*) for information. Cameras, recorders, and sketch pads are prohibited in all cases. Another good resource for information is the *Hopi Cultural Center* (Second Mesa, tel. 520/734–2401), which has a group of shops, a pueblo-style museum, a good restaurant serving American and Native American dishes, and an immaculate motel.

Hubbell Trading Post National Historic Site (AZ 264, 1 mi west of Ganado, tel. 520/755–3475). Established in 1878 by John Lorenzo Hubbell, this is the oldest continuously operating trading post on the Navajo Reservation. Exhibits at the visitor center illustrate the post's history, and Hubbell's house, now a museum, contains fine examples of Native American artistry. Beautifully crafted Navajo rugs are expensive, but you won't find a better selection than the one here.

Lake Powell. With more than 1,900 miles of shoreline, Lake Powell, which stretches through northern Arizona and southern Utah, is the heart of the 1,255,400-acre Glen Canyon National Recreation Area. The jade-green lake, created by the construction of the Glen Canyon Dam in 1953, is encircled by immense red cliffs and extends through an otherworldly landscape of eroded canyons nearly devoid of vegetation. The most popular destination on the lake is *Wahweap*, a vacation village 5 miles north of Glen Canyon Dam; for information on boat rentals, water sports, camping, or other lodging, contact AraMark Leisure Services (Box 56909, Phoenix 85079, tel. 800/528–6154) or Glen Canyon National Recreation Area (Box 1507, Page 86040, tel. 520/608–6200). Well worth booking is the half-day boat trip from Wahweap to *Rainbow Bridge National Monument*, where the world's largest natural stone bridge, a massive 290-foot red sandstone arch, straddles a cove of the lake. Information about, and a view of, the 710-foot *Glen Canyon Dam* is available at the Carl Hayden Visitor Center (U.S. 89, tel. 520/645–2511).

Monument Valley Navajo Tribal Park (3½ mi off U.S. 183, 24 mi north of Kayenta, tel. 801/727–3353). You'll recognize the soaring red buttes of Monument Valley from such Westerns as *Stagecoach, She Wore a Yellow Ribbon,* and *How the West Was Won.* You can take a 17-mile self-guided tour through the heart of the 30,000-acre Monument Valley Navajo Tribal Park, but the road is unpaved and rutted; consider booking one of the many guided van tours. There are operators in and around the visitor center, which also has a crafts shop and exhibits devoted to the Native American history of the area.

Navajo National Monument (HC 71, Box 3, Tonalea 86044, tel. 520/672–2366). The largest Native American ruins in Arizona, two 13th-century Anasazi pueblos, Keet Seel and Betatakin, stand under the overhang of soaring orange-and-ocher cliffs. During the summer, national park rangers escort tours to these sites, reached via AZ 564 off U.S. 160; call 520/672–2367 for reservations and information.

Navajo Reservation. Some 100,000 members of the Navajo Nation live here on the largest Native American reservation in the United States, spread over the northeastern corner of Arizona as well as parts of Utah and New Mexico. In Window Rock, the tribal capital, located near the New Mexico border, visit the *Navajo Tribal Museum* (AZ 264, next to Navajo Nation Inn, tel. 520/871–6673), a small space devoted to the art and culture of the region, with an excellent selection of books, and the adjoining *Navajo Arts and Crafts Enterprise* (tel. 520/871–4090), which sells local creative works. Among the other attractions on the reservation are Canyon de Chelly, Hubbell Trading Post, Monument Valley Navajo Tribal Park, and Navajo National Monument, all detailed above.

Oak Creek Canyon. The winding, wooded 16-mile stretch along Rte. 89A, following Oak Creek through the red cliffs north from Sedona to Flagstaff, is among the most scenic routes in the country. Seven miles north of Sedona, you'll see a sign for *Slide Rock State Park* (tel. 520/282–3034), a good spot for a picnic and hike back into the forest. Take along an extra pair of old pants if you'd like to plunge down a natural rock slide into a swimming hole.

Petrified Forest National Park (Box 2217, Petrified Forest 86028, tel. 520/524–6228). Some 225 million years ago, this stark desert was the floor of an ancient sea; now there are tree trunks fossilized into colorful pieces of petrified wood here. The park covers nearly 100,000 acres; the section north of the highway contains the *Painted Desert*, a moonscape of warm pastels and earth tones. Drive about 25 miles east of Holbrook on I-40 to reach the visitor center.

Sedona. A stunning setting—red sandstone formations with clear blue sky and dark green forests as a backdrop—has drawn visitors to Sedona in droves in the past decade. The most popular way to explore the region is on a Jeep tour along U.S. 89A, one of the two main drags; this section of Sedona, called Uptown, also has a number of tacky souvenir outlets and New Age shops. More expensive boutiques and art galleries are concentrated along AZ 179. Two miles west of Sedona on U.S. 89A is the turnoff for the 286-acre *Red Rock State Park Center for Environmental Education* (tel. 520/282–6907), an ideal spot to enjoy the red rock formations and beautiful Oak Creek. The five park trails, all fairly short, are well marked.

Sunset Crater Volcano National Monument (Rte. 3, tel. 520/526–0502). Fifteen miles north of Flagstaff, off U.S. 89, a loop road leads east to a black-and-rusty-red, 800-square-mile volcanic field created in AD 1065 when Sunset Crater erupted; it's particularly beautiful in winter when the many pine trees are topped with snow. Drive 20 miles north of the visitor center along AZ 545 to reach the entrance of the associated **Wupatki National Monument** (tel. 520/679–2365). Some 2,700 identified sites—including an ancient three-story structure with more than 100 rooms—contain evidence of Native American settlement from AD 600 until AD 1300 in this area; families from the Sinagua, Anasazi, and perhaps other Indian cultures are believed to have lived here harmoniously.

Walnut Canyon National Monument (take I-40 east of Flagstaff for 7 mi to exit 204, drive 3 mi south, tel. 520/526–3367). Sinagua Indians built nearly 300 cliff dwellings in this peaceful pine-dotted gorge more than 1,000 years ago. Paved trails lead right up to the ruins.

Restaurants

Known for drive-through service, Flagstaff nevertheless has some sophisticated but reasonably priced restaurants. Among them are **Cottage Place** (tel. 520/774–8431), which offers Continental cuisine with many innovative touches in a series of pretty, intimate dining rooms, and **Sakura Restaurant** (tel. 520/773–9118), catering to the town's many Japanese tourists, with excellent sushi and *teppan* grill specialties. Low-key and more typically Western, the **Horseman Lodge & Restaurant** (tel. 520/526–2655) serves unpretentious American fare in a room with knotty-pine beams and a stone fireplace, while the small, colorful **Café Olé** (tel. 520/774–8272) is good for home cooked Mexican food. The **Beaver Street Brewery and Whistlestop Cafe** (tel. 520/779–0079) is known for its burgers, salads, wood-fired pizzas, and nine types of beer.

Yuppie-oriented Sedona has many good upscale eateries including **Renés** (tel. 520/282–9229), which serves Continental cuisine in a romantic setting decorated with many nice works of art. The **Cowboy Club** (tel. 520/282–4200), in Sedona's oldest commercial building, hollers cowboy through and through. The sweet, healthy Buffalo sirloin is delicious; the tough rattlesnake is for more daring cowpunchers. Moderately priced, tasty Southwestern fare is served at the **Heartline Café** (tel. 520/282–0785), which has a light-filled dining room and a rose-bedecked patio.

Spectacular views combined with good food are hard to come by, but three restaurants in northern Arizona fill the bill: **El Tovar Hotel** (tel. 520/638–2631), overlooking the South Rim of the Grand Canyon; the **Grand Canyon Lodge** (tel. 520/638–2611), facing the North Rim; and the **Rainbow Room in Wahweap Lodge** (tel. 520/645–2433), with vistas of Lake Powell. All three dining rooms serve a variety of American food with Southwestern accents.

Most of the restaurants in sparsely populated Indian country are of the fast-food variety, but three places that serve good standard American fare along with some Native American dishes are the **Navajo Nation Inn** (tel. 520/871–4108) in Window Rock, **Goulding's Lodge** (tel. 801/727–3231) near Monument Valley, and the **Holiday Inn** (tel. 520/674–5000) just outside Canyon de Chelly.

Tourist Information

Grand Canyon Chamber of Commerce (Box 3007, Grand Canyon 86023, tel. 520/638–2901). **Flagstaff Visitors Center** (1 E. Rte. 66, Flagstaff 86001, tel. 520/774–9541 or 800/842–7293). **Hopi Tribe Office of Public Relations** (Box 123, Kykotsmovi 86039, tel. 520/234–2441). **Navajoland Tourism Department** (Box 663, Window Rock 86515, tel. 520/871–6659). **Page/Lake Powell Chamber of Commerce** (Box 727, Page 86040, tel. 520/645–2741). **Sedona–Oak Creek Canyon Chamber of Commerce** (Box 478, Sedona 86339, tel. 520/282–7722 or 800/288–7336). **Williams Chamber of Commerce and Visitor Center** (200 W. Railroad Ave., Williams 86046, tel. 520/635–1418).

Reservation Services

Arizona Association of Bed & Breakfast Inns (Box 7186, Phoenix 85011, tel. 800/284–2589). **Arizona Trails Bed and Breakfast Reservation Service** (Box 18998, Fountain Hills 85269, tel. 602/837–4284 or 888/799–4284, fax 602/816–4224). **Mi Casa Su Casa B&B Reservation Service** (Box 950, Tempe 85280, tel. 602/990–0682, 800/456–0682 reservations only, fax 602/990–3390).

Apple Orchard Inn

656 Jordan Rd., Sedona 86336, tel. 520/ 282–5328 or 800/663–6968, fax 520/204– 0044

Although only a half mile from Uptown Sedona, the Apple Orchard Inn, which is on the edge of town, feels like it's in the country—deer and wild pigs frequent the property's two acres and you'll often hear coyotes howling late into the night. When former owner, Bill Pritchard, a retired Sedona fire chief, purchased the building in 1996, he stripped it to its bare red rock structure and re-created a childhood memory of a Sedona home using native stone, antiques, and Western furniture. Bob and Paula Glass then took over in October 1997; they replaced much of Bill's firehouse memorabilia with their own (Bob is a former hospital CEO and race car driver, Paula is a former flight attendant and offshore powerboat racer).

Guest rooms are simple, with lots of amenities, including VCRs and refrigerators. All but one have king-size beds. In the Sedona Room, an image of Bell Rock has been carved into the flagstone of the armoire and headboard, with a cow-skin rug leading from the bed.

In summer, you can eat breakfast on the outdoor patio and enjoy a magnificent view of Wilson mountain. Hearty breakfasts, prepared by professional chefs, might include French toast custard soufflé with smoked bacon and maple syrup, fresh fruit, scones, and fresh-ground roasted coffee. They will also cook dinner upon request.

▥ *7 double rooms with baths. TVs/ VCRs, phones, refrigerators in all rooms, Jacuzzi tubs in 6 rooms, fireplaces in 2 rooms, hiking. $135–$195, full breakfast. MC, V. No smoking, no pets, no children under 10.*

Birch Tree Inn

824 W. Birch Ave., Flagstaff 86001, tel. 520/774–1042 or 888/774–1042, fax 502/ 774–8462

This 1917 white clapboard house is in a residential neighborhood across the street from a grassy city park and the Coconino National Forest. Joseph Waldhaus, a former mayor of Flagstaff, lived here during the 1930s. Used as a fraternity house in the 1970s, the by-then well-worn property was rescued in 1988 by four friends from California, who turned it into a bright, clean bed-and-breakfast. The two couples, Donna and Rodger Pettinger and Sandy and Ed Znetko, take turns running the inn.

A wraparound porch runs the length of their spacious house. Inside, a handsome pool table and stand-up piano sit in a bay-windowed game room. The adjoining light-blue living room, which has a stained-oak floor and brick fireplace, is a great place for lounging.

The guest rooms are upstairs. You can see the San Francisco Peaks from both windows of the corner Wicker Room, decorated in blue and white. The Pella Room, named for a town in Iowa with many residents of Dutch descent, has a delft-blue ceiling, a hand-stitched tulip quilt, Dutch lace curtains, a brochure for an Iowa tulip festival on the bureau, and two pairs of wooden shoes on the floor.

The Southwest Suite, occupying the northeastern corner, has a king-size bed with stucco headboard and large bath with separate tub and shower; it's the only room with carpeting rather than hard-wood floors. Carol's Room, facing out to the pine forest above Thorpe Park, is done in hunter green and beige, with a Shaker pine queen-size bed and matching bureau and end table. The Wagner-Znetko Room, decorated in ivory and emerald green, seems reminiscent of grandma's attic, with an 80-year-old rocking chair, an ancient sewing machine, and black-and-white family photos.

Afternoon refreshments are served in the parlor (lemonade and crackers in summer, hot spiced cider and cookies in winter); a full breakfast is served in either the sunny dining room or on the long veranda. The hosts have rotating breakfast menus, all included in their 95-page bed-and-breakfast cookbook. Popular recipes include baked French toast stuffed with cream-cheese-and-pineapple filling and homemade praline sauce; or spicy ranchero-style potato casserole, made with chilies, cheese, and turkey breakfast sausage.

▦ *7 double rooms with baths, 2 doubles share bath, 1 suite. TV in living room. $55–$109, full breakfast, afternoon refreshments. AE, MC, V. No smoking indoors, no pets, no children under 10.*

Boots and Saddles

2900 Hopi Dr., Sedona 86336, tel. 520/ 282–1944 or 800/201–1944, fax 520/204–2230

This intimate bed-and-breakfast owned by John and Linda Steele is an economical alternative to Sedona's expensive B&Bs. Although rooms are on the smaller side, the rustic mountain feel of this cedar A-frame cabin makes it a healthy choice.

Guest rooms have been individually decorated in the Western tradition. Upstairs, the Bunk House Room was built using Kansas barnwood; rusted-iron wall lamps with Western-style motif cutouts glow over each side of the bed. The downstairs Wrangler Room is filled with furniture made from old corral fencing; horseshoe racks and barbed wire line the bathroom's walls. The small Lariat Room has a queen-size bed and chairs of lodgepole pine and a cathedral window with sweeping views of the Mongollan rim.

Come morning, Southwest enchiladas with blue-corn muffins, cowboy beans, and fruit tacos are among the items that may be laid out in the common room for breakfast. Afterwards, you can relax in the small sitting room, which has a fireplace and board games, or take a hike from the property's edge.

▦ *4 double rooms with baths. TVs, phones, outdoor hot tub. $69–$129, full breakfast, afternoon refreshments. AE, D, MC, V. No smoking, no pets, no children under 6.*

Briar Patch Inn

HC 30, 3190 N. Hwy. 89A, Sedona 86336, tel. 520/282–2342, fax 520/282–2399

Shaded by a canopy of sycamore, juniper, canyon oak, pine, elm, and cottonwood trees, 17 individual log cabins nestle on the floor of Oak Creek Canyon, just north of Sedona. The murmur of the spring-fed creek blends with the rustle of the leaves and chirping of the birds to create a relaxing, peaceful ambience on this wooded, 9-acre property. It isn't hard to believe that the Briar Patch Inn has been called a "healing, magical oasis."

In the early 1880s, this was the site of a goat barn, and there's still a resident goat, along with a friendly sheep and some chickens. The cabins were built during the 1940s to provide a summer getaway from the heat of urban Phoenix; at an elevation of 4,484 feet, this area is always temperate. The place became a bed-and-breakfast in 1983.

June through September, guests enjoy the quiet strains of a violinist and classical guitarist who play by the creek during breakfast. Sunday afternoons bring outdoor chamber music concerts on the lawn. The library is stocked with volumes on Native American culture and the history and geography of the Southwest. Innkeepers JoAnn and Ike Olson also like to schedule small workshops on the creative arts here: Navajo weaving, Native American arts, painting, photography, philosophy, self-healing, and more.

The cabins are rustic cozy, with log walls, beam or plank ceilings, Southwestern furnishings, and private patios or decks. All except the three on the creek—Deck House, Creekside, and Kingfisher—have fireplaces, and a supply of aromatic, shaggy-bark cedar firewood is stacked outside the front door. One of the newest cabins, Eagle, has a Native American theme, featuring a lodgepole-pine bed, table, and chairs; polished clear-pine floors; and an armoire, paneling, and bath done in knotty pine. One windowed wall faces the tree-shaded creek. Blue Jay, the oldest cabin on the property, has the smallest windows.

Iced tea, coffee, and cookies are always available in the main building. In the morning, a heart-healthy buffet breakfast includes home-baked seven-grain bread or muffins, granola, yogurt, fresh eggs, hot apple sauce from local apples, and seasonal juices and fruits. Guests can take a tray to their room, dine at private tables in the main building, or eat at tree-shaded picnic tables overlooking the creek.

🏨 *13 2-person cabins, 4 4-person cabins. Kitchens in 12 cabins, masseuse available. $145–$265, full buffet breakfast. MC, V. No smoking indoors, no pets.*

Canyon Villa Bed & Breakfast Inn

125 Canyon Circle Dr., Sedona 86351, tel. 520/284-1226 or 800/453-1166, fax 520/284-2114

Opened in 1992, Canyon Villa combines the personal comforts of a traditional inn with the amenities of a first-class resort. Innkeepers Chuck and Marion Yadon researched the business for 18 months, visiting B&Bs from New England to California, before distilling their knowledge into this elegant two-story accommodation.

The site at the edge of the Coconino National Forest has uninterrupted views of Sedona's main attractions: the red sandstone cliffs of Castle Rock, Bell Rock, and Courthouse Butte. This is prime property, and staying at Canyon Villa is very much like visiting the mansion of a wealthy Arizona rancher. Guests' spaces include a well-stocked library: a beam-ceiling, skylit modern living room with a glass-enclosed fireplace; and a 32-foot heated swimming pool in the garden. Snacks and beverages are set out each afternoon in the dining room.

A broad stairway covered with thick carpeting leads to the five upstairs guest rooms, all with large windows and glass French doors to capitalize on the breathtaking scenery; the less expensive room on the ground floor has less stunning views. All the rooms are named after the flowering cacti and shrubs found in the Sedona area and have private baths, balconies or patios, wall-to-wall carpeting, individual heating and cooling units, telephones, cable TV, 10-foot ceilings with fans, and eclectic Southwestern decor; the larger ones also have double sinks and fireplaces.

Santa Fe–themed Ocotillo has a wrought-iron four-poster bed and a fireplace. The bed in Manzanita, done in blue, is also a four-poster. The corner Strawberry Cactus Room, with white wicker furniture and a blue carpet, has views from two sides and a bath with a stained-glass window. The Spanish Bayonet is perfect for honeymooners, with its private balcony, fireplace, and bathtub two steps from the king-size bed.

Two long tables, each with eight purple-accented place settings, fill the huge, carpeted dining room, where Marion's catering background is revealed at breakfast time. Marion, Chuck, and hired help (there is a staff of 11) serve a nutritious breakfast of fruit, just-baked bread, and an entrée such as chili-cheese quiche, pumpkin pancakes, or sour cream waffles; a drawback for people traveling alone is that they may be assigned to a seat for the meal.

🏨 *11 double rooms with baths. Whirlpool tubs, robes, and pool towels in rooms. $135–$215, full breakfast, afternoon snacks. MC, V. No smoking, no pets.*

Casa Sedona

55 Hozoni Dr., Sedona 86336, tel. 520/282–2938 or 800/525–3756, fax 520/282–2259

John and Nancy True left Pasadena in 1994 to take over Casa Sedona, a relaxing Southwestern-style B&B with excellent service and first-rate amenities. The owners took two years to visit various inns in the Southwest before settling on this beautiful spot with panoramic views of the red rocks.

Guest rooms all have terry-cloth robes, fireplaces, and outdoor terraces. If you stay in sea-themed Cielo Mar, you can enjoy spectacular sunrises over Cathedral Rock from the room's balcony. Rose-color Panache, with a wrought-iron king-size bed and jetted tub, gets great sunset views. The Sunrise Room has a sleigh bed under a canopy drape and an antique oak secretary against the wall.

In the common room, Colonial-style pieces blend nicely with the Southwestern furniture. Breakfast is served next to the library, which has some interesting Native American artwork; or on the terrace, where there's a porch swing and outdoor hot tub. For the main breakfast course, the hosts alternate between egg dishes (such as *juevos rancheros*), and sweet dishes (oatmeal pancakes with a homemade berry sauce). A fruit plate, homemade granola, and fresh juice are always served.

🏨 *16 double rooms with baths. Phones, refrigerators. $120–$195, full breakfast. MC, V. No smoking anywhere on premises, no pets.*

Cathedral Rock Lodge

61 Los Amigos La., Sedona 86336, tel. 520/282–7608, fax 520/282–4505

This 1948 dark red lodge with stone terraces and landscaped green lawn resembles a rural farmhouse, yet it's on an acre in the stunning red rock country of Sedona, not on a Wisconsin cornfield. Mature trees—elm, Arizona cypress, and cottonwood—a playhouse deck, picnic tables, and barbecue grills make this a perfect place for families to enjoy an Arizona outdoor experience.

The homey living room, furnished in comfortable contemporary style, has a picture window facing Cathedral Rock, a flagstone fireplace, pine paneling, a beamed ceiling, and rather bland carpeting. Guest rooms are country cozy with family antiques, handmade quilts, and bathroom floors made of Douglas fir. The upstairs Amigo Suite has a wonderful 4-foot cactus in the corner, a sitting room furnished in lodgepole pine, a kitchenette, sleeper couch, and private deck. As shadows grow over the valley at sunset, Cathedral Rock lights up in deep red and creates a spectacular sight. There's also a cottage with a full kitchen, an African-themed bedroom, and a fantasy bath with a claw-foot tub. A wooden ladder leads to a sleeping loft.

Innkeeper Carol Shannon rotates six breakfast menus; all include freshly ground coffee, fresh fruit and juice, and homemade bread and jam.

🏨 *2 double rooms with baths, 1 suite, 1 cottage. TV/VCR in living room, nearby stable, homemade jam on departure. $75–$135, full breakfast (Continental breakfast in cottage), evening refreshments. MC, V. No smoking indoors, no pets, 2-night minimum on weekends.*

Coyote Pass Hospitality

Contact Will Tsosie Jr., Box 91-B, Tsaile 86556, tel. 520/724-3383, fax 520/724-3258

You're not likely to encounter a more unusual place to stay than this roving bed-and-breakfast run by the Coyote Pass clan of the Navajo Nation. In northeastern Arizona, where lodging options are limited, this one also gives outsiders the chance to experience Native American hospitality.

It isn't for everyone: Guests sleep on a mattress on the dirt floor of a hogan (cone-shape log-and-earth Navajo dwelling), use an outhouse, and eat a traditional Navajo breakfast—perhaps blue-corn pancakes with Navajo herbal tea—prepared by a member of the clan on a wood-burning stove. But for those who don't mind roughing it a bit, this is a rare chance to be immersed in Navajo culture in beautiful surroundings. The location of the guest lodgings depends on the season, but most of the hogans are near the Canyon de Chelly. Guided hikes, nature programs, and meals are also available; Will Tsosie Jr., the knowledgeable coordinator of the program, is happy to tailor a visit to guests' interests.

🏠 *Hogans accommodate 1–15 people. Guided tours, full meal service available. $85 first person, $10 each additional person, full breakfast. No credit cards. No smoking indoors.*

Cozy Cactus Bed & Breakfast

80 Canyon Circle Dr., Sedona 86351, tel. 520/284-0082 or 800/788-2082, fax 520/284-4210

Set on the edge of the Coconino National Forest, this 1983 ranch-style complex looks directly up at some of Sedona's most scenic red rock formations; from the house it's an easy hike up—about 200 yards—to touch the base of Castle Rock.

The living room of the house is filled with theatrical memorabilia from the Broadway careers of innkeepers Lynne and Bob Gillman. A 1930s grandfather clock here is typical of the family treasures scattered throughout the five cozy guest rooms. Two pairs of rooms each share a sitting room with a fireplace and kitchen. The Wyeth Room has a mahogany four-poster bed and reproductions of Andrew Wyeth paintings; the Nutcracker features an 1890s Swedish high-back mahogany bed and a display case filled with carved Bavarian nutcrackers.

Served in the open country kitchen at a knotty-pine table, breakfast might consist of red raspberry wholewheat buttermilk pancakes, made without sugar, or custard French toast with baked stuffed pears or baked apples in cranberry sauce.

🏠 *5 double rooms with baths. Cable TV in living room. $95–$115, full breakfast, afternoon beverages. AE, D, DC, MC, V. No smoking indoors, no pets.*

The Graham B&B Inn

150 Canyon Circle Dr., Sedona 86351, tel. 520/284-1425 or 800/228-1425, fax 520/284-0767

Carol and Roger Redenbaugh view their bed-and-breakfast as original art—a chance to create a mood by offering their guests uniquely themed rooms and warm, personalized service in an enchanting setting. This may well be Sedona's best inn, and it claims to have the highest annual occupancy of any B&B in the country.

Spacious accommodations in the main inn feature antiques, original artwork, fresh flowers, and thick robes, as well as modern amenities like TVs, VCRs, and video libraries. Every item in the room matches the theme; for example, seashells are sprinkled throughout the soft blue and peach San Francisco Room, where a hot-air balloon floats over the chaise, a cable car and crystal dolphin rest on the California dresser, and a birdhouse, shaped like a lighthouse, sways gently over the private balcony.

Next to the main inn, the Adobe Village houses the Graham's most distinctive suites. The four lavish casitas range in style from elegant to rustic, artsy to adventurous—yet each is intensely romantic. The owners spared no expense in endearing them with full-size Jacuzzis, waterfall showers, two fireplaces each, entertainment centers with VCRs and CD-stereos, and private decks (all have magnificent views of the surrounding red rock landscape). The elegant Sunset Casita, decorated in light clay colors, has floor-to-ceiling windows, a massive fireplace, and some striking Indian sculpture. Its iron bed holds up 9-foot posts that branch out like wild trees. The cowboy-themed Lonesome Dove, with its hardwood floors, red rock fireplace, barnwood cabinetry, and high-poster bed, sends you back to a simpler time. The lone cactus has a country guitar as its only friend, and an old saloon door opens to an immense lantern-lit bathroom that glows over the four-person Jacuzzi. Upon arrival, you'll be greeted by the smell of freshly baked bread and the melancholic songs of Randy Travis.

Breakfast may be savored in the dining room, outside on the deck, or in your casita. Popular entrées include German pancakes, maple bread pudding, and *huevos rancheros*. In the morning, Carol also gives newly arrived guests an orientation on the area. Some of the best assets of this contemporary, two-story inn are outside: a heated pool and spa; a walled, landscaped lawn and garden; and a broad deck for outdoor dining.

🛏 *5 double rooms with baths, 1 suite, 4 casitas. TV/VCR, phones, pool, bicycles, kitchenettes and Jacuzzis in casitas. $109–$187, Sedona Suite $229, casitas $269–$369, full breakfast, afternoon refreshments. D, MC, V. No smoking indoors, no pets, 2-night minimum on weekends.*

The Inn at Four Ten

410 N. Leroux St., Flagstaff 86001, tel. 520/774–0088, or 800/774–2008, fax 520/774–6354

Now a friendly bed-and-breakfast, the Inn at Four Ten was built in 1907 by Tom E. Pollock, a wealthy banker and cattle rancher, as the manor house of his grand estate; its extensive grounds included a stable and separate quarters for the grooms. After Pollock died, the property was split up and some years later, the main building became a fraternity house.

After completing extensive renovations, including the installation of an all-white commercial kitchen, the Inn at Four Ten opened for business in 1991. Howard and Sally Krueger, who bought the inn in 1993, upgraded the rooms, making them some of the most luxurious in Flagstaff. Guests step from a broad front porch to an open living room with polished-oak floors, bookcases, door frames, ceiling beams, and a tile fireplace. South-facing windows in the adjoining dining room let in the soft morning light, while a small courtyard and garden beckon guests to relax outside.

A great deal of detail went into the decoration of the guest rooms. The elegant Tea Room, with hunter green and rose carpeting, has a floor-to-ceiling mahogany bookcase, a wrought-iron kingsize bed, and a 7-foot walnut burl armoire; polished-oak doors lead directly into the living room. Also downstairs, the Southwest Room is Santa Fe style all the way with a Saltillo-tile floor, kiva fireplace, and lodgepole-pine bed imported from New Mexico.

Upstairs, the Conservatory resembles Beethoven's private studio; a bust of the great composer rests on a mahogany secretary, white sheet music doubles for wallpaper, and an antique music stand waits patiently near the fireplace. The two rooms of the Dakota suite are dressed in cowboy decor, with log beds and barn-wood walls.

You can eat breakfast in the sunny dining room or under the gazebo in the garden. Sally's cooking has been praised in a national B&B recipe contest; favorites include fresh fruit with cinnamon and honey followed by stuffed French toast with cream cheese and orange marmalade.

🏨 *9 double rooms with baths. Coffeemakers, mini-refrigerators, kitchenettes in 4 rooms, Jacuzzis in 2 rooms, fireplaces in 7 rooms. $110–$155, full breakfast, afternoon tea and snacks. MC, V. No smoking, no pets.*

The Inn on Oak Creek

556 Hwy. 179, Sedona 86336, tel. 520/282–7896 or 800/499–7896, fax 520/282–0696

One of Sedona's newest and most luxurious B&Bs, the Inn on Oak Creek opened in late 1996. The young energetic owners, Rick Morris and Pam Harrison, left the corporate world behind to create their dream home, and great attention to detail has brought them to their goal.

Of the 11 carefully designed rooms, seven have private decks that face Oak Creek; all have fireplaces, cotton waffle-weave robes, marble bathrooms, and whirlpool tubs. The Rested Rooster Room, dressed in country French fabrics, has roosters everywhere: on the pillow shams and on the mantle top, posing in wall paintings and hopping along the wallpaper. An adjoining "Hen House" with a trundle bed can be added to make it a suite. Likewise, the Golf on the Rocks Room, decorated with Scottish plaid, attaches to the Pro Shop—it's a golfer's dream suite. The Hollywood Out West Room commemorates the 43 Westerns filmed in Sedona with items such as original playbills, a star-patterned antique reproduction quilt, a Winchester ammunition box and lariat, and John Wayne and Maureen O'Hara director's

chairs. The inn's most romantic room must be the Rose Arbor Room, with soft floral prints and panoramic views of Sedona's red mountains.

Rick and Pam serve gourmet breakfasts in the dining room, which has pine tables and fresh flowers; or, in summer, you can eat on the outdoor deck. Professionals bake the pastries and main dishes—like French toast with a fresh berry sauce, kiwis, and bacon—leaving the owners free to chat with guests. Come evening, tasty hors d'oeuvres are set out in the intimate sitting room with a red rock fireplace. You can wander the parklike grounds that extend to a creek, which flows from springs in the canyon. Here you can fish or wade by the water's edge. You might also select a film from the video library before retiring for a peaceful Arizona night.

🏨 *11 double rooms with baths, TVs, VCRs, phones. Trout fishing with permit. $140–$215, full breakfast. AE, D, MC, V. No smoking, no pets, 2-night minimum on weekends.*

Jeanette's Bed-and-Breakfast

3380 E. Lockett Rd., Flagstaff 86004, tel. 520/527–1912 or 800/752–1912

Jeanette's bed-and-breakfast, built in 1996, re-creates the elegance of a Victorian mansion with modern-day amenities. The house is filled with Jeanette's many acquired objects, including the sitting room's fireplace, a 1912 red Divan couch, a 1935 stand-up radio, and white lace curtains. A collection of ancient-looking irons and typewriters lie at the top of the stairs. Jeanette, who never wavers in her Victorian character, will happily recount stories of all her collectibles, and which great aunt or grandmother might have handled them over the years.

In fact, all rooms have been named after family members, and black-and-white family photos adorn many dresser tops.

Mamie's Room, furnished with two walnut beds pushed together to make a king, has a beautiful English mahogany armoire. The bathroom has a pedestal sink and a 1914 claw-foot tub. Toiletries in all bathrooms include a bar of Jeanette's glycerine soap, made in house. In Emelia's Room, an old traveling trunk rests at the base of a queen-size bed and an oak settee with beautiful inlaid carvings sits against the wall. There's a fireplace as well, and a burgundy-colored bathroom with a stunning ceramic sink, oak washstand, and claw-foot tub. Aunt Stella's Room, which has a great view of Eldon mountain (part of the San Francisco peaks), is dressed in hues of pale green. There's a four-poster queen-size bed with a chenille spread; a separate sitting room has a fainting couch.

Breakfast is served in the dining room at a six-person table. Jeanette makes everything from scratch, including eggs Benedict with whipped yams and four-mushroom stuffed plum tomatoes.

If she's not already in a Victorian costume, ask Jeanette about her vintage clothing collection. You may also want to inquire about her seminars, which cover subjects such as dolls or French cooking. Additionally, if you're looking for an extra romantic atmosphere, let Jeanette know in advance and she'll help arrange some extra touches—perhaps chocolate-dipped strawberries will be in order!

▥ *4 double rooms with baths. $65–$85, full breakfast, afternoon refreshments. MC, V. No smoking indoors, no pets.*

Lantern Light Inn Bed & Breakfast

3085 W. Hwy. 89A, Sedona 86336, tel. 520/282–3419

This European-flavored inn in Sedona, formerly part of a residential complex built in 1970, marked time for a while as a music museum. A new section was added before the place opened as a B&B in 1990.

The inn lies on one of Sedona's two main roads, but privacy is preserved by a cul-de-sac driveway fronted by a landscaped dirt mound. Wrought-iron gates lead into a plant-filled breezeway, and etched-glass doors open into the subdued living room overlaid with bookcases and rich Oriental rugs. The hospitable innkeepers Ed and Kris Varjean serve breakfast—perhaps Belgian waffles or eggs Benedict—on a large table in the adjacent dining room.

The country French–style Red and Blue rooms face south to a fenced, tree-shaded garden; they share a deck facing the courtyard. Across the breezeway is the spacious Ryan Room, with Oriental rugs, a king-size bed and sofa bed, tiled kitchenette, and sitting area.

▥ *2 double rooms with baths, 1 triple with bath. TV, refrigerator in 2 rooms, Shiatsu massage. $90–$125, full breakfast. No credit cards. No smoking indoors, no pets.*

The Lodge at Sedona

125 Kallof Pl., Sedona 86336, tel. 520/204–1942 or 800/619–4467, fax 520/204–2128

Barb and Mark Dinunzio were on a hiking trip from Phoenix when they found this gracious Sedona home in 1991. Its rustic charm convinced them to try running a B&B. They were able to purchase the two-story mountain ranch–style lodge in 1993 and spent six months converting it into a European-style country inn and landscaping its 2½ acres of lawns and pine trees.

Beamed ceilings, red rock, and wall-to-wall oatmeal carpets lend an organic feel to the common rooms, which include a sitting room, a game room and library, and a fireside room with wing chairs. Guest rooms each have distinctive motifs, from Italian to Western, Renaissance to Southern. The Master Suite has its own private entrance, a large stone fireplace, brick archways, and a king-size bed. Beamed ceilings and a vintage claw-foot tub add to the charm of the Renaissance Room, which has a four-person Jacuzzi on an outdoor private deck.

A gourmet breakfast, prepared by a chef from Maryland's *L'Academie de Cuisine*, is served in a sunlit dining room, which has long window-walls overlooking the backyard and the red rocks in the distance. The menu might include mixed fresh fruits with a brown sugar cream, cranberry scones, quiche Lorraine, pumpkin muffins, or poached eggs with spinach and bacon.

▦ *10 double rooms with baths, 3 suites. Jacuzzi in 6 rooms, fireplace in 3 rooms, TV in parlor, library, spa, concierge services. $120–$225, full breakfast, evening hors d'oeuvres. MC, V. No smoking indoors, no pets.*

Saddle Rock Ranch

255 Rock Ridge Dr., Sedona 86336, tel. 520/282–7640, fax 520/282–6829

On a hill overlooking the valley, Saddle Rock commands a spectacular, 17-mile panoramic view of Sedona and the surrounding mountains. Built as the base for a 6,000-acre horse ranch, the house opened as a B&B in 1988. Its original rugged red sandstone and adobe brick exterior echo the Old West, as do its beamed ceilings, polished flagstone floors, and superb Western art collection. Many Westerns have been filmed from this location, including *Angel and the Bad Man* (1937) with John Wayne and *Broken Arrow* (1947) with Jimmy Stewart.

Innkeepers Fran and Dan Bruno were once executives with Ritz Carlton hotels, and their expertise shows. For example, they furnished the Saddle Rock Suite with a white stone fireplace and an English-style, white birch canopy bed.

The wood-paneled Honeymoon Cottage, once the ranch's bunkhouse, has flagstone floors, a massive lodgepole pine four-poster bed covered with an antique white quilt, a claw-foot tub, and a pedestal sink.

The tasty dishes that are freshly baked for breakfast may be relished out by the pool or in the sunny, rock-walled breakfast room. Morning birdseed scattered outside the window attracts a covey of bold and hungry quail. The hosts will help plan day trips—they'll even lend you coolers to take along.

▦ *3 double rooms with bath. Terry robes and pool towels, concierge service, pool and spa. $125–$150, full breakfast, afternoon snacks and beverage. No smoking, no pets, no children under 14, 2-night minimum stay, 3-night minimum during spring and fall.*

Territorial House

65 Piki Dr., Sedona 86336, tel. 520/204–2737 or 800/801–2737, fax 520/204–2230

Owners John and Linda Steele have created a friendly atmosphere here, which makes this inviting ranch house particularly popular with families. Hiking, biking, and bird-watching in Sedona's red rock mountains are only steps away. If you'd rather just hang out, you can relax by the stone fireplace in the sitting room and watch an old Western, or enjoy the crisp mountain air out on the veranda. A dip in the hot tub also provides a pleasant respite. Guest accommodations have private baths and king- or queen-size beds, and each hides an angel somewhere in the room–to ensure a heavenly stay, of course.

The romantic Red Rock Crossing Room has a four-poster canopy bed and a Precious Moments figurine collection in a display case. There's also a jetted bath and a private deck. Upstairs, Native American pictures decorate the walls of the intimate Indian Garden Room, which has a sloping ceiling and a private balcony. Two separate sleeping rooms make up Schnelby Station, which has a shared bath and fireplace. One of the rooms has a king-size bed under a barn-wood headboard, antique dressers, highback wicker chairs, and fireplace; the other houses a queen and twin bed with sage-green and red-bandanna pillows, a card table next to a knotted pine wall, and a kid's closet hidden by outhouse doors. These two rooms can be rented separately or together.

Breakfast is shared around the dining room's harvest table or outside on the veranda. A house specialty is the "six-shooter": a potato and egg casserole served with homemade bread or cranberry poached pears. In the afternoon, snacks are set out, including Linda's homemade gingerbread.

▥ *4 double rooms with baths, 3 with TV/VCR. Hot tub, bicycles, TV/VCR in living room. $109–$159, full breakfast, afternoon snacks. AE, D, MC, V. No smoking indoors, no pets, 2-night minimum on weekends.*

Central Arizona

Maricopa Manor B&B

Including Phoenix, Prescott, and the White Mountains

Great desert meets great mountain range in central Arizona, providing a stunning variety of natural environments within easy touring distance. The region also combines some of the oldest dwellings in the western hemisphere with the homes of contemporary Native American tribes and America's newest, fastest-growing major urban center, metropolitan Phoenix.

In the middle of central Arizona, at the northern tip of the Sonoran Desert and ringed by mountain ranges, lies the 1,000-square-mile Valley of the Sun, so dubbed because of its 330-plus days of sunshine a year. The valley, formed by the Salt River, was farmed by the Hohokam Indians from 300 BC, but abandoned around AD 1450. It was not widely inhabited again until 1867, when a U.S. Army officer decided to reopen the canals the Hohokam had built in order to help feed the men and horses stationed at nearby Fort McDowell. The 300 people who settled here were prescient in naming their new town, which they predicted would rise "like a phoenix" from the ashes of a vanished civilization.

East of Phoenix loom the barren peaks of the Superstition Mountains, so called for their eerie habit of seeming just a few miles away and luring unwary prospectors to a dusty death. Beyond them, the White Mountains, with altitudes of 7,000 to 8,000 feet and Ponderosa pine forests, provide a cool retreat in summer and skiing on an Apache-owned resort in winter.

To the north of Phoenix, behind the dusty Hieroglyphic Mountains (misnamed for Hohokam petroglyphs found here), rises the gigantic Mogollon Rim, an escarpment almost as wide as Arizona; it got its name for posing an overwhelming mogollón (obstruction) to Spanish-speaking explorers probing northward. Here the slopes are green with pine trees, and the alpine meadows lush with grasses and aspens. After gold was found in the area in the early 1860s, President Lincoln sent the Arizona Territory's first governor to found the capital at Prescott and secure mineral riches for the union.

A number of the stately Victorian homes from Prescott's Territorial days have been carefully restored and turned into bed-and-breakfasts, and the White Mountain towns are scattered with rustic lodges and inns. Phoenix has not widely awakened to the B&B phenomenon, though a few choice lodgings are found here. Scottsdale has more than a dozen B&Bs and private home-stay accommodations, but zoning regulations prevent them from being "visible" to the public: no advertising, no phone-book listings, no signs out front. They can, however, be found through the reservation services listed below.

Places to Go, Sights to See

Arcosanti (35 mi southeast of Prescott, off I–17, tel. 520/632–7135). For a glimpse of the future, tour architect Paolo Soleri's visionary city, a prototype combination of architecture and ecology ("arcology") designed to one day house 7,000 people. Visitors are also welcome to the *Cosanti Foundation* (6433 Doubletree Ranch

Rd., Scottsdale, tel. 602/948–6145), which operates Soleri's studio and the gallery where his famous wind-bells are cast and sold.

Arivaipa Canyon Wilderness. Eleven miles south of Winkelman on Rte. 77, an unpaved road heads east 8 miles to this designated "primitive area." The 4,044-acre wilderness includes a wild stretch of Arivaipa Creek and 6,145-foot Holy Joe Peak.

Besh-Ba-Gowah Archeological Park. An unusual stone-and-mud building with 300 rooms is the centerpiece of this ruined 14th-century village at the southern edge of Globe. A small museum explains the history of this site, occupied by the Salado Indians from 1225 to 1400. Contact the Globe-Miami Chamber of Commerce (*see* Tourist Information, *below*) for details.

Boyce Thompson Southwestern Arboretum (Hwy. 60/70, between Florence Junction and Superior, tel. 520/689–2811). Founded in the early 1920s along the riparian habitat of Queen Creek, this desert garden now has 35 acres of unusual cacti, succulents, and water-efficient trees. The visitor center is on the National Register of Historic Sites.

Casa Malpais National Historic Landmark (2 mi northwest of Springerville). The Mogollon mountain tribe occupied this rocky site ("House of the Badlands") for some 200 years, abandoning it around 1400. In 1883, archaeologists discovered that volcanic caves here contained Indian burial places. The caves, or fissures—controversially described as "catacombs"—are sacred to Hopi and Zuni tribes and thus off-limits to visitors, but the public can observe the excavation of the 15-acre site, which includes a masonry pueblo, a steep basalt staircase, and a Great Kiva made of volcanic rock. Stop in first at the *Casa Malpais Museum* (318 Main St., tel. 520/333–5375) in Springerville for information.

Downtown Phoenix. At the renovated east end of downtown Phoenix, from 6th and 7th streets between Monroe and Adams, *Heritage Square* is a block of turn-of-the-century houses in a parklike setting; the queen is the Rosson House (6th and Monroe Sts., tel. 602/262–5029), an 1895 gingerbread Victorian in the Eastlake style. The *Phoenix Museum of History* (105 N. 5th St., tel. 602/253–2734) offers a healthy dose of regional history from the 1860s (when Anglo settlement began) through the 1930s. The *Arizona Science Center* (600 E. Washington St., tel. 602/716–2000) has lively "please touch" exhibits as well as a planetarium and a 50-foot-high projection screen.

Fort Apache Cultural Center. Just outside the town of Whiteriver, on the Fort Apache Indian Reservation, are the remains of the U.S. military post established in 1870 to keep peace between settlers and tribes in the area. A museum housed in the three-room cabin of General George Crook provides a look back at U.S. Cavalry and Apache tribal history. For information, call the Tribal Offices in Whiteriver, tel. 520/338–4346.

Globe. In the southern reaches of Tonto National Forest and dotted with majestic cypress trees, Globe is the most cosmopolitan of the old mining towns east of Phoenix. It's a good area for antique shopping, and quilting is a local cottage industry. The Gila County Courthouse, built in 1888, now houses the *Cobre Valley Center for the Arts* (tel. 520/425–0884), an art gallery, crafts shop, and performing arts theater. Contact the Globe-Miami Chamber of Commerce (*see* Tourist Information, *below*) for pamphlets detailing a self-guided *walking tour of the historic downtown area*, and a *drive-yourself mine tour*, including six mine sites in the area dating from 1910 to the present.

Heard Museum (22 E. Monte Vista Rd., Phoenix, tel. 602/252–8848). The collection of primitive and modern Native American art in the Spanish Colonial–style adobe Heard mansion is probably the most extensive in the nation. Live demonstrations of Native American art forms are presented daily.

Jerome. When the copper mines closed in 1953, the community on the steep side of Mingus Mountain once known as the Billion Dollar Copper Camp saw its population drop from 15,000 to 50. But hippies discovered the ghost town during the 1960s and it is gradually reviving as an artists' colony. Set at 5,000 feet, the town has views 50 miles across the Verde Valley. *Jerome State Historic Park* (Douglas Rd., tel. 520/634–5381), occupying the mansion of James "Rawhide Jimmy" Douglas Jr., Jerome's mining king, displays artifacts from the town's mining heyday.

Montezuma Castle National Monument (east of I–17, between Camp Verde and McGuireville, tel. 520/567–3322). Archaeologists estimate that this five-story Indian cliff dwelling, set high into a sheer, limestone cliff face, is more than 700 years old. A visitor center provides information on the valley's natural and human history.

Prescott. Much of the 19th-century history of this former capital of Arizona Territory has been preserved, with more than 400 buildings listed on the National Register of Historic Places. Numerous Queen Anne–style homes dot the neighborhoods around the imposing 1916 courthouse. Among the town's other sights are the old taverns on Montezuma Street's *Whiskey Row*, the *antiques shops* along Cortez Street, and the *Sharlot Hall Museum* (415 W. Gurley St., tel. 520/445–3122), 3 acres of historical displays in a series of buildings including the 1864 Governor's Mansion. Three smaller galleries are also worth exploring: the *Bead Museum* (140 S. Montezuma, tel. 520/445–2431), the *Phippen Museum of Western Art* (4701 Hwy. 89 N., tel. 520/778–1385), and the *Smoki Museum* (147 N. Arizona St., tel. 520/445–1230), which focuses on Native American artifacts and crafts.

Scottsdale is shopper's heaven, its downtown filled with nationally known art galleries and lots of fashionable boutiques. *Old Scottsdale* has become touristy, but its rustic storefronts and wooden sidewalks give visitors a taste of life here 80 years ago. The art galleries and antiques shops are concentrated on *Main Street*, and the 40-year-old stretch of *Fifth Avenue* is the place to find everything from cacti to handmade Indian jewelry.

Sunrise Park Resort (off AZ 260 on AZ 273 between Springerville and Pinetop/Lakeside, Greer 85927, tel. 800/554–6835), the state's largest ski area, has five day lodges, 11 lifts, and 65 trails on three mountains rising to 11,000 feet.

Owned and operated by the White Mountain Apache Tribe, the resort is one of the most successful Native American business enterprises in the United States.

Taliesin West (12621 Frank Lloyd Wright Blvd., Scottsdale 85261, tel. 602/860–8810 or 602/860–2700). Frank Lloyd Wright's winter home, studio, and school in the desert, Taliesin is also one of the master architect's prototypes for "the natural house." Tours of this National Historic Landmark and its grounds are available daily.

Tonto National Monument (50 mi north of Payson, on Hwy. 87, tel. 520/467–2241). Northwest of Globe-Miami, just south of Theodore Roosevelt Lake, two important 14th-century cliff dwellings have been preserved. The 1,120-acre monument and visitor center reveal what life was like here in the rugged desert for the Salado Indians more than 600 years ago.

Tuzigoot National Monument (Camp Verde, tel. 520/634–5564). On the crest of a hill overlooking the Verde River, in the valley below the old mining town of Jerome, is the stone ruin of an Indian fortress. Its 100 rooms were constructed during the 13th century by the Sinagua Indians. A museum exhibits artifacts of the period.

Verde River Canyon Excursion Train (300 N. Broadway, Clarkdale 86324, tel. 800/293–7245). Starting from Clarkdale, in the valley below Jerome, the Verde Canyon Railroad runs north along the Verde River 22 miles to Perkinsville. The four-hour excursion uses old mining company tracks that once linked Jerome with Prescott and offers a leisurely, scenic round-trip. Sights along the way include eagles, Sinagua Indian ruins, old mining camps, red rock cliffs, and wildflowers.

White Mountains Trailsystem. A partnership project of the U.S. Forest Service, Arizona Game and Fish Department, Navajo County, the city of Show Low, the town of Pinetop-Lakeside, the White Mountain Horsemen's Association, and the Audubon Society of the White Mountains, the system is composed of some 180 miles of multiuse—equestrian, hiking, and mountain bike—loop trails along the Mogollon Rim. For a detailed map, send $3.95 to Chilton-Larson Publishing, Inc., Box 34, Pinetop 85935.

Restaurants

For travelers with deep pockets and a taste for fine dining, there are a number of innovative, upscale establishments in Phoenix. Vincent Geurithault is one of the handful of originators of Southwestern cuisine, and **Vincent's on Camelback** (tel. 602/224–0225) is the place to experience his art. Another leader of Southwestern cuisine, chef Mark Ching, presides at the **Compass Room** (tel. 602/440–3166), Arizona's only rotating dining room, at the top of downtown's Hyatt Regency Hotel. Seven casual **Garcia's restaurants** (tel. 602/272–5584 in Phoenix; call for other locations), spread across the valley from Glendale to Chandler, serve good Arizonan versions of Mexican dishes. Inexpensive restaurants in the area include **Chianti** (tel. 602/957–9840), serving reliable Italian standards in a crowded but efficient poster-hung room.

Prescott has the only other concentration of decent restaurants in central Arizona, many within walking distance of the central Court House Square. For romantic and delicious Continental dining, try the lovely deco **Peacock Room** (122 E. Gurley St., tel. 520/778–9434) in the Hassayampa Inn. The classy fern-and-brass **Murphy's** (tel. 520/445–4044) has an award-winning kitchen that turns out prime rib and pasta and a dozen seafood dishes. The eclectic menu at the **Prescott Brewing Company** (130 W. Gurley St., tel. 520/771–2795) includes healthy and flavorful dishes along with great handcrafted beers.

In a former bordello in tiny Jerome, the **House of Joy** (tel. 520/634–5339) attracts patrons from all over the region, perhaps as much for its legendary setting as for its classic Continental cuisine. Reserve far in advance: It's open only for dinner on Saturdays and Sundays.

Tourist Information

Arizona Office of Tourism (1100 W. Washington St., Phoenix 85007, tel. 602/542–8687 and 800/842–8257, fax 602/542–4068). **Globe-Miami Chamber of Commerce** (Box 2539, Globe 85502, tel. 520/425–4495 or 800/804–5623). **Jerome Chamber of Commerce** (Box K, Jerome 86331, tel. 520/634–2900). **Phoenix & Valley of the Sun Convention & Visitors Bureau** (One Arizona Center, 400 E. Van Buren St., Suite 600, Phoenix 85004, tel. 602/254–6500, fax 602/253–4415). **Pinetop-Lakeside Chamber of Commerce** (Box 266, Pinetop 85935, tel. 520/367–4290). **Prescott Chamber of Commerce** (117 W. Goodwin St., Box 1147, Prescott 86302, tel. 520/445–2000 or 800/266–7534). **Scottsdale Chamber of Commerce** (734 Scottsdale Mall, Scottsdale 85251, tel. 602/945–8481 or 800/877–1117). **Show Low Chamber of Commerce** (Box 1083, Show Low 85901, tel. 520/537–2326). **Springerville-Eager Chamber of Commerce** (Box 31, Springerville 85938, tel. 520/333–2123). **White Mountain Apache Tribal Headquarters** (Box 700, Whiteriver 85941, tel. 520/338–4346).

Reservation Services

Arizona Association of Bed & Breakfast Inns (Box 7186, Phoenix 85011, tel. 800/284–2589). **Arizona Trails Bed and Breakfast Reservation Service** (Box 18998, Fountain Hills 85269, tel. 602/837–4284 or 888/799–4284, fax 602/816–4224). **Mi Casa Su Casa B&B Reservation Service** (Box 950, Tempe 85280, tel. 602/990–0682, 800/456–0682 reservations only, fax 602/990–3390).

Bartram's White Mountain Bed & Breakfast

Rte. 1, Box 1014, Lakeside 85929, tel. 520/ 367–1408 or 800/257–0211

A road leading out of Lakeside dead-ends at the edge of an Apache Indian reservation. Turn right and you're in the driveway of a gray 1940s-era ranch house, where you'll be greeted by two resident collies, two potbellied pigs, a number of cats, a parrot, and chickens cackling contentedly in the back coop. Innkeepers Petie and Ray Bartram opened this country-comfortable inn in 1987; the house has a fresh, new feeling thanks to their expert use of cheerful colors and fabrics.

Every room has a private entrance. The Blue Room has a queen-size bed with white wood-paneled walls, a lace-covered vanity, and a private patio. In the Peach Suite, double doors close off a separate children's room with two daybeds. The Jenny Lind Room is furnished with some antique pieces and Tiffany-style lamps. Plants and flowers fill every nook and cranny of the Garden Room, which has a beautiful green canopy bed.

Petie is justifiably proud of her seven-course breakfasts; among her entrées are cinnamon toast stuffed with cream cheese, asparagus quiche, and smoked turkey eggs in puff pastry.

▥ *4 double rooms with baths, 1 suite. TV, VCR in living room. $85, full breakfast. No credit cards. No smoking indoors, no pets.*

The Coldstream Bed & Breakfast

Box 2988, Pinetop 85935, tel. 520/369– 0115

You'd never suspect that this handsome two-story home was actually built 7 miles away in the 1920s. It was the res-idence of a lumber mill owner in nearby McNary and then the official company guest house before it was upped and moved to this wooded site near the Pinetop Country Club in 1980.

Innkeepers Cindy and Jeff Northrup and manager Nicole Edington took three years, 1994 to 1997, to completely remodel the inn. The decor comfortably blends "north woods country" design with modern amenities. A fireplace warms the spacious, carpeted living-dining area and the billiard table is pleasantly diverting. Guest rooms are named after 19th-century White Mountain lumber camps. The McNary and Cooley suites, with pine-paneled walls and polished wood floors, are upstairs.

Breakfast is served in the dining room or in a sunny nook between the kitchen and the flagstone patio. A popular entrée is crepes Romeo and Juliet with cream cheese and strawberries.

▥ *3 double rooms with baths (1 across hall), 2 suites. Terry robes, TV with VCR, pool table, bicycles, enclosed outdoor spa, horse boarding. $95–$135, full breakfast, 4 PM social tea. MC, V. No smoking indoors, no pets, no children under 11.*

The Cottages at Prescott Country Inn

503 S. Montezuma St. (U.S. Hwy. 89), Prescott 86303, tel. 520/445–7991, fax 520/717–1215

With an artful application of paint, white lattices, trees, and flowers, what was once a sterile 1940s motor court with 12 cottages has been converted into an inviting complex of one-, two-, three-, and four-room suites. The apartment-like rooms are furnished in an eclectic country style, with hand-quilted gingham comforters, fresh flowers and potted plants, nostalgic prints, and lots of knickknacks. A private spa-solarium surrounded by poinsettias and ferns has been added and can be used by appointment. Continental breakfast, delivered to your room in a country basket in the evening, includes juice, breads, rolls, and muffins. All rooms have coffeemakers. A nice touch: when you get up in the morning, you'll find your windshield has been washed.

Owners Morris and Sue Faulkner also rent out their former residence—the Prescott Lakes Suites. This house stands alone on a hill overlooking Granite Dells. The entire upstairs, with a living room, full kitchen, and master bedroom, is rented as the "Master Suite", while the downstairs, with two bedrooms, a den, and a kitchen, is rented as the "King Suite." Guests are on their own for food in this spacious, quiet house.

🏨 *2 1-room units, 7 2-room units, 2 3-room units, 1 4-room unit. TV, phone, refrigerator, private entrance in rooms, off-street parking, outdoor barbecue. $89–$129, Continental breakfast, complimentary lunch or dinner at a Prescott restaurant. Prescott Lakes Suites: Master Suite $179; King Suite $149. D, MC, V. No smoking, no pets.*

Greer Lodge

Box 244, Greer 85927, tel. 520/735-7216, fax 520/735-7720

An alpine lodge that could have come straight from the drafting board of a Hollywood set designer, this 1948 building in the White Mountains is made entirely of polished logs, exposed inside and out. The spacious lobby is replete with deer antlers, a black bearskin, wagon-wheel chandeliers, lodgepole-pine furniture, and plank floors. A stone fireplace crackles with juniper logs.

The backdrop—pine-studded Greer Valley, at an elevation of 8,500 feet, with deer and elk grazing in the meadows—is equally picture perfect. The Little Colorado River, stocked with trout and dammed here and there by beaver colonies, meanders through the grounds.

The rooms pick up the rustic theme, with knotty pine or polished log walls, oak or pine plank floors, and cheerful chintz curtains and bedspreads; each has a private bath and individual electric heat controls. First choice are the corner rooms, such as Nos. 2, 4, and 5, which have views of both the valley and the wooded mountains. On the third floor, under the peaked roof, is a romantic pine-paneled room with a clear view to the south. In addition to the accommodations in the lodge, there are similarly furnished rooms in the Little Lodge, a four-bedroom log cabin with a kitchen and a deck overlooking the river; and rooms in a variety of smaller cabins, some with kitchens and fireplaces.

Breakfast, lunch, and dinner are served in the skylit solar-heated dining room, open to the public. It's surrounded by glass, and every table overlooks the creek, three ponds, an expansive lawn populated with ducks, and the wooded hills beyond. Breakfast possibilities include Belgian waffles with strawberries, biscuits and gravy, and blueberry pancakes. At lunchtime, salads, burgers, and hot and cold sandwiches are available.

No license is required to fish in the Lodge's two fishing ponds, but there is a fee. If you catch something in the larger fly-fishing pond, you have to throw it back, but you can keep whatever bites in the smaller bait-fishing pond.

🏨 *7 double rooms with baths, 2 suites in Lodge, 2 1-bedroom cabins, 5 2-bedroom cabins, 1 4-bedroom cabin. Fruit basket upon arrival, cable TV in lounge, bar, restaurant, fly-fishing classes Apr.–Oct. Lodge $120, Little Lodge $35 per person (8-person minimum), cabins $75–$110, full breakfast option. AE, D, MC, V. No pets, 2-night minimum on weekends, 3-night minimum on holidays.*

Hassayampa Inn

122 Gurley St., Prescott 86301, tel. 520/ 778–9434 or 800/322–1927, fax 520/445– 8590

Prescott is rightfully proud of this exacting restoration of its downtown 1927 Spanish Colonial Revival hotel. Named for the nearby river where prospectors discovered gold in 1863, the three-story Hassayampa Inn has preserved its unique Western Roaring Twenties atmosphere.

The lobby is rich in glazed tile. The massive, faux-beamed ceiling is ornately hand-painted, and plush tapestry chairs and couches complement the antique grand piano and giant golden radiators set against the walls. Delicate bamboo sprouts from 3-foot-high ceramic pots and classical music plays softly.

The rooms are furnished with original or period pieces and have wall-to-wall carpeting, brass bedside lamps, and lace curtains. Included in the room rate are a complimentary cocktail in the cozy bar and lounge and a full breakfast—whatever you like from the menu of the elegant Peacock Room, Prescott's finest restaurant.

🏨 *58 rooms with baths, 10 suites. TV, phones in rooms, restaurant, lounge, bar. $99–$129 rooms, $135–$175 suites, full breakfast, afternoon cocktail. AE, D, DC, MC, V. No pets.*

Hillside Hideaway Bed and Breakfast

621 Hillside La. (HC 66 Box 2695), Pinetop 85935, tel. 520/367–0212

This romantic escape in Pinetop's residential community has but two guest rooms and a spacious lodge-style living room. Cokie Lukavsky has furnished her home with many loving touches, including a lighted pinecone wreath that hangs over the grand stone fireplace, a

wrought-iron chandelier extending from the open-beam pine ceiling, and a teapot collection sitting on the shelves.

The Enchanted Woods Room, colored in forest green and white, has a four-poster ponderosa pine bed and furnishings carved in bark. The Sunshine Garden Room, adorned with pale yellow prints and white wicker furniture, can accommodate up to four people with its queen and sofa beds. Cokie always places fresh flowers in both rooms.

Cokie admits she's not the best cook, but she sets a cute table and ensures that fresh fruits and juices, as well as a meat or egg dish, is on the menu. The dining room has a nice view of the back yard's pine trees, fishpond, and porch swing.

🏨 *2 double rooms with baths. TVs, phones, refrigerators, TV/VCR in living room, library in loft. $85–$95, full breakfast, evening snacks. No credit cards. No smoking indoors, no pets, no children under 12.*

Juniper Well Ranch

Box 11083, Prescott 86304, tel. 520/442– 3415

This 50-acre horse ranch is set in a peaceful valley in the midst of Prescott National Forest, 25 minutes north of Prescott. At night, not a light can be seen in surrounding hills, which are home to some 1,000-year-old alligator-bark junipers. A distant rock outcropping hides a fort built more than 800 years ago by the Prescott Indians.

Two cozy, 22 × 24-foot lodgepole-pine cabins sit on the property. Each has a covered porch, exposed log walls, wall-to-wall carpeting, full kitchen, bath with ceramic tile tub, and a woodstove with a supply of aromatic juniper firewood. One cabin, with a Western flavor, has a loft with a double bed reached by a ladder, a queen-size bed, and some English oak antiques. The other is decorated in a more romantic style with lace curtains and floral patterns. In 1994 the original ranch house was opened up to guests. Done in Western motifs, with a 6-foot-high wood-burning stove, it can comfortably accommodate 10. You may even see one of the occasional animals that comes to visit the front porch.

🏠 *2 cabins, 1 2-bedroom ranch house. Hot tub, barbecue pits. Cabins: $105, full breakfast. Ranch house: $100 for 4 people, $10 per additional person, breakfast not included. AE, D, MC, V. No smoking indoors, small pets permitted.*

Log Cabin Bed-and-Breakfast

3155 N. Hwy. 89, Prescott 86301, tel. and fax 520/778–0442 or 888/778–0442

The country-themed Log Cabin, which is in the Granite Dells area near Prescott, opened in May 1996 after the property's many rocks were dynamited out of existence. The rustic cabin is surrounded by miles of desert hills and lonely red rock, while peeled pine logs shelter the guests inside.

Old mining cars and wagon wheels greet you in the driveway, and once inside the living area, you'll find a stone fireplace, stand-up piano, and room to kick off yer' shoes. Hosts Valerie Ewalt and Lorna Mildbrand serve a full breakfast in the adjacent dining room, which has two round tables with ruffled cloths.

The cabin has four rooms. The Cozy Fireside, with its slanted skylit roof, has a sleigh bed covered with a down-filled comforter, a gas log fireplace, and an original claw-foot tub. The Bird's Nest Room, decorated in hues of navy and burgundy, has a queen-size brass bed and bent willow furniture; in contrast, Granny's Attic is decorated with white wicker furniture. Sweet Solitude has a rod-iron canopy bed and a day bed with a trundle.

🏠 *4 double rooms with baths. TV/VCR in common room, hot tub. $85–$105, full*

breakfast. MC, V. No smoking, 5-day advance-reservation required.

Lynx Creek Farm

Box 4301, Prescott 86302, tel. 520/778–9573

There are more than 200 fruit trees, including seven varieties of apple, at this 25-acre property on a hilltop east of Prescott. The farm overlooks Lonesome Valley and the Blue Hills; in addition, there's a menagerie of chickens, pigs, parrots, goats, cats, and dogs on the property. At the bottom of the hill, Lynx Creek meanders through a shady grove of tall cottonwood trees. This idyllic setting is equally suited to honeymooners and families, offering privacy as well as plenty of space and activities for restless children.

Built in the early 1980s, the farm was bought by Greg and Wendy Temple in 1985 and turned into a bed-and-breakfast. Across the driveway from the main house, where Greg and Wendy live, is a guest house with two rooms; each has a wood-burning stove and there's a shared hot tub on the viewside deck. The cozy pine-paneled Sharlot Hall Room, named for a Prescott pioneer woman, is filled with antiques, books, and memorabilia. One of the room's two king-size beds is set in a low-ceiling loft reached by ladder—an ideal space to stow the kids. The White Wicker Room next door is light, lacy, and romantic, with wicker furniture and a queen-size bed with a striking gauze canopy.

In 1992 Greg added a handsome log cabin with four inviting rooms. All have wall-to-wall Berber carpets, king-size beds, and private hot tubs on outdoor decks with valley views. The Old West–style Chaparral Room is decorated with beat-up saddles, antlers, and a hand-stitched quilt, while the more romantic Country Garden Room features lots of plants and whitewashed log-beam ceilings. A living room with a kitchenette can be connected to any of the rooms to create a two-room suite; two daybed couches open up into four single beds for extra family members.

Mornings bring guests to the breakfast room of the main house, decorated with blue ribbons that the Temples were awarded for their apples, or to the wide deck overlooking the creek below. Large breakfasts usually feature organically homegrown fruits, quiches made with fresh eggs, homemade yogurt, fresh-baked muffins, breads, and coffee cakes. On request, a Continental breakfast-in-a-basket will be delivered to your door.

🏠 *4 double rooms with baths, 2 suites. Terry robes and coffeemakers in rooms, playground, basketball, volleyball, horseshoes, hiking. $75–$145, full breakfast, afternoon refreshments. AE, D, MC, V. No smoking indoors.*

Maricopa Manor Bed and Breakfast Inn

15 W. Pasadena Ave., Phoenix 85013, tel. 602/274–6302 or 800/292–6403, fax 602/266–3904

Business travelers appreciate this all-suite facility, centrally located near downtown Phoenix and just minutes from the Heard Museum, the Herberger Theatre, and the America West Arena. Innkeepers Paul and Mary Ellen Kelley raised 12 children in this 1928 residence, on a quiet, palm-shaded street, before turning it into an elegant executive retreat.

The immaculate Spanish Colonial-style home is decorated with fine art and stocked with countless books. Visitors have the run of the high-ceiling family room, living room, dining room, and outdoor patio. Stressed guests can let off steam by soaking in the hot tub in the gazebo out back or floating in the heated pool with Mexican fountains.

The accommodations have every amenity offered by the posh Phoenix resorts—fresh flowers, expensive toiletries—and even some they don't have: an array of paperbacks in each room and rubber duckies in the bathtub.

The Victorial Suite is in the main house. Set off the family room, it is done in satin, lace, and antiques; the private bath is across the hall. The other accommodations are arrayed outside in adjoining buildings. A private entrance leads to the Library Suite, with volumes of leather-bound books, a desk, and a canopied king-size bed.

In an adjoining guest house with its own carport and a gated driveway are two more spacious suites. Reflections Past has a fireplace, antique mirrors, and king-size bed with a tapestry canopy. Reflections Future, done in black and white with a Chinese flavor, has a living room, a full kitchen with breakfast area, and a small study with a desk and phone.

A Franklin stove sets the tone for the traditional American decor in the Palo Verde Suite, which has two bedrooms and an enclosed sunporch. The large Master Suite features a three-sided fireplace that separates the living room from the mahogany-furnished bedroom; there's also a double whirlpool bath.

Breakfast—orange juice, hot coffee, a fresh fruit plate, homemade bread or pastries, and a hot cheese miniquiche—is delivered to your door, at the hour you specify, in a wicker picnic basket.

🏠 *4 1-bedroom suites (1 with private bath across the hall), 1 2 bedroom suite. Hot tub, pool, bathrobes, cable TV, phone in all rooms. $89–$199, full breakfast. AE, D, MC, V. No pets.*

The Marks House

203 E. Union St., Prescott 86303, tel. 520/778–4632

The mayor of Territorial Prescott and a man with successful interests in ranching, mining, and wholesale liquor, Jake Marks spared no expense when it came to building a house for his wife, Josephine. Redwood was imported from California; the glass in the turret windows was curved to match the rounded sills; the cast copper door hinges were engraved with decorative designs; and parquet floors were laid in the formal dining room. In all, it took two years to construct this two-story Queen Anne-style mansion on Nob Hill, overlooking the central Court House Square; it was completed in 1884.

Restoration on the building, which served for a time as a boardinghouse and a rest home, began in 1980; it debuted as a bed-and-breakfast in 1987. Today it is listed on the National Register of Historic Homes and owned by Beth Maitland, known for creating the role of Traci on CBS's *The Young and the Restless*. Her parents, Dotti and Harold Viehweg, manage the inn and continue to improve it.

Like the rest of the house, the bay-windowed living room is furnished with antiques from the 1870s through the 1890s and wallpapered with a reproduction Victorian print; filled to the rafters with lacy doodads and knickknacks, it hosts a boutique for decorative items. The formal dining room, which enjoys a view out over Court House Plaza, has room for three linen-covered tables and matching oak sideboards.

The jewel in this B&B's crown is the Queen Anne Suite adjoining the circular turret; it's furnished in white wicker and has a claw-foot tub in the bath. The view north from the curved windows sweeps over the tall trees surrounding the Court House, across the city to majestic Thumb Butte in the distance. Princess Victoria, also upstairs, is done in mauve and lavender with floral patterns; an unusual, hammered copper tub in the bath was salvaged from an 1892 bathhouse in New York State. All the rooms have featherbeds, which would be too comfortable to abandon if it weren't for Dotti's wonderful cooking.

Breakfast is served family style at an hour that guests agree upon in advance. Popular entrées include blackberry dumplings made from an old family recipe, a deep-dish egg casserole with meat, and French toast.

🏨 *2 double rooms with baths (1 adjoining), 1 1-bedroom suite, 1 2-bedroom suite. Welcome mineral water in rooms, gift shop. $75–$135, full breakfast, afternoon hors d'oeuvres. D, MC, V. No smoking indoors, no pets.*

The Meadows

Box 1110, Pinetop 85935, tel. 520/367–8200, fax 520/367–0334

Looking just like a New England country inn, the Meadows sits in a flower-filled field amidst the largest continuous stand of ponderosa pine in the world. Completed in 1993 in a modified Victorian style, the inn opened in November 1994 to set a new standard of accommodations for the White Mountains. Owner and Executive Chef Steve McBrayer serves three gourmet meals a day in the Dining Room, which is open to the public; his fresh, innovative menus are complemented by selections from the comprehensive wine cellar.

The interior is subdued French Country, with white walls and forest green carpeting. Juniper logs burn in the brick fireplace of the loft-ceiling living room, and the cozy upstairs library has books, games, and cable TV. The one suite, No. 7, has a white beehive fireplace, brass bed, and kitchenette, all under a tower ceiling. Upstairs, No. 1 includes an antique bed with a brass and porcelain headboard, as well as a large bathroom occupied by a claw-foot tub. Another of the upstairs corner rooms, No. 2 features wicker furniture with lavender, white, and green quilts and wallpaper.

Guests select their breakfasts in the evening from daily menus and may enjoy them in the sunny breakfast room.

🏨 *6 double rooms with baths, 1 suite. Small complementary bottles of wine in rooms, restaurant, room service, hot tub. $69–$145, full breakfast option, afternoon refreshments. No smoking indoors, no pets, 2-night minimum on weekends, 3-night minimum on holidays.*

Mount Vernon Inn

204 North Mt. Vernon Ave., Prescott 86301, tel. 520/778–0886, fax 520/778–7305

Having escaped the windy winters of Chicago, Jerry and Michelle Neuman bought this Victorian residence, which is on a quiet street four blocks from the center of Prescott, in 1996. The inn, whose beautifully restored rooms remain true to their original 1900 style, has been placed on the National Register of Historic Places.

As you enter Mount Vernon, the parlor and sitting rooms greet you with original Douglas fir floors, 10-foot ceilings, bay windows, pocket doors, Victorian couches, and a fainting chair. An old grandfather clock stands still in time while a crystal chandelier preserves the inn's refined gracefulness.

The stairway hall, decorated with black-and-white family photos, leads to four light-filled rooms, dressed in pretty but not overly fussy florals and Victorian antiques. The Arcana room, off the street, stays quietest. Guests who stay in the main house receive a full breakfast with fresh fruit, homemade breads, and a hot entrée.

Families and those wishing to stay longer term may opt for one of the cottages. The Carriage House, with an upstairs sleeping loft and a downstairs room, and the Studio, with two full baths, comfortably accommodate four. The Doll House—the name aptly describes its dimensions—is a private little aerie for two. Because there are individual kitchens in all three cottages, guests fend for themselves for the morning meal.

🏨 *4 double rooms with baths, 3 cottages with baths. Phones in all rooms, TVs and kitchens in cottages. $90, full breakfast, afternoon refreshments. Cottages $100–$120, breakfast not included. D, MC, V. No smoking indoors, children in cottages only.*

Noftsger Hill Inn

425 North St., Globe 85501, tel. 520/425–2260

Frank and Pamela Hulme are busy these days removing wax from acres of white maple hardwood floors. They're in the process of converting the Noftsger Hill School, built in 1907 and overlooking the mining town of Globe, into a bed-and-breakfast. The inn opened in April 1993; all the accommodations are decorated with local antiques and have Western themes. The living room, formerly the school hallway, is furnished with a five-piece antique living room set, Oriental rugs, and a piano.

Three of the completed guest rooms are huge—23 × 30 feet with high ceilings, fireplaces, and the original slate blackboards, as well as panoramic views of the Pinal Mountains. In one, there's an antique king-size bed, fireplace, and large sitting area. The smaller guest room used to be a school office.

A "miner-size" breakfast, which might include Mexican quiche with green chilies, is served in the dining room (converted from a classroom) at a formal antique oak table.

🏨 *3 triple rooms with baths and 1 double with bath. Wheelchair ramp. $55–$75, full breakfast. MC, V. No smoking indoors, no pets.*

Paisley Corner
Bed & Breakfast

Box 458, Springerville 85938, or 287 N. Main St., Eagar 85925, tel. 520/333-4665

You'll see a Ford Model A, a Texaco gas pump, and a vintage street clock in the yard as you drive up. The old memorabilia gives this imposing two-story red-brick mansion, occupying a corner lot on the main street of little Eagar, a certain haunting character. Innkeepers Cheryl and Cletus Tisdell worked three years to restore the 1910 Historical Landmark to its pre–World War I grandeur, and probably surpassed it. They used the hammered-tin ceilings from the old Fox Theatre in Phoenix to create wainscoting, borders, and ceilings throughout the house.

Opened as a bed-and-breakfast at the end of 1991, the mansion boasts furnishings authentic to the early 20th century. An enameled wood-burning stove and formal walnut table dominate the dining room. The two front rooms retain their original stained-glass windows. In the "ice cream parlor," across the front hall from the living room, Cletus shows off his two jukeboxes, which play 78 rpm records; his working antique Coke machine; and his collection of American memorabilia.

The names given the guest rooms, all upstairs, were popular ones for women at the turn of the century. Each room has wall-to-wall Irish rose carpeting and a lazily rotating ceiling fan. Fanny's black-and-gold wrought-iron bed fronts a three-faced dressmaker's mirror and a maple vanity in an unusual cattail design; the spacious bathroom, with a clawfoot tub and 19th-century pull-chain commode, is next door. In Miss Lily, most aptly called a boudoir, mauve wallpaper in a rose pattern wraps around a lace-covered, white-and-brass bed that reposes regally on a step-up platform with formidable wooden banisters.

Entry to spacious Mabel Joy is through a pair of etched-glass doors with porcelain handles secured by a pink satin rope; the room has dark-green wallpaper with a hammered-tin border, as well as a massive, carved-oak canopy bed and matching beveled-glass vanity. Fontanille, a two-bedroom suite, has an artificial fireplace with tiger-oak columns and an ornate 1820s carved-walnut bed with an 8-foot-high headboard.

Cheryl's full breakfasts are prepared on a 1910 gas stove and served on rose-patterned china set on a lace tablecloth. Fresh-ground coffee precedes fresh juice, fruit, potatoes, and home-baked breads or muffins. The main dish may be quiche; a rich breakfast casserole of bacon, hard-boiled eggs, and sour cream; or French toast with real maple syrup.

🛏 *3 double rooms with baths, 1 2-bedroom suite. Welcome basket, TV in living room. $65–$85, full breakfast. No credit cards. No smoking indoors, no pets.*

The Pleasant Street Inn
Bed & Breakfast

142 S. Pleasant St., Prescott 86303, tel. 520/445-4774

The original 19th-century home on this corner lot in Prescott's Victorian neighborhood burned down years ago, but in 1990 an enterprising contractor moved a 1900 New England–style home onto the site. The B&B that Jean Urban opened here *feels* new because of the soft, gray wall-to-wall carpet, the plastered walls, and the traditional style of the rose and light blue furnishings. It's also sunny and bright, a nice alternative to some of the Victorian inns.

But there are many traditional touches. In the comfy living room, with a bay window overlooking a lush lawn, a fireplace burns aromatic cedar logs. An oak table shares the dining room with a dark-pine sideboard. Breakfast, which always includes fresh fruit and homemade breads, is served here or on the south-facing terrace.

Rooms are pretty, with floral-print quilts. The Pine View Suite enjoys corner light, a bay window, and a fireplace. The Terrace suite maintains a separate sitting room with an Oriental touch, a rose-colored bedroom, and an outdoor terrace. The Garden Room has white wicker furnishings and lace curtains.

▦ *2 double rooms with baths, 2 suites. Fresh flowers, ceiling fans/evaporative cooling in rooms. $85–$125, full breakfast, afternoon hors d'oeuvres. MC, V. No smoking indoors, no pets.*

Red Setter Inn

Box 133, Greer 85927, tel. 520/735–7441, fax 520/735–7425

Ken Conant and Jim Sankey packed their corporate suitcases and kissed Los Angeles goodbye in order to open this widely acclaimed '40s-style lodge in Arizona's White Mountains. Antiques fill every nook and cranny of this three-level inn, built with hand-peeled lodgepole pine. A marvelous toy collection is displayed in the high-ceiling Gathering Room, and you'll find wood-cased radios in many guest quarters. Downstairs, there's an antique Bally's mini–bowling alley and old pinball machine in the game room, which always has popcorn and sodas waiting for the inn's adults-only guests. There's a formal living room near the entrance with a fireplace and overstuffed lodge couches. Because of the Red Setter's size—there are many common areas—it feels roomy and comfortable even when there's a full house.

Nine individually decorated rooms promise one thing in common: a figurine or book about a red setter stemming from Jim's love for the breed. Beyond that, some rooms have views of the Little Colorado River, and some have fireplaces and Jacuzzi tubs. The four downstairs rooms lead to a common deck

from which you step down to the river, just 25 feet away. On the main floor, a room equipped for people with disabilities has a Western-style queen-size bed, dormer window, and private deck with a telescope leading to the front of the house. Upstairs, spacious Room 9 has two double beds with country quilts separated by a room divider. In Room 4, a queen-size sleigh bed, Jacuzzi tub, fireplace, vaulted ceilings, and private deck make for a romantic escape.

A considerable breakfast of pancakes and sausage, egg frittatas, quiche, or eggs Benedict is served in the lodge's skylit dining room. Guests who stay two or more nights are entitled to a sack lunch with deli sandwiches and cookies, which they can take to explore the beautiful surrounding area. When they return, afternoon refreshments will welcome them back to their home-away-from-home.

▦ *9 double rooms with baths. Ceiling fans, private balconies. $120–$160, full breakfast. AE, MC, V. No smoking, no pets, no children under 16, 2-night minimum on weekends.*

White Mountain Lodge

Box 143, Greer 85927, tel. 520/735–7568 or 888/493–7568, fax 520/735–7498

This 1892 landmark lodge in the tiny White Mountain town of Greer enjoys a panoramic view of Greer Valley. The Little Colorado River runs along the foot of the property, which is about 15 minutes from the Sunrise Ski area.

The living room in the main lodge has a stone fireplace under a beamed ceiling, Southwestern furniture, and walls decorated with Native American pottery and crafts. A dining room table seating 12 takes full advantage of the view a picture window affords. The full breakfast varies daily but includes homemade coffee cakes, muffins, donuts, and bread.

The seven guest rooms in the lodge are on the cozy side; most are pine paneled, and all have wall-to-wall carpeting, floral print bedspreads or country quilts, and individual electric heating units. The upstairs rooms lie under low, slanted-pine ceilings. Innkeepers Charlie Bast and Mary Lawrence also have three cabins with kitchens for rent, ideal for families and those who prefer to do their own cooking and housekeeping.

🏨 *5 double rooms with baths, 1 triple, 1 quad, 3 cabins. TV with VCR in Entry room, guest fax and refrigerator. $65–$85, full breakfast; $80–$95 for cabins. D, MC, V. Small pets welcome, 2-night minimum weekends, 3-night minimum on holidays.*

Tucson and Environs

El Presidio B&B

The second-largest city in Arizona, Tucson is at once a bustling center of business and a laid-back university and resort town. Its year-round population of 665,000 swells in the winter, when snowbirds from the North come to enjoy the city's warm sun and warm hospitality. The town is flanked by vast preserves of huge saguaro cactus, but the desert here is literal, not cultural: Tucson is among only 14 cities in the United States that can claim a symphony and opera, theater, and ballet companies; Tucson also boasts a planetarium and one of the best photography centers in the country.

The region's earliest known citizens, the Hohokam Indians, lived in the fertile farming valley in AD 100, though other Native American artifacts in the area can be traced as far back as 2,000 years. At the end of the 17th century, Jesuit missionary Father Eusebio Francisco Kino rode north on horseback from Mexico to preach Catholicism to the peaceful Pima and Tohono O'Odham Indians who had settled along the banks of the Santa Cruz River. He noted in his diary in 1692 that he had arrived in the town of Stkjukshon, meaning "spring at the base of black mountain." The name was corrupted by Spanish explorers who built the presidio (fortress) of San Agustín del Tuguisón in 1776 to keep Native Americans from reclaiming the city.

Rebuilt by Franciscans in the 18th century, the lovely Spanish-Moorish-style Mission San Xavier del Bac still stands at the outskirts of Tucson on the site of Father Kino's original mission church and still serves the Tohono O'Odham Indians, whose vast reservation—only that of the Navajo Nation is larger—spreads out to the west of Tucson. But Father Kino's original route north has become I-19, along which the border town of Nogales, the artists' center of Tubac, and the huge retirement community of Green Valley now thrive. And the black mountain for which Tucson was named, probably the dark volcanic cone near downtown known as Sentinel Peak, is more popularly known as "A" mountain because University of Arizona students annually whitewash the large "A" cut into its side.

For much of this century, Tucson was called the "Dude Ranch Capital of the West." Bed-and-breakfasts are a more recent development but are taking off rapidly. Some of the inns in town look back to Territorial times when settlers built elaborate Victorian homes—albeit out of adobe brick— and tried to pretend they weren't in the desert; other, more contemporary inns have been set deliberately in remote areas, built with natural materials to capitalize on the landscape's unique beauty. In summer, when temperatures can linger around 101°F, some of the bed-and-breakfasts close; others drop their rates.

Places to Go, Sights to See

Arizona–Sonora Desert Museum (2021 N. Kinney Rd., tel. 520/883–1380). You can see birds, animals, and plants from southern Arizona and northern Mexico all displayed in carefully re-created natural habitats at this museum, which is considered one of the top 10 zoos in the world. All the desert creatures are here too, from scorpions and rattlesnakes to javelina, mountain lions, and hummingbirds. Allow at least half a day to see it all.

Biosphere 2 (35 mi north of Tucson on Hwy. 77, tel. 520/825–6200 or 800/828–2462). This once-controversial science project hit the news in 1991 when eight "Biospherians" were sealed inside the giant 3-acre terrarium in order to study the environment—and, if necessary, to prepare to colonize other planets. The project achieved respectability in 1995 when Columbia University signed a five-year contract to manage and direct all of Biosphere's scientific, educational, and visitor-center operations. Guided walking tours, which last about two hours, don't enter most of the sealed sphere, but the living quarters of the Biospherians were opened to the public in late 1996, and indoor and outdoor observation areas let you peer in at the rest.

Colossal Cave (Old Spanish Trail, 22 mi southeast of Tucson, tel. 520/647–7275). The largest dry cavern in the United States, with a steady temperature of 72°F, Colossal Cave has never been fully explored. Treasure is said to be hidden in its dark recesses.

De Grazia's Gallery in the Sun (630 N. Swan Rd., tel. 520/299–9191). From the metal mineshaft doors at the entrance to the polished saguaro tiles in the floor, the sprawling, single-story museum and gallery of one of Arizona's best known artists, Ted De Grazia, is as appealing as the paintings on the walls. Built by the artist with the help of Native American friends, it uses only materials from the surrounding desert. Adjacent to the museum is the *Mission in the Sun*, a hand-built adobe chapel covered with De Grazia murals. Close to the chapel is the artist's grave, frontier style, covered by a mound of rocks.

El Presidio District. The area surrounding the original Spanish presidio, or fort, was the center of Tucson for a long time; now this downtown district is home to many museums, art galleries, theaters, and boutiques. The Spanish Colonial-style *Pima County Courthouse*, built in 1927 on the site of the original single-story adobe courthouse of 1869, is perhaps Tucson's most beautiful historical building. The nearby *Tucson Museum of Art and Historic Block* (140 N. Main Ave., tel. 520/884–7379) houses an impressive collection of pre-Columbian art and a permanent display of 20th-century Western art. You can join a free docent tour of the historic buildings in the museum complex, including the Casa Cordova, the Fish House, the Corbett House, and the Stevens Home. Contact the Museum of Art for more information.

Golf. Pima and Santa Cruz counties have some of the best desert courses in the country—and more than 300 days of sunshine to play on them. *The Tucson & Southern Arizona Golf Guide*, published by Madden Publishing, Inc. (send $5 to Box 42915, Tucson 85733, tel. 520/322–0895), describes and rates all the local courses. For a personalized golf package based on your budget, interests, and experience, you might contact **Tee Time Arrangers** (tel. 800/742–9939).

Mission San Xavier del Bac (Mission Rd., just outside of Tucson, tel. 520/294–2624). The beautiful "White Dove of the Desert," established in 1783 by Franciscan missionaries on the site of an older Jesuit mission and finished 14 years later, is the only Spanish mission in the United States still serving its original, Native American parishioners. Its wealth of painted statues, carvings, and frescoes has earned San Xavier the designation "Sistine Chapel of the United States."

Old Tucson Studios (201 S. Kinney Rd., tel. 520/883–0100). This film set–cum–theme park, seriously damaged by fire in 1995, reopened after some $13 million of renovations in early 1997. Many of the adobe structures that were used as movie backdrops (the studio was built for the 1940 motion picture *Arizona*) still stand, but the complex was redesigned with wider streets, larger buildings, and a more logical layout. The scheduled gunfights, live shows, rides, restaurants, and shops have all returned in full force.

Pima Air Museum (6000 E. Valencia Rd., tel. 520/574–0462 or 520/574–9658). The dry desert air is kind to old aircraft: They never rust. Come here to see 180 planes representing more than 80 years of U.S. aviation history. Also run by nonprofit Pima Air Museum foundation is the **Titan Missile Museum** (exit 69 off I-19, 25 mi south of Tucson, tel. 520/791–2929), the only one of 54 Titan II sites left intact when the SALT II treaty with the Soviet Union was signed. Visitors can descend into the command post, where a ground crew of four lived, and look at the 114-foot, 165-ton, two-stage liquid-fuel rocket. Now empty, it originally held a nuclear payload with 214 times the explosive power of the bomb that destroyed Hiroshima.

Sabino Canyon (5900 N. Sabino Canyon Rd., tel. 520/749–2327). Part of Coronado National Forest, but filled with desert flora and fauna, this is a good spot for hiking, picnicking, or enjoying the waterfalls, streams, and natural swimming holes on a hot day. No cars are allowed; a narrated tram ride (45 minutes round-trip) takes you to the top of the canyon. Nighttime tram tours are offered when there's a full moon.

Saguaro National Park. Probably the only national park that has a city in the middle of it—Tucson separates the east section of the park from the west—this one is also unique in the United States as a habitat for the towering saguaro (pronounced *suh-WAR-oh*) cactus. These slow-growing plants—they can take up to 15 years to add 1 foot and may live more than 200 years—are protected by state and federal laws: Enjoy, but don't disturb them. The 21,000-acre portion on the far west side of town (tel. 520/733–5100) is the more visited one, but it's rarely crowded, and you'll practically have the scenic trails on the 62,000-acre east side (tel. 520/296–8576) to yourself if you go during the week.

University of Arizona. The original land for this 325-acre university was "donated" by a couple of gamblers and a saloon owner in 1891, but Territorial funds were used to construct the first building, Old Main. Among the many interesting museums on campus are the *Center for Creative Photography* (1030 N. Olive Rd., tel. 520/621–7968), housing one of the world's largest collections of 20th-century photographs; the *Arizona Historical Society's Museum* (949 E. 2nd St., tel. 520/628–5774), with fascinating displays of Arizona history and an excellent historical archive; and the *Grace H. Flandrau Science Center and Planetarium* (Cherry Ave. and University Blvd., tel. 520/621–4515), where attractions include a 16-inch public telescope, a flashy multimedia show, an interactive meteor exhibit, and, in the basement, the impressive Mineral Museum.

Restaurants

Tucson's excellent range of restaurants includes everything from low-key, authentic Mexican cafés to upscale resort dining rooms. The best of the upper range include **Janos** (tel. 520/884–9426), serving cutting-edge Southwestern cuisine in an elegant historic adobe, and the **Ventana Room** (tel. 520/299–1771) in the posh Ventana Canyon Resort, where the fine Continental food is matched only by the views of the desert or of Tucson in the distance. **Anthony's** (tel. 520/299–1771) in the Catalinas has equally impressive desert views and a high-quality, though rather more traditional, Continental menu. At the more moderately priced **Café Terra Cotta** (tel. 520/577–8100), you can enjoy Southwest-inspired specialties on the outdoor terrace or in a colorful indoor dining room. The **Cottonwood Café** (tel. 520/326–6000) also has an innovative Southwestern menu and offers the similarly difficult choice of eating on the patio or indoors. In a comparable price range, **Vivace** (tel. 520/795–7221) serves fine northern Italian food in a chic (if not overly quiet) setting. The pretty, romantic **Bocatta** (tel. 520/577–9309) adds a bit of a French twist to its own northern Italian selections. For outstanding regional Mexican cuisine at reasonable prices, you can't beat **Café Poca Cosa** (tel. 520/622–6400). Sooner or later, all locals head for the Mexican-American enclave of **South Tucson**, where it's hard to go wrong with any of the low-priced places you'll find on Fourth Avenue south of 22nd Street.

Tourist Information

Metropolitan Tucson Convention & Visitors Bureau (130 S. Scott, Tucson 85701, tel. 520/624–1817 or 800/638–8350).

Reservation Services

Arizona Association of Bed & Breakfast Inns (Box 7186, Phoenix 85011, tel. 800/284–2589). **Bed & Breakfast Southwest** (2916 N. 70th St., Scottsdale 85251, tel. 602/995–2831 or 800/762–9704, fax 602/874–1316). **Mi Casa Su Casa B&B Reservation Service** (Box 950, Tempe 85280, tel. 602/990–0682, 800/456–0682 reservations only, fax 602/990–3390). **Old Pueblo HomeStays RSO** (Box 13603, Tucson 85732, tel. and fax 520/790–2399 or 800/333–9776). **Premiere Bed & Breakfast Inns of Tucson** (316 E. Speedway Blvd., 85705, tel. 520/628–1800 or 800/628–5654, fax 520/792–1880).

Adobe Rose Inn

940 N. Olsen Ave., Tucson 85719, tel. 520/ 318–4644 or 800/328–4122, fax 520/325– 0055

There are lots of reasons to like the Adobe Rose: the quiet, central location, which is near the University of Arizona but not close enough to be subject to its traffic; the clean-lined Santa Fe–style house, constructed in 1933 of adobe bricks 1 foot thick; the courtyard with a palm-fringed pool and a bougainvilla-draped deck; and innkeeper Diana Graham, a special education teacher who left the field after 14 years to avoid burnout. Her former profession shows in her patience in answering guest questions, but her cheerful manner hints that she's happy to be spending more time talking with adults.

Accommodations consist of three double rooms in the main house, an adjoining cottage, and, around the corner, an upstairs suite that includes a kitchenette. All are decorated in vibrant, desert colors and furnished with lodgepole pine pieces created specifically for the inn. Some lovely original details remain, too: Rainbow's End has a kiva fireplaces and stained-glass windows, while Arizona offers a huge hand-tiled tub depicting the red rocks of Sedona.

🏠 *3 rooms with bath, 1 cottage, 1 suite. TV in all rooms, pool. $65–$115, full breakfast. AE, D, MC, V. No smoking indoors, no pets.*

Bienestar

10490 E. Escalante Rd., Tucson 85730, tel. 520/290–1048, fax 520/290–1367

In 1963, when a member of the Dewars family decided he needed a bit more than Scotch to keep warm, he built a winter home in Tucson, five minutes from Saguaro National Park East. Since 1996, the low-slung hacienda-style house has been the domain of two sisters, Peggy

Muller and Angela Telfer, but there are still plenty of good spirits to go around.

Peggy, an RN with a holistic background, makes sure breakfasts are healthful as well as delicious, using whole grains and free-range eggs in her recipes. She can also arrange for a massage therapist. However, you'll probably feel most the tension naturally melt away as you gaze out the windows that overlook 6 acres of mature desert.

Lovely Mexican antiques and Native American art lend the house a Southwest feel. All the accommodations, done in deep desert tones, have at least one special feature: The suite has two fireplaces, the casita features a fireplace and kitchen, and the room boasts a bay window with a view of the Santa Rita Mountains.

🏠 *1 room with bath, 1 suite, 1 casita. TV and phone in suite and casita, pool, hot tub, library with piano, gift shop. $85–$125, full breakfast, afternoon high tea. D, MC, V. No smoking, no pets (except horses; trailer space available), 2 night minimum on weekends during high season.*

The Cactus Quail

14000 N. Dust Devil Dr., Tucson 85739, tel. 520/825–6767

About 9 miles north of Tucson, in a residential enclave, the Cactus Quail has one of the most impressive vistas you could hope to find. The contemporary Southwest-style bed-and-breakfast looks out over the Sonoran Desert and directly at the Santa Catalina Mountains, larger than life and pasted against an endless sky. Best of all, the view will never be obstructed because the land belongs to Catalina State Park. In the foreground, large-eared rabbits and other desert creatures keep guests entertained, as do the horses, dogs, and cats that belong to the inn's proprietors, Marty and Sue Higbee.

On the walls of the smallish Pueblo Room, Tucson artist D. Lawrence West painted ancient Native American cliff dwellings that he saw first in a dream; he designed the Hacienda Room, which shares a bath with Pueblo, to resemble a Mexican village. The Bunkhouse, with a private bath and an upstairs sleeping loft, has a more unadorned Western theme. All are luxurious, with not only beautiful, high-quality furnishings but also plush robes and cable TV with VCR.

🏠 *2 rooms share 1 bath, 1 room with private bath. VCR library, fireplace in living room, arrangements made for horseback riding and Jeep tours. $95–$110, full breakfast. MC, V. No smoking, no pets.*

Casa Alegre Bed and Breakfast Inn

316 E. Speedway Blvd., Tucson 85705, tel. 520/628–1800 or 800/628–5654

When innkeeper Phyllis Florek decided to open a bed-and-breakfast, she searched from Napa Valley to the Caribbean for the right building in the ideal climate. Her choice was a 1915, stuccoed, bungalow-style home near the University of Arizona in Tucson. In 1991, after thoroughly renovating it, she opened her "Happy House."

The house features a volcanic stone fireplace in the living room, hardwood floors, Oriental rugs, dark-wood door frames and cabinets, and a swimming pool and hot tub in the back garden. The most spacious accommodation is the corner Saguaro Room. It has its own fireplace, windows on three sides, a lodgepole-pine bed, and saguaro rib curtain rods. The Hacienda Room has a handsome Mexican wood armoire and a headboard originally hand-carved for a Mexican priest. There are three spacious guest rooms in the 1923 Buchanan House, which is next door.

A full breakfast—perhaps hot bread pudding with strawberries or green chili quiche—is served in the dining room or on the covered back patio.

🏠 *5 double rooms with bath. TV in all rooms, fireplace in one room, 2 common rooms with fireplaces, pool, hot tub. $80–$105, full breakfast. D, MC, V. No smoking indoors, no pets.*

Casa Tierra Adobe Bed & Breakfast

11155 W. Calle Pima, Tucson 85743, tel. 520/578–3058, fax 520/578–3058

You won't find a better place to experience the magic of the Sonoran Desert than Tucson's Casa Tierra (Earth House), an environmentally conscious B&B near Saguaro National Park and the Arizona–Sonora Desert Museum. The last leg of the trip here is via dirt road. Innkeeper Karen Hymer-Thompson reports that guests often arrive asking, "Why don't you get that road paved?" They leave saying, "I'm glad you're a little hard to reach."

The adobe hacienda that Lyle Hymer-Thompson built on the couple's 5 acres couldn't be more suited to the landscape, with its vaulted brick entryways, central courtyard, viga and latilla ceilings, handmade ceramic lights, Mexican furniture, and brightly painted Talavera tiles. Three colorful Southwestern-style guest rooms all have private entrances and patios. A short path leads to an outdoor Jacuzzi ramada (a roofed structure without walls), where guests can watch the sun set or the moon rise. Huge picture windows in the dining room allow them to enjoy Karen's fresh-ground coffee and home-baked goodies while gazing at saguaro cactus and desert critters.

🏠 *3 double rooms with baths. Microwaves, mini-refrigerators in rooms, outdoor Jacuzzi, access to barbecue and coffeemaker. $85–$95, full breakfast. No credit cards. No smoking indoors, no pets. Closed June–Aug.*

Catalina Park Inn

309 E. 1st St., Tucson 85705, tel. 520/792–4541 or 800/792–4885, fax 520/792–0838

Some people are perpetual tinkerers, always aiming at perfection. Mark Hall and Paul Richard, who moved from San Francisco to Tucson in 1994 so that they could afford to open up an inn that met their high standards, fit this profile to a tee. Although their bed-and-breakfast appears completely and beautifully finished, they're constantly on the lookout for ways to improve it. Right now, for example, a pool with a small bathhouse is in the works.

Mark and Paul had a wonderful base from which to begin: a centrally located two-story residence graced with neoclassic symmetry. Because the place had only been in three other hands since it was built in 1927, many of the original details were left intact. These include the extensive wood trim made from amapa, a blond mahogany brought in from the interior of Mexico, and the Art Nouveau lotus-pattern tiles used as borders in many of baths. An overhang on the second floor and French doors in the upstairs rooms, where most of the guest quarters are located, were designed so that the house could stay relatively cool, even in pre-air-conditioned Tucson summers.

To the upper level rooms in the main house, Mark and Paul added a downstairs unit, converted from a family game room. You can still see the shallow closets that used to hold pool cues, as well as the scored concrete floor, very much in vogue again in the Southwest. A huge closet made from a Kentucky cedar closet was the perfect spot to install a raised whirlpool tub. The last project, transforming the old garage, introduced two more rooms, one with a wood-burning fireplace, and both with private entrances. All the accommodations are decorated in a distinctive style that makes extensive use of antiques but is never overly fussy. There is a nice contrast in the Oak Room, for example, between its ornate four-poster bed and plush tapestry chairs and a rough-hewn wood desk.

Breakfast is as gracious as you might expect, served on fine china in either a cozy separate nook or, for the more social, in a larger dining room. Fresh fruit, yogurt, muesli, and home-baked goods supplement such entrées as stuffed French toast or delicate, raspberry-topped pancakes.

🏨 *6 rooms with bath. TV, telephone, robes, hair dryer, iron and board in all rooms, fireplace in 1 room, private balconies in 2 rooms, fireplace in living room, gardens. $90–$115, full breakfast. MC, V. No smoking indoors, no pets.*

El Presidio Bed & Breakfast Inn

297 N. Main Ave., Tucson 85701, tel. 520/623–6151 or 800/349–6151, fax 520/623–3860

Listed in the National Register of Historic Places, this gracious 1880s Territorial-style home has 21-inch-thick walls made of adobe brick and a 17-foot ceiling with hand-hewn beams in the *zaguan* (center hallway). Broad windows look onto a cobblestone courtyard banked with geraniums, snapdragons, and rosebushes and shaded by mature trees that attract hummingbirds and cactus wrens.

Each of the three suites here has a different theme. The Victorian Suite, in the main house, has a parlor decorated with white wicker furniture, a kiva fireplace, and a braided rug. The Gate House, with a huge blue wicker bed and a private entrance, has the feel of a French country manor. The brick veranda of the Carriage House is topped by a Mexican-tile roof. Inside is a kitchenette with a stocked refrigerator, a living room, and a rose-themed bedroom.

Elaborate breakfasts, which vary daily, are served at a handsome walnut dining table that can expand to seat 10. Innkeeper Patti Toci's lemon muffins, topped with lemon streusel, are made with lemons picked from a tree outside the window.

🏨 *3 suites. TV, phone, bathrobes in each room, kitchen in 2 suites stocked with beverage and fruit, TV in sitting room. $95–$115, full breakfast. No credit cards. No smoking indoors, no pets.*

Elysian Grove Market

400 W. Simpson, Tucson 85701, tel. 520/ 628–1522

In 1924 Jose Trujillo built his grocery store in Barrio el Hoyo, at the shady, downhill end of this typical Mexican neighborhood. During the 1960s, the stuccoed, Territorial adobe shop was converted to residential use, and in 1993 the B&B opened. (In 1994, this was a location for the film *Boys on the Side*.)

Innkeeper-decorator Debbie LaChapelle lives in one unit, and the other two comprise her Mexican barrio–flavored B&B. Her collection of 18th–20th-century Mexican and American fine art, folk art, and antiques furnishes the inn.

Both suites have sleeping quarters on two levels: in a wine-cellar type area and on the ground floor opening onto the garden—a mix of verbena, lantana, aloe vera, and prickly pear shaded by mature mesquite and tamarisk trees and a chinaberry. The rooms have 12-to-16-foot ceilings with hammered tin (one patched with an old license plate), brown stucco walls, oak floors, and Mexican tile baths with showers and pull-chain toilets.

Debbie serves Colombian coffee with her Mexican-style light breakfasts. She also will conduct a walking tour of the historic neighborhood, now gradually being restored.

🏨 *2 2-bedroom suites, 1 with full kitchen. Fireplace, fridge, microwave, phone, radio, and tapes. $75, Continental breakfast. No credit cards. No smoking indoors, no pets.*

Hacienda del Desierto

11770 Rambling Trail, Tucson 85747, tel. 520/298–1764 or 800/982–1795, fax 520/ 722–4558

It's a family affair here. The distinctive, high-ceiling home that Rosemary and David Brown built grew, as the Brown children grew, into a little desert complex. Because the additions to the house were designed to provide privacy as well as space, Hacienda del Desierto is the perfect place to bring *your* family, too.

The house is an amalgam of local history, incorporating wood from a renovated Tucson hospital, timbers from abandoned telephone poles, and ceramic roof tiles from Mexico, but the result couldn't look more unified. As you walk through tall, rough-hewn wooden doors into a Spanish-style courtyard, you almost feel as though you're entering a religious retreat. Abundant ivy, hanging plants, and mature trees help create a serene atmosphere, as do shaded wraparound porches.

Which is not to suggest there's no action here. Although the Browns no longer keep pigs, horses, and chickens, you'll be entertained by several friendly cats and a herd of visiting javelinas. (Sticks are provided in order to keep these somewhat stinky wild pigs from poking their noses into your business.) The inn's 16-acre spread is less than a mile from Saguaro National Park East, so hiking and desert biking are also options.

Lovebirds will like the romantic Rose Room, with its fluffy pillows and appropriately reddish-hued decor, but a pull-down Murphy bed means there's always room for one (or two) more. The Patio Suite has a double hide-a-bed in its separate living room, along with a lovely view of the courtyard. Largest of all, the two-bedroom Casita features a hot tub looking out on the Santa Rita mountains.

All the units are equipped with kitchen facilities (full-size in the case of the Casita), TV, VCR, and a gas or wood-burning stove; all have carpeting and private entrances, too. Exposed adobe brick walls and Mexican tile are among the many touches that lend Southwest character.

A buffet of fruit, yogurt, cold cereals, baked goods, and hard boiled eggs is laid out in the courtyard, cozy dining area, or great room, depending on the weather and guests' inclinations.

🏠 *1 room with bath, 1 suite, 1 casita. Kitchenettes, gas or wood-burning stoves, TV/VCRs, film library, hot tub. $85–$130, Continental breakfast. No credit cards. No smoking indoors, no pets, 2 night-minimum stay in casita. Closed June–Aug.*

The Jeremiah Inn

10921 E. Synder Rd., Tucson 85749, tel. 520/749-3072

"Oh, that I had in the desert a lodging place for travelers," lamented the prophet Jeremiah. When former Seattleites Bob and Beth Miner had similar yearnings along these lines, they were well equipped to fulfill them. A contractor and landscape architect, Bob knew how to design the ideal bed-and-breakfast. Jeremiah might not have had an outdoor pool and spa in mind, but guests are glad that the Miners did.

In 1995 the Miners began welcoming visitors to their 3.3-acre patch of desert, which is close to some of the best outdoor recreational areas in Tucson, including Mount Lemmon and Sabino Canyon. Nearby Agua Caliente Park is unique for its hot springs, and the Raven golf course is a hit with duffers.

The three guest rooms have comfortable, if fairly nondescript, contemporary-style furnishings; two have sleeper sofas in addition to queen-size beds. Comments on follow-up surveys show that guests are very happy with the accommodations, as well as with the hosts' gracious hospitality and their generous breakfasts.

🏠 *3 rooms with bath. Color TV and telephone in all rooms, TV/VCR in living room, guest refrigerator, pool. $70–$100, full breakfast, afternoon snack. MC, V. No smoking indoors or outdoor public areas, no pets.*

La Posada del Valle

1640 N. Campbell Ave., Tucson 85719, tel. and fax 520/795-3840

Built as an elegant residence in 1929 by southwestern architect Josias T. Joesler, who combined Santa Fe Territorial with Spanish Colonial elements to create his signature style, La Posada del Valle (Inn of the Valley) sits on the edge of a quiet neighborhood near the university. This classic adobe is surrounded by walled, landscaped flower gardens and an abundance of orange trees. Innkeepers Karin Dennen, and her daughter Claudia, are originally from South Africa.

The high-ceiling living room is dappled with sunlight; a tall white bookcase, filled with books on Southwestern history, art, and culture, lines one wall. Afternoon tea is served here, in front of the copper-hooded adobe fireplace. The dining room, where guests enjoy a full breakfast, has a picture window facing north to the Santa Catalina Mountains.

Each of the guest rooms is named after a famous woman of the Roaring Twenties: Karen Blixen, Isadora Duncan, Sophie Tucker, Claudette Colbert, and Pola Negri. Decor and furnishings successfully re-create the ambience of the period.

🏠 *4 double rooms with baths, 1 cottage. TV and private entrance in all rooms, phones in 2 rooms, Tucson Racquet Club privileges available. $90–$135, full breakfast. MC, V. No smoking, no pets.*

Mi Gatita

HCR 70, Box 304a, 14085 Avenida Haley S., Sahuarita 85629, tel. 520/648-6129

You never know what to expect at this bed-and-breakfast in Sahuarita, some 25 minutes south of Tucson. Ron White, cowboy poet and the world's last mule skinner, may come riding up on Yaqui, his dancing horse. Ron is a local celebrity who appeared on the Johnny Carson show, but he hasn't let it go to his head; if you ask nicely, he'll get Yaqui to do a little two-step (or is that four-step?) for you.

One of Rusty's two-legged pals is Bill Lambert, who built the house Mi Gatita now occupies on land that used to be part of the Navarro Ranch, deeded to its owner by the King of Spain. In keeping with the Hispanic spirit of the place, Lambert designed the former ranch house along Mexican lines, with lots of niches, courtyards, and gardens, as well as private entrances. Among the many interesting items he acquired during his travels—he finally sold the place in order to indulge his wanderlust—are the carved Tarahumara columns that buttress the portico.

Current owners Jean and Bentley Pace have added their own character, not only by adopting three desert cats—one of whom, Jean claims, gave them the original tour of the house—but also with their creative furnishings. The San Blas room has a carved wooden bed (from which there's a wonderful view of Tucson), as well as an antique hatstand and Mexican equipale (pigskin) furniture. The more casual two-bedroom San Carlos/Cozumel Suite also has Mexican touches, including a piñata that none of the guests has smashed (yet). In both rooms you'll find books and games, fresh flowers, terry robes, and Sees candy.

The chocolate is but a hint of the culinary delights to come. Chile relleno puffs or oat waffles with hot ginger peach topping are among Jean's delicious, elabo-rate breakfast entrées. Bentley makes a mean cup of coffee, but it's his tour-guiding skills that especially endear him to guests. He's an expert on the San Xavier Mission, only 10 minutes away, and familiar with all the natural attractions in the area.

🏠 *1 room with bath, 1 suite. Fireplace in 1 guest room and in common room. $85, full breakfast, afternoon snack. No credit cards. No smoking indoors or in common outdoor areas, no pets, no children under 14.*

The Peppertrees Bed and Breakfast Inn

724 E. University Blvd., Tucson 85719, tel. and fax 520/622-7167 or 800/348-5763

Early settlers who came to the Arizona Territory at the turn of the century tried to create pockets of civilization in what was then a dusty desert outpost. Some 80 years later, perhaps in a similar spirit, Marjorie Martin brought antiques from her family home in the English Cotswolds to furnish her 1905 redbrick Victorian. After a careful restoration, she opened the Peppertrees in 1988. The classic residence is two blocks from the main gate of the University of Arizona and near the Fourth Avenue shopping district.

To check into the inn, guests enter the main house. Rooms with 12-foot-high ceilings and pine floors covered with Oriental carpets highlight Marjorie's furnishings, most of which date back to the last century. The mahogany-and-glass bookcase in the living room contains the family's Royal Doulton china.

Penelope's Room has windows on three sides; the one to the south looks out on a mature pomegranate tree and landscaped patio. It's decorated in Victorian style, with a white wrought-iron bed, a frilly rose-patterned comforter, and a 150-year-old mirrored mahogany dresser.

Adjacent to the main house is a 1917 Bungalow-style home with a large, comfortable living room and two bedrooms decorated with mahogany furniture, frilly, patterned comforters, and lace curtains. Behind the main house, across a cozy garden with a splashing Mexican-tile fountain, are two fully equipped guest houses. Each duplex unit, furnished in contemporary style, has two bedrooms upstairs with a shared bath. Downstairs are a half-bath, living room, dining area, full kitchen, and private patio.

A gourmet cook, Marjorie published her *Recipes from Peppertrees Bed and Breakfast Inn*. Breakfast is served buffet-style in the dining room or, on those perfect southern Arizona mornings, outdoors on the patio. There is always fresh fruit and home-baked breads or scones and a main dish such as blue-corn pancakes or savory French toast filled with cream cheese and orange. Special diets can be accommodated with advance notice, and picnic baskets may be ordered for day excursions.

🏨 *3 double rooms with baths, 2 2-bedroom duplex guest houses. TV, phones, washer/dryers in guest houses. $78–$165, full breakfast. D, MC, V. No smoking, no pets indoors.*

Quail's Vista Bed and Breakfast

826 E. Palisades Dr., Tucson 85737, tel. 520/297-5980

Built in 1987 on the brow of a hill looking out on the rugged west face of the Santa Catalina Mountains, Quail's Vista enjoys one of the most spectacular views in southern Arizona. Among the other nice features of this Santa Fe–style solar adobe B&B are a cactus garden, a flagstone terrace where families of quail gather, and a redwood deck. Innkeeper Barbara Jones, a licensed tour guide, can direct guests to all the best places to see in Tucson.

Inside the house, peeled spruce columns support the beamed ceiling and low, rounded walls; brick floors, a kiva fireplace, Native American pottery, Mexican blankets, and local artwork in the public areas are also in keeping with the Southwestern theme. Guest rooms feature Saltillo-tile floors, white-oak closets, and bright, Mexican-tile baths. Grandma's Room has a Victorian theme, with an antique queen-size bed and framed heirloom portraits. The largest room, the Queen Master Suite, has a kiva fireplace, separate tub and shower rooms, and a spectacular view of the mountains. Breakfast is a buffet of fruit, cold cereals, pastries, and coffee.

🏨 *1 double room with bath, 2 doubles share bath. TV and VCR in living room, outdoor hot tub, nearby country club privileges (extra). $65–$85, Continental-plus breakfast. No credit cards. No smoking indoors, no pets.*

Rancho Quieto

12051 W. Fort Lowell Rd., Tucson 85743, tel. 520/883-3300

When watercolorist Corinne Still bought Rancho Quieto (pronounced Kay-ET-o) in 1990, she had in mind an artist's retreat. As it turned out, the Southern Arizona Watercolor Guild sometimes has its "paint outs" here, but the less artistically talented portion of the populace also has the chance to stay at this unique 40-acre bed-and-breakfast, only a few minutes from Saguaro National Park West.

It was designed in 1970 by local landscape architect Mervin Larson, best known in Tucson for the real-looking boulders he made for the Arizona-Sonora Desert Museum (which adjoins this property). To the mature desert foliage he added fruit trees—orange, tangerine, lemon, lime, grapefruit, tangelo, and fig—six types of palms, ironwoods and he even imported a stand of bamboo from the San Diego Zoo. The centerpiece of this little portion of paradise is the swimming pool that resembles a natural rock grotto; it's fed by a waterfall created by pumped and recirculated well water. A gently bubbling outdoor spa looks enough like a genuine hot spring to make Mother Nature do a double take.

The house, which draws from a variety of Southwest and Mexican styles, is as dramatic as the setting; a saguaro rib ceiling and beams made of redwood collected from old railroad bridges and trestles are among its interesting details. Decorating the tremendous sunken living room was one of Corinne's many artistic outlets, and she's demonstrated that she's no slouch, either, when it comes to creating illusions: Because she couldn't afford a Navajo rug large enough to fit the large space above her fireplace, she simply painted one on the wall. Her country-hearty breakfasts are served in the adjacent dining room.

You might be tempted to settle in here for a while. The three split-level suites in the main house and the separate guest house all have full kitchens, wet bars, and fireplaces; Suite II also features a Jacuzzi tub for two in a paradisiacal plant-filled bathroom. Individually chosen by Corinne, the contemporary Southwest furnishings have an artistic flair. And you'll never tire of watching the sunset from your private patio or deck.

🏠 *3 suites, 1 guest house. Guest phone, kitchens, fireplaces, TV, pool, piano in living room, barbecues, horseshoes. $125–$150, full breakfast. No credit cards. No pets. Closed June–mid-Sept.*

Rimrock West Hacienda

3450 N. Drake Pl., Tucson 85749, tel. 520/749–8774

Scenery—a panoramic view of Tucson—and solitude—20 acres of desert—are what innkeeper Mae Robbins and her husband Val provide for guests. Bobcats, coyote, javelina, and quail are frequent visitors to their 1960s-era adobe ranch house.

The beamed ceiling of the comfortable living room spans white-painted adobe walls, thick white carpeting, overstuffed couches, and an adobe fireplace, which burns massive pecan logs in winter. The art is mostly by Val, Mae, and their artist-son Christopher, who share a studio next door.

Both the queen room and the twin room have thick white Berber carpeting, modern pastel Southwestern decor, and mountain views. They open onto a sunny brick courtyard landscaped with oleander, aloe vera, and a splashing Mexican fountain. A kidney-shape pool occupies its own walled and landscaped enclosure.

Breakfast is usually served on the patio's cowhide Mexican tables and chairs. Mae offers a choice of cereals, eggs, pancakes, and fruit with her specialty hot muffins.

🏠 *2 double rooms with baths, 1 cottage with kitchen. Air-conditioning, ceiling fans, TV, pool. $95–$140, full breakfast. No credit cards. No smoking, no pets, no children under 16.*

The Triangle L Ranch Bed & Breakfast

Box 900, Oracle 85623, tel. 520/896–2804

Buffalo Bill is said to have been a regular visitor to this cattle and sheep ranch, homesteaded in the 1890s. The original 2,700 acres have been reduced to 80, but innkeepers Tom and Margot Beeston got the best part of the land, at a temperate elevation of 4,500 feet and with the largest oak trees in Oracle—a town 35 miles north of Tucson and now best known as home to Biosphere 2.

Guest accommodations are in four private cottages, dating from the 1880s to the 1920s and restored and furnished with period antiques. The Guest House is an ivy-covered adobe with a screened sleeping porch shaded by giant oaks. The three-bedroom Hill House has a front deck and views of the Santa Catalina Mountains as well as wrought-iron beds, a fully equipped kitchen, and a bath with a claw-foot tub and a shower.

Activity is centered in the main ranch house. Breakfast is prepared in a large, turn-of-the-century kitchen and includes homemade breads and muffins. The 15-foot table in the formal dining room and the matching sideboard are early-19th-century pieces that Margot inherited from her great grandmother.

🏨 *4 cottages. Kitchens in 2 cottages, fireplace in 1 cottage. $80–$110, Continental-plus breakfast. D, MC, V. No smoking indoors, no pets. Closed June–Aug.*

Southern Arizona

Mine Manager's House Inn

For many people, the question, "Why visit Southern Arizona?" can be answered in two words: Cochise County. The name alone evokes every dime-novel image of the Wild West— ferocious Indian wars, vast land grants, huge mineral stakes, and savage shoot-'em ups. But it all really happened in a southeast Arizona setting little different from the one visitors see today. Abandoned mining towns and sleepy Western hamlets dot a lonely landscape of rugged rock formations, deep pine forests, dense mountain ranges, and scrubby grasslands.

South of Sierra Vista, just above the Mexican border, a stone marker commemorates the spot where the first Europeans set foot in what is now the United States. In 1540, 80 years before the Pilgrims landed at Plymouth Rock, Spanish conquistador Don Francisco Vasquez de Coronado led one of Spain's largest expeditions from Mexico along the fertile San Pedro River valley, where the little towns of Benson and St. David are found today. They had come north to seek the legendary Seven Cities of Cibola, Indian pueblos rumored to have doors of polished turquoise and streets of solid gold.

But the real wealth of the region lay in its rich veins of copper and silver, not tapped until more than 300 years after the Spanish marched on in disappointment. Then all hell broke loose. Fortune seekers who rushed to the region to get in on a sure thing were met by the Chiracahua Apaches, led by Cochise and Geronimo. From rugged mountain hideaways, the Indian warriors fought off encroaching settlers and the U.S. cavalry sent to protect them.

Although the search for mineral booty in southeastern Arizona is much more notorious, the western side of the state wasn't entirely untouched by the rage to plunder the earth. The leaching plant built by the New Cornelia Copper Company (later Phelps Dodge) in 1917 transformed the sleepy desert community of Ajo into one of the most important mining districts in the state. And, in fact, its future potential for producing wealth for Phelps Dodge has been much in the news these days: The mines, closed in 1985, will be working again by the end of this century.

But today Southern Arizona is mainly mining the new lode of tourism. The bed-and-breakfast inns springing up throughout the area are a good barometer of the degree to which they've hit pay dirt. Many of the places here are not luxurious, but most are very comfortable—and where else can you fulfill your frontier fantasies by staying in a former four-room schoolhouse, a mine manager's house, or a branch of the county jail?

Places to Go, Sights to See

Ajo. About halfway between Tucson and the California border, Ajo was a thriving Phelps Dodge copper mining town for many years. It looked as though it might be abandoned when the company shut down operations in 1985, but many retirees were lured here by a temperate climate and low-cost housing. The 1997 announcement of the reopening of the mines by 1999 should bring about renewed growth. On Indian Village Road, at the outskirts of town, the *New Cornelia Open Pit Mine Lookout Point* provides a panoramic view of the town's huge open-pit mine, almost 2 miles wide. The white, Santa Fe–style mansion of John Campbell Greenway, who laid out the town in 1916 for the Calumet and Arizona Mining

Company, sits on a rocky ridge overlooking the mine and the lonely grave where he was buried in 1926. Nearby, the *Ajo Historical Society Museum* (160 Mission St., tel. 520/387–7105), set in St. Catherine's Indian Mission, has collected a mélange of articles relating to the town's past from locals. Some of the historical photographs are fascinating.

Amerind Foundation (Dragoon, exit 318 off I-10, tel. 520/586–3666). Hidden in the oaks and boulders of Texas Canyon is a striking Spanish-style museum devoted to Native American culture, founded in 1937 by amateur archaeologist William Fulton, whose collection of mostly Southwestern art is housed in the adjacent Fulton-Hayden Memorial Art Gallery. The setting, the house, and the quality of the displays make this well worth a short detour.

Benson. Once the hub of the Southern Pacific Railroad and a stop on the Butterfield Stagecoach route, Benson has for many years been a fairly sleepy little town. With the start-up in 1995 of the *San Pedro & Southwestern Railroad* (796 E. Country Club Dr., tel. 520/586–2266 or 800/269–6314), a scenic ride through the San Pedro Riparian Preserve that includes lunch at the ghost town of Fairbanks, Benson began to draw a few more visitors. And more recently, the town has begun annexing property along Highway 90 and building additional chain hotels in anticipation of the long-awaited opening of *Kartchner Caverns State Park,* delayed at least a year from the originally announced date of November 1997. For directions and information about the opening date, contact the Benson–San Pedro Valley Chamber of Commerce (*see* Tourist Information, *below*).

Bisbee. Dominated for many years by the Phelps Dodge Corporation, Bisbee went into decline when its last mine closed in 1975, but was revitalized in the 1980s as an artists' community. At the edge of town, visitors can still see the huge hole left by the *Lavender Pit Mine* and descend for a fascinating tour of the *Copper Queen Mine* (1 Dart Rd., tel. 520/432–2071). Across the street, housed in the former Phelps Dodge general office, the *Mining and Historical Museum* (Queens Plaza, tel. 520/432–7071) houses photographs and artifacts from the town's mining heyday. Behind the museum is the venerable *Copper Queen Hotel,* built a century ago (*see* review, *below*), and, adjacent to it, *Brewery Gulch,* where excess beer used to flow down the street and into the gutter. Bisbee's *Main Street* is lined with appealing crafts shops, boutiques, and restaurants, many of them in well-preserved turn-of-the-century brick buildings.

Chiracahua National Monument (Dos Cabezas Route, near intersection of U.S. 666 and AZ 181, tel. 520/824–3560). Here vast outcroppings of volcanic rock worn by erosion into pinnacles and spires are set in a forest where autumn and spring occur at the same time. During the last century, the beautiful but rugged landscape was the home territory of Chief Cochise and his Chiracahua Apache tribe, who dubbed it "Land of the Standing-Up Rocks." In 1862, U.S. troops built a fort designed to help protect stage routes from attacks by the Apache. On AZ 186, just north of Chiracahua National Monument, the *Fort Bowie National Historical Site* (tel. 520/847–2500), which includes the Butterfield Stage Stop, is testament to this historical period.

Douglas. Founded in 1902 by Dr. James Douglas to serve as the copper smelting center for the mines in nearby Bisbee, Douglas doesn't seem to have changed much since the 1950s; it's often used as a location for Hollywood films set in even earlier times. There's not much yet to see inside, but the *Douglas/Williams House Museum* (10001 D Ave., tel. 520/364–7379), opened in 1991 by the Arizona Historical Society, is the 1909 home of "Rawhide" Jimmy Douglas, son of the man for whom the town is named. "Texas" John Slaughter, sheriff of Cochise County from 1886 to 1890 and U.S. marshal, retired to *Slaughter Ranch/San Bernardino Land Grant* (17 mi east of Douglas, tel. 520/558–2474) after his law-enforcement adventures in Tombstone and Bisbee were over. A visit to the preserved ranch and a videotape of Slaughter's life and times provide a glimpse of the wild and woolly Old West. The center of town in Douglas has long been—and continues to be—the *Gadsen Hotel* (1046 G Ave., tel. 520/364–4481), built in 1907. This National Historic Monument, which has a 42-foot stained-glass window depicting a desert landscape, served as the location of *The Life and Times of Judge Roy Bean*.

Fort Huachuca (Sierra Vista, 80 mi south of Tucson, tel. 520/533–3536). Established as a frontier outpost by the U.S. Army in 1877 to control the Indians, Fort Huachuca hosts one of this country's finest museums of military history. Displays document the all-black units, called Buffalo Soldiers, who helped fight the Native Americans after the Civil War. Civilians may visit, but they must register at the main entrance, Buffalo Soldier Gate, and show vehicle registration and driver's license.

Ghost Towns. A number of the smaller mining communities of Cochise County died when their veins of ore ran out, and their adobe buildings gradually melted back into the desert under the summer monsoons. Some of what are termed ghost towns in the area are only heaps of rubble, but others give strong evidence of better days. At *Gleeson*, marked by a turnoff just east of Tombstone on AZ 80, some building ruins and an old cemetery can still be seen. To the west of Tombstone, on AZ 82, *Fairbanks* has had a bit of a resurgence since it became a stop on the San Pedro & Southwestern Railroad (*see* Benson, *above*). The onetime rail and stage-coach stop is being restored by the Bureau of Land Management; you can wander around a number of ramshackle buildings that date back to 1882, including a post office and a general store established by the Goldwater brothers. *Charleston*, where the San Pedro train turns around, once saw more action than Tombstone, some 9 miles away. Outlaws Johnny Ringo and the Clanton brothers used to hang around the town's four 24-hour saloons, and Curley Bill Brocius, shot dead by Wyatt Earp, is said to be buried there, though no grave site was ever found. A few holdouts remain in *Dos Cabezas*, 15 miles southeast of Willcox, enough to keep the post office open; the 1885 Wells Fargo station still stands. A tunnel through the mountaintop connects the eastern and western halves of the abandoned town of *Hilltop*, farther southeast of Willcox. The gold camp of *Pearce*, 1 mile off Rte. 191, 29 miles south of Willcox, also has a post office and one viable store; the ruins of the mill, the mine, and many old adobes are very much in evidence. Six miles northwest of Portal in the Chiricahua Mountains, *Paradise* was active in the 1900s, and a few old-timers still live here. Look for the old town jail among the ruined buildings.

Kitt Peak National Observatory (56 mi southeast of Tucson, off AZ 286, tel. 520/325–9200 for recorded tour information, tel. 520/620–5350 for visitors center). This cluster of 19 telescopes in the Quinlan Mountains, on the Tohono O'Odham Indian Reservation, includes the largest solar telescope in the world. The visitors center has films and tours of the mountaintop complex. Nighttime dinner and stargazing tours are offered; call for details.

Nogales. Many visitors to Tucson take the easy 63-mile drive down I-19 to Mexico's lively border town of Nogales, a good place to shop for souvenirs— everything from stuffed armadillos and cowboy boots to handcrafted tiles and pottery—or to have a good Mexican meal. Most Americans park in one of the many lots on the U.S. side (about $4 a day) and walk across the border.

Organ Pipe Cactus National Monument (visitor center 32 mi southeast of Ajo, off AZ 85, tel. 520/387–6849). The largest gathering spot north of Mexico for the many-armed cousin of the saguaro, Organ Pipe has two scenic loop drives, one 21 miles long, the other 53 miles long, both on winding, graded dirt roads; stop at the visitor center for a map. The latter trail leads to Quitobaquito, a desert oasis with a flowing spring.

Patagonia. Art galleries and boutiques coexist with real Western saloons in this little, tree-lined town some 82 miles south of Tucson, surrounded by rolling hills and choice cattle-grazing land. At the *Patagonia-Sonoita Creek Preserve* (tel. 520/394–2400), 750 acres of riparian habitat are protected along the Patagonia-Sonoita Creek. More than 260 bird species have been sighted here, along with deer, javelina, coatimundi, desert tortoise, snakes, and more.

Ramsey Canyon Preserve (90 mi southeast of Tucson, off AZ 92, tel. 520/378–2785). Designated the first U.S. National Natural Landmark, in 1965, this 300-acre preserve with well-marked trails is home to more than 170 species of birds, dozens of species of butterflies, deer, snakes, frogs, and mountain lions.

Texas Canyon (63 mi east of Tucson off I-10). You don't have to get off the freeway to see Texas Canyon, a striking gathering of huge boulders that appear to be delicately balanced against each other, but a rest area here with bathrooms and picnic tables is a good place to stop for lunch.

Tombstone. Every Sunday and sometimes on Saturday, the fatal 1881 gunfight between Wyatt Earp and Doc Holliday and the Clanton gang is reenacted by professional stuntmen on *Allen Street*, the main tourist drag of Tombstone. You can see the graves of some of the losing gunmen at the *Boot Hill Graveyard* at the northwestern corner of town, facing U.S. 80. At the *OK Corral* (Allen St., bet. 3rd and 4th Sts., tel. 520/457–3456), the site of the shoot-out, a recorded voice-over details the infamous event; the history of the entire town is dramatically narrated by Vincent Price at the adjoining *Historama*. You can step back into time at the *Bird Cage Theater* (6th and Allen Sts., tel. 520/457–3421), where a honky-tonk piano once played and performers such as Lillian Russell trod the creaky boards; and at the beautiful mahogany bar of the *Crystal Palace* (Allen and 5th Sts., tel. 520/457–3611). For the least touristy look at the town's history, visit *Tombstone Courthouse State Historic Park* (Toughnut and 3rd Sts., tel. 520/

457–3311); the courthouse, built in 1882, is filled with fascinating artifacts of the town in the days when it was the seat of Cochise County.

Tubac. The military garrison established here in 1752 to protect early Spanish settlers and the peaceful Pima and Tohono O'Odham Indians from Apache raids is the oldest European settlement in Arizona. It was from here that Juan Bautista de Anza led 240 colonists across the desert, an expedition that resulted in the founding of San Francisco in 1776. Today, the little town is a popular art colony with more than 70 galleries, studios, and shops; contact the Tubac Chamber of Commerce (tel. 520/398–2704) for information on the annual *Tubac Festival of the Arts,* held in February. The *Tubac Presidio State Historic Park and Museum* (center of town, tel. 520/398–2252) preserves relics and history of the early colony, and the first 3 miles of the *de Anza National Historic Trail,* along the Santa Cruz River from Tumacacori to Tubac, was dedicated in 1992. The conquistador's march along the trail is reenacted with great pageantry during the last week of October.

Tumacacori National Monument (50 mi south of Tucson on I-19, tel. 520/398–2341). Around 1800, on the tree-shaded banks of the Santa Cruz River, the Franciscans built the mission of San Jose de Tumacacori. The friars fled in 1848 as a result of fierce Indian raids; legend has it that the silver church bells they buried nearby have never been recovered.

Willcox, once the Cattle Capital of the country, is also the hometown of cowboy singer and actor Rex Allen, whose life and times are detailed at the *Rex Allen Arizona Cowboy Museum* (155 N. Railroad Ave., tel. 520/284–4583); the Cowboy Hall of Fame in the back of the museum salutes the Arizona cattlemen. Also in town is the *Museum of the Southwest* (1550 N. Circle Rd., tel. 520/384–2272), a room in the visitor center focusing on Willcox history as well as on rancher and Native American life in the late 1880s and early 1900s. Adjacent to the museum, *Stout's Cider Mill* (tel. 520/384–2272) is a good place to pick up some dessert for the road; with an excellent climate for growing apples at an elevation of 4,167 feet, Willcox is now the apple pie center of Arizona.

Wineries. The term "Arizona wine country" may sound like an oxymoron, but the soil and atmospheric conditions in the Santa Cruz Valley, southeast of Tucson, are ideal for growing grapes. The growers in the scenic ranching region, all found near where Routes 82 and 83 intersect, include *Callaghan* (3 mi south of Elgin, tel. 520/455–5650), *Sonoita Vineyards* (3 mi southeast of Elgin, tel. 520/455–5893), the kosher *Santa Cruz Winery* (154 McKoewn Ave., Patagonia, tel. 520/394–2888), the *Village of Elgin Winery* (Elgin, tel. 520/455–9309), and *Arizona Vineyards* (1830 Patagonia Hwy., 4 mi northeast of Nogales on Rte. 82, tel. 520/287–7972).

Restaurants

As Bisbee continues to be discovered by visitors, dining quality and options are steadily improving. The small northern Italian–style menu at stylish **Cafe Roka** (tel. 520/432–5153) emphasizes pastas; portions are generous and the entrée price

($9–$16) includes soup, salad, and a palate-cleansing sorbet. Also reasonably priced, **Stenzel's** (tel. 520/432–7611), set in a wooden cabin, is known for its seafood, but its meats and pastas are well prepared too. A jewel in the town's gourmet crown is the **High Desert Inn**; *see* the listing *below*, for details. Tombstone's restaurants are geared for the eat-and-run, modest-budget tourist trade. At the **Nellie Cashman Restaurant and Pie Salon** (tel. 520/457–3950)— the oldest restaurant in Tombstone, opened in 1882—the menu is basic American with a variety of burgers, hot and cold sandwiches, steaks, fried chicken, and some Mexican entrées; there are often lines to get in.

Arizona wine country is home to some surprisingly sophisticated but moderately priced restaurants. In tiny Sonoita, **Karen's Wine Country Cafe** (tel. 520/455–5282) could be straight out of Sonoma, California, with its pretty country French-style patio and innovative menu featuring salads and pasta dishes—and of course a good selection of wines by the glass. Also in Sonoita, **Er Pastaro** (tel. 520/455–5821), a low-key place, serves every type of pasta imaginable, as well as a nice selection of Italian wines. Patagonia also has a couple of excellent eateries: **Marie's** (340 Naugle Ave., tel. 520/394–2812), opened in early 1997, serves creative Mediterranean fare in a series of colorful, French Impressionist–pretty dining rooms. New owners of **Ovens of Patagonia** (corner 3rd Ave. and AZ 82, tel. 520/394–2483), long known for its fine quiches and salads, have expanded both the menu (there's a snazzy Cuban-Mexican influence now) and hours (it's open for dinner on high-season weekends). Restaurant hours are limited throughout the area; be sure to call ahead before you do any driving.

Tourist Information

Ajo Chamber of Commerce (AZ 85, just south of the plaza, 321 Taladro, Ajo 85321, tel. 520/387–7742). **Benson–San Pedro Valley Chamber of Commerce** (226 E. 4th St., Box 2255, Benson 85602, tel. 520/586–2842). **Bisbee Chamber of Commerce** (7 Main St., Box BA, Bisbee 85603, tel. 520/432–5421). **Douglas Chamber of Commerce** (1125 Pan American Way, Douglas 85607, tel. 520/364–2477). **Graham County Chamber of Commerce** (1111 Thatcher Blvd., Safford 85546, tel. 520/428–2511. **Patagonia Visitors Center** (Box 241, 315 McKoewn Ave., 85625, tel. 520/394–0060). **Sierra Vista Chamber of Commerce** (21 E. Willcox, Sierra Vista 85635, tel. 520/458–6940 or 800/288–3861). **Tombstone Office of Tourism** (Box 917, Tombstone 85638, tel. 520/457–3548 or 800/457–3423). **Tubac Chamber of Commerce** (Box 1866, Tubac 85646, tel. 520/398–2704). **Willcox Chamber of Commerce & Agriculture** (1500 Circle I Rd., Willcox 85643, tel. 520/384–2272 or 800/200–2272).

Reservation Services

Arizona Association of Bed and Breakfast Inns (Box 7186, Phoenix 85011, tel. 800/284–2589). **Bed & Breakfast Southwest** (2916 N. 70th St., Scottsdale 85251, tel. 602/995–2831 or 800/762–9704, fax 602/874–1316). **Mi Casa Su Casa B&B Reservation Service** (Box 950, Tempe 85280, tel. 602/990–0682, 800/456–0682 reservations, fax 602/990–3390).

Amado Territory Inn

*Box 81, 3001 E. Frontage Rd., Amado
85645, tel. 520/398-8684 or 888/398–8684,
fax 520/398–8186*

Blending old-style architecture with modern conveniences, the Amado Territory Inn resembles a ranch house from the late 1800s on the outside. Inside, a soaring pitched ceiling and lots of contemporary Southwest art remind you that this place was actually built closer to the end of the current century—1996, to be exact.

The location mixes two worlds, too. The town of Amado consists of a few stores, two cowboy bars, and a post office, but it's bisected by busy I-19. Even though the inn is directly off the frontage road, it feels worlds away. It's part of a beautifully landscaped complex that includes a fine Greek-southwestern–style restaurant, a plant nursery, a naturopathic healer, and a silversmith.

Rooms, furnished with pieces handcrafted in Mexico, are all on the second floor; some have balconies. On the first floor, adjacent to a lounge with a huge fireplace, the dining room looks out on the Santa Rita Mountains. Liz Lazich, one of the two friendly innkeepers, is a gourmet chef. She might start your day with a wonderfully light mushroom-and-cheese strudel.

▦ *9 double rooms with bath. TV lounge, restaurant next door. $65–$125, full breakfast included. MC, V. No smoking indoors, no pets.*

The Bisbee Grand Hotel

61 Main St., Box 825, Bisbee 85603, tel. 520/432–5900 or 800/421–1909

This 1906, two-story rooming house for copper miners burned down in 1908 and had to be rebuilt. In 1986, an antiques dealer from Texas transformed it into a flamboyant, Old West–Victorian hotel. Bill Thomas and his late wife Gail later purchased it and opened it as a B&B in July of 1989.

Today, with its broad staircase, skylight, balcony overlooking Main Street, ornate chandeliers, red carpets, and red-flocked wallpaper, it recalls nothing so much as a historic bordello; the high-ceiling rooms heighten that impression. The Garden Suite is filled with a forest of faux plants, a trickling fountain, sinful red carpeting, and a 6-foot walnut bed suitable for Adam and Eve. In the red-ceiling Oriental Room lined with black Cantonese wallpaper, the focus is on the ornate, 19th-century, carved teak Chinese wedding bed.

A full breakfast, featuring custom-blended Bisbee Grand Coffee, is served in the lobby, on the landing, or outside on the balcony.

▦ *4 double rooms with baths, 4 doubles share 3 baths, 3 suites. Ceiling fans, sinks in all but 1 room, claw-foot tubs in suites, off-street parking. $55–$78 rooms, $95–$110 suite, full breakfast. D, MC, V. No smoking, no pets, 2-day minimum stay on holiday and special-event weekends.*

Casa de San Pedro

8933 S. Yell La., Hereford 85615, tel. 520/366–1300, fax 520/366–9701

Everything's up-to-date in Hereford, a sleepy town near Sierra Vista—or at least it is at the Casa de San Pedro. Everything seems like new at the hacienda-style inn built adjacent to the San Pedro Riparian National Conservation area in 1995. Even the bird-watching is high-tech: A computer with Robert Tory Peterson software in the high-ceiling common room lets avian admirers check their daily sightings against the lists of the departed master.

Guest quarters, arranged around a tiled central courtyard, are bright and modern, too, with handcrafted wooden furnishings from northern Mexico lending local character. Each room is individually decorated. In one there's a bed with a saguaro rib headboard, for example, while another has a cheerful Western-pattern bedspread and curtains.

Because the place is so new, the surrounding landscape is still a bit sparse, but hiking trails just beyond the house lead directly into the lush nature preserve. Breakfasts are designed to be as healthy or indulgent as you like; they're light on cheese and eggs, and meat is served on the side.

🛏 *10 rooms with private bath. Guest services area with house phone, refrigerator, and microwave, library, gift shop, guest laundry for longer stays. $95 double, full breakfast. MC, V. No smoking indoors, no pets, no children under 12, minimum stay some holiday weekends.*

The Clawson House

116 Clawson Ave., Box 454, Bisbee 85603, tel. 520/432–5237 or 800/467–5237

The Clawson House sits regally atop Castle Rock, the craggy buttress of Tombstone Canyon, and surveys Old Bisbee. Once the home of S. W. Clawson, the superintendent of the Copper Queen Mine, it was built in 1895 on the only flat acre in town, an executive fortress overlooking its fiefdom.

In 1988 Californians Wally Kuehl and Jim Grosskopf purchased the proud old redwood structure and spent two years restoring and furnishing it with the art and antiques they had collected during the previous 30 years. Many of the fittings are original to the house, including the etched Italian crystal windows, glass French doors, creaky oak floors, and crystal chandeliers. The Oriental carpets in the living room, the fireplace in the grand parlor, and the white-paneled china cabinet in the formal dining room all reflect the fussy glory of the period, as do the stuffed animal heads, mounted horns, ceramics, and other assorted collectibles that fill practically every inch of

surface. Nor are the walls left bare: Both public areas and guest rooms are lined with Currier & Ives prints, framed battle scenes, landscapes, and portraits of long-lost Victorians.

But if you tire of Victorian clutter, all you need do is step out to the sunporch for the world to open up. To the south you can look out over the once-wild and bawdy Brewery Gulch, past the raw, gaping, Lavender Pit Mine to the silhouette of the San José Mountains in northern Mexico on the distant horizon. To the north, the eye follows Tombstone Canyon, lined with 19th-century homes and the occasional giant cottonwood trees, to the crest of the Mule Mountains.

Upstairs, two spacious, well-lighted rooms share a bath that still has the original floor tiles and claw-foot tub. The downstairs bedroom has a 6-foot mahogany bedstead with mirrored mahogany vanity to match, a ruby-domed gas chandelier converted to electricity, and a standing lamp with a tasseled, red velvet shade.

Jim's elaborate breakfasts are served in what was originally the water tower, now a cozy dining nook attached to the modern kitchen. A fresh fruit compote with lemon yogurt might be followed by home-baked zucchini-pineapple bread and Swiss cheese and chili quiche, still hot from the oven.

🛏 *1 double room with bath, 2 doubles share bath. Cable TV, off-street parking. $65–$75, full breakfast. AE, D, MC, V. Smoking in designated areas only, no pets, no small children.*

Copper Queen Hotel

11 Howell Ave., Drawer CQ, Bisbee 85603, tel. 520/432–2216 or 800/247–5829

Built by the Copper Queen Mining Company (which later became Phelps Dodge) in 1902, the imposing five-story brick hotel was once *the* gathering spot for politicians, mining officials, and celebrities, among them John Wayne, Teddy Roosevelt, and General "Black Jack" Pershing. More recently, it's hosted Hollywood types who've discovered Bisbee as a Wild West TV and movie location.

The rooms all have high ceilings with circulating fans, tall windows, and roomy private baths. Some are tiny, however, and the walls are thin. A modernization program has restored some of their former sheen and added modern amenities, but don't expect to be as wowed as the turn-of-the-century crowd was.

The white-pillared Copper Queen Dining Room, just off the lobby, serves three meals a day in an atmosphere of faded period luxury. The Copper Queen Saloon recaptures the days of World War I, when copper prices were high and Bisbee was booming.

⊞ *45 double rooms with baths. Telephones, radios, and color TVs in rooms, no-smoking rooms available, restaurant, bar, pool, gift shop. $72–$100, breakfast not included. AE, D, MC, V.*

The Duquesne House Bed and Breakfast

357 Duquesne St., Box 772, Patagonia 85624, tel. 520/394–2732

Don't be startled when you enter this unusual, tree-shaded Eden in tiny Patagonia and see a 21-foot-long snake. Innkeeper Regina Medley is an artist who works with textiles; her reptile and other soft sculptures and artwork enliven various parts of her tin-roofed adobe inn, as do the creations of other local artists.

Buttresses and plastered Santa Fe benches have been added to the B&B, built as a boardinghouse for miners more than 90 years ago, and burned adobe bricks replaced the original wood floors, but the 17-inch-thick adobe walls, narrow doors, and lintels are all original. The Western period furniture through-

out the house was collected in the Patagonia area. Each of its four high-ceiling guest units has its own private street entrance. The rooms are not luxurious, but creative-minded visitors find that such details as hand-painted scrollwork and colorful tiles compensate.

Regina's breakfasts, served buffet style, may be enjoyed in your room, on the flower-filled screen porch, or at the hostess's table in the dining room, part of a Santa Fe–style great room.

⊞ *3 suites, 1 efficiency apartment. Radios and ceiling fans in all rooms, woodburning stove in 2 rooms, kitchenette and TV in apartment, common area with TV and house phone. $70–$85, full breakfast. No credit cards. No smoking, no pets.*

Grapevine Canyon Ranch

Box 302, Pearce 85625, tel. 520/826–3185 or 800/245–9202, fax 520/826–3636

You expect Jack Palance to gallop up to the gates of this guest ranch in the Dragoon Mountains, about 80 miles southeast of Tucson, and take you out to round up some doggies. You will have the chance to watch—and, in some cases, take part in—real cowboy activities at the working cattle ranch next door. This is the place to come if you've ever had fantasies of riding off into the sunset: Horses for all levels of experience are on hand. There are also lots of hiking trails on quintessential Western terrain, and the ranch is a good base from which to explore Douglas, Tombstone, Bisbee, and Chiracahua National Monument.

Accommodations, located in either cabins, casitas, or a lodge house, vary: Some are rather plain, while others have striking contemporary southwestern furnishings. All have spacious decks and porches. Three hearty meals are served buffet style in the rustic dining room, where a fire blazes on cool evenings.

🏨 *3 2-person cabins, 2 casitas for up to 3 people, 4 casitas for up to 5 people, 3-bedroom lodge for up to 9 people. Pool, hot tub, games room, TV/video room, gift shop, coin laundry, unscheduled live entertainment. $170 per person, 3 meals included. AE, D, MC, V. No pets, 4-night minimum in peak season, 2-night minimum off-season.*

The Guest House Inn

700 Guesthouse Rd., Ajo 85321, tel. 520/ 387-6133

Like virtually every other building in Ajo, this one was built by the Phelps Dodge Corporation; it was designed in high style in 1925 to accommodate executives visiting the copper mine. Abandoned when the mine closed in 1985, the inn was purchased three years later by Norma Walker, who used to work here as a housekeeper.

The four original VIP guest rooms, now beautifully remodeled, all have different themes. The Ajo Room features Santa Fe–style decor, while the Old Pueblo Room emphasizes Ajo's Spanish Colonial heritage. The Bisbee Room has twin brass beds and Victorian furnishings, and the Prescott Room boasts a four-poster bed and fittings reminiscent of Arizona's Territorial days.

The B&B's pride is the stately dining room with its formal, 20-foot carved walnut table where breakfast is served; specialties include pecan waffles with berries and cream, and blueberry French toast. A longtime Ajo resident, Norma can direct you to all the best places for bird-watching in the area.

🏨 *4 double rooms with baths. Individual heating/cooling controls in rooms, fireplace and TV in common room, patio. $69–$79, full breakfast. AE, DC, MC, V. No smoking, no pets.*

High Desert Inn

Box 145, 8 Naco Rd., Bisbee 85603, tel. 520/432-1442 or 800/281-0510

Bisbee is nothing if not adaptable. The little hillside town looked like it might go under in 1975, when Phelps Dodge shut down the copper mine, but many miners liked the place well enough to hang around. They were soon joined by hippies, who opened crafts shops and started an annual poetry festival. Now there's a new wave of urban refugees, who enjoy Bisbee's tranquility but also want a bit of the consumerist good life.

Count Margaret Hartnett in the latter category. The Cordon-Bleu trained chef, who had been cooking for some major political movers and shakers in New York City, was on a trip out West when, as she puts it, "I got off I-10 in New Mexico and found myself in Bisbee an hour later." It was love at first sight. She bought a house within a week, and then convinced her other love (now husband), actor Darrell Dixon, to come out and open up a restaurant and inn with her.

Using a lot of elbow grease and imagination, the couple set to work on restoring the 1908 county jail, little more than four walls and a lot of turn-of-the-century electricity when they acquired it in 1992. It took them 10 months to gut and restore the neoclassic-style building, but the metamorphosis was little short of amazing: The inn that opened in 1994 at the edge of Bisbee's historic district offers the most up-to-date and stylish accommodations in town—not to mention some of the best food.

No attention to detail was spared: All five rooms feature handmade wrought-iron beds imported from Paris, covered by 200-count cotton sheets. Craftsman-style end tables were handcrafted in Bisbee to match the beds' higher-than-standard-size frames. Modern amenities include data-compatible phones with built-in answering machines, not available anywhere else in town; the rooms also have cable TV. The chic Continental restaurant, which doubles as an art gallery, is only open for dinner Thursday through Saturday; seasonally changing dishes might include baked Brie and goat cheese followed by French-trimmed pork chops.

🏠 *5 double rooms with baths. Coffee bar in lobby. $65–$90, breakfast not included. D, MC, V. No smoking, no pets. Closed 1st 3 weeks in June.*

Main Street Inn

26 Main St., Box 454, Bisbee 85603, tel. 520/432–5237 or 800/467–5237

A place with a history of hospitality, the Main Street Inn was built as a hotel in 1888 and later served as a boardinghouse for copper miners. More than a century later, the building is open to the public again.

The lodging's nine guest units are on the second floor, as are a living room, TV room, kitchen, and glassed-in back porch. The somewhat creaky wooden floor is covered with wall-to-wall carpeting. The high-ceiling rooms are done in southwestern style; some have skylights and exposed brick walls, and those facing Main Street feature distinctive bay windows.

🏠 *3 double rooms share 2 baths, 4 doubles share 2 baths, 1 2-bedroom suite. Off-street parking. $45–$65 rooms, suite $95, Continental breakfast. AE, D, MC, V. Smoking in designated areas only, no pets.*

The Mine Manager's House Inn

1 Greenway Dr., Ajo 85321, tel. 520/387–6505, fax 520/387–6508

The imposing, 5,000-square foot mansion that once belonged to the superintendent of the Phelps Dodge copper mine overlooks the entire town from its site atop the highest hill in Ajo. The public

areas include a library/sunroom, a spacious living room, and a formal dining room with a view out over the town. A hot tub in the back is wonderful for soaking tired muscles after a day of desert travel.

Each of the five individually decorated rooms has high ceilings and ceiling fans. The Greenway Suite, also called the "honeymoon suite," is the largest one and boasts a marble bathtub and vanity, and pretty floral drapes. The Nautical Room has two queen-size brass beds and a 180-degree view out over the town; parts of an old schooner, including the steering wheel, are worked into the decor.

Breakfasts are served on linens and fine china in the superintendent's light-filled formal dining room. The meal may feature eggs Benedict or waffles, in addition to coffee, fresh juices, and seasonal fruits.

🏠 *2 double rooms with baths, 3 suites. TV and VCR in living room, library, guest coin laundry, outdoor hot tub, barbecue grill, off-street parking. $72–$105, full breakfast. MC, V. No smoking indoors, off-site pet boarding.*

The OK Street Jailhouse

9 OK St., Box 1152, Bisbee 85603, tel. 520/432–7435, 800/821–0678 message phone, fax 520/432–7434

If the narrow building at No. 9 OK Street, one block from Bisbee's Brewery Gulch, looks formidable, that's because it was built in 1904 as the downtown branch of the Cochise County Jail. The first story is faced with stone blocks, the second with brick; the walls and floors are of thick, poured concrete, and the windows are barred with solid iron grilles. It took a clever entrepreneur to turn the place into a cheery and wonderfully original two-story suite.

The downstairs jailer's office is now the small entry area. The drunk tank, framed by floor-to-ceiling cell bars, houses a small modern kitchen, a half bath, and a contemporary-style living room with a couch that folds out into a queen-size bed. Upstairs, in the heavily barred cell once used for serious offenders, is a bedroom with a queen-size bed, small sitting area, and modern bathroom with shower and Jacuzzi tub. Guests have the entire building to themselves for the duration of their self-imposed sentence; advance arrangements are made to pick up the key from managers Reg and Doris Turner.

🏠 *1 duplex suite. Phone, TV. $100 (each additional night $75, 1 week $450), no breakfast. MC, V. Pets accepted with advance notice only.*

Olney House Bed & Breakfast

1104 Central Ave., Safford 85546, tel. 520/428-5118 or 800/814-5118

George Olney was a sheriff of Graham County in the Wild West days of the 1870s. Unable to budget a salary, the county fathers agreed to pay him $2.50 for every arrest. Within two years he had amassed $30,000. Much of these earnings were spent on this classic, two-story example of Western Colonial Revival, completed in 1890. From the bay windows on the second floor, with a 180-degree view of Safford and the verdant Gila River Valley, Sheriff Olney could look for local desperados.

In 1988 the National Park Service announced that 20 Safford buildings had qualified for listing in the National Register of Historic Places: the 1920 Arizona Bank, the 1920 Southern Pacific Railroad Depot, a 1915 schoolhouse, a 1920 hotel, and 16 private residences. The oldest of these was the Olney House.

Innkeepers Patrick and Carole Mahoney, from San Francisco, spent four years renovating the redbrick, 14-room mansion. In 1992 they opened it as Graham County's first B&B. The home boasts 12-foot ceilings (now with circulating fans); five fireplaces with unusual, ceramic-tile detailing; polished oak and maple floors; and lots of elegant wood paneling. The bright corner dining room fills with morning light from three wide, 7-foot windows. Many of the furnishings are treasures brought back by the Mahoneys from travels in Southeast Asia. Upstairs there are three corner bedrooms.

A huge pecan tree shades two cottages in the back. Other trees on the landscaped corner lot include willows, cottonwood, Italian and Arizona cyprus, native pine, ash, and paloverdes. Each year the Mahoneys harvest fresh fruit from their apple, plum, and peach trees to make jams.

The breakfast coffee beans, ground fresh daily, are from Graffeo in San Francisco. The dill and cilantro in the omelets and potatoes are picked from the garden. Guests have a choice of muesli with yogurt, honey, and fruit; oatmeal with pecans, wheat germ, honey, and fruit; or a cheese omelet spiced with roasted New Mexico chilies (mild, medium, or hot).

🏠 *3 double rooms share bath, 2 cottages. TV, cable, fireplace in living room, spa. $70, full breakfast. MC, V. No smoking indoors, no pets.*

Ramsey Canyon Inn

31 Ramsey Canyon Rd., Hereford 85615, tel. 520/378-3010

When guests talk turkey around the breakfast table at the Ramsey Canyon Inn, you can take that literally: Wild toms often strut their stuff in full view of the visitors. But it's the hummingbirds—all 14 species that visit the Nature Conservancy's Mile Hi/Ramsey Canyon preserve, adjacent to the inn—who are the stars. Some true devotees also come to see the elegant Trogon, a rare species that has successfully nested in the area.

But this scenic, tree-filled gorge in the Huachuca Mountains, 10 miles south of Sierra Vista, is not only a haven for bird-watchers; at 5,400 feet, it's also one of the most temperate spots in the nation, with an annual average high of 75°F and average low of 50°F. You can walk the shaded paths of the preserve and see all kinds of wildlife—coatimundi, deer, and the endangered Ramsey Canyon frog.

The inn is almost as interesting as its setting. The front section, built of native stone and wood in 1963, incorporates local Arizona history with planks from the old post office at Fort Huachuca, the train station at Fairbank, and the Lavender Pit Mine in Bisbee. The 1988 addition at the back of the house includes the six guest rooms, named by owner Shirlene DeSantis after her favorite hummingbirds. These accommodations, furnished in country Victorian style, enjoy the soothing ripple of a year-round stream, as do two separate housekeeping cottages (those who stay there don't get breakfast but have their own kitchens).

Not only the rooms, but every area of the house is filled with fascinating collectibles. On the staircase leading up to the guest rooms you can see antique tobacco artifacts, including an ad for Lucky Strikes featuring Ronald Reagan. In the kitchen the focus is naturally on food-related items, and the old jars and containers often fascinate guests who remember them from their childhood.

If your fortifying breakfast—perhaps stuffed French toast or blue-corn pancakes served with jam from the inn's own orchard—doesn't hold you through the afternoon, there are always two fresh-baked pies waiting for you in the kitchen.

🏠 *6 double rooms with baths, 2 housekeeping cottages. Fireplace in living room, gift shop. $90–$105 rooms, full breakfast; cottages, accommodating up to 4 people, $95–$115, no breakfast. No credit cards. Smoking on patio only, no pets.*

San Pedro River Inn

8326 S. Hereford Rd., Hereford 85615, tel. 520/366–5532

Walter Kolbe is proof that you *can* go home again. When, after 25 years of living in Illinois, he decided he wanted to return to the ranch country of southern Arizona where he grew up, he was hard pressed to figure out how he and his wife, May, could make the move financially feasible. Enter Walt's sister, Beth, who works for the Nature Conservancy in Tucson. The story goes that the non-profit group needed to sell off 20 acres of land adjoining the San Pedro Riparian National Conservation area, and they were hoping to find someone who would turn the former dairy farm into a low-impact business—say, a bed-and-breakfast. Walt and May jumped at the chance, and the rest is hospitality history.

The inn's four separate guest houses are perfect for a variety of visitors. Proximity to the preserve makes this place ideal for groups of bird-watchers—a banding seminar was once offered here—while families appreciate the full kitchens and barbecue grills of each house, as well as the on-site laundry facilities. There are even jungle gyms and swings. This is a spot where you'll want to settle in and relax for a spell, maybe fish from the shores of one of the two ponds or picnic under a spreading willow tree. You can even bring your pets, if you're willing to leave them outdoors in the large, coyote-proof pen that a former owner built for his Barbados sheep.

Furnishings in the houses are low-key and country comfortable; you don't come here for glitz but for peace and quiet (although the media-addicted can tune into noncable TV). With the fully supplied kitchen—baked goods, fresh fruit, and juice—you can keep pretty much to yourself if you like, but then you'd miss the sing-alongs May sometimes leads in the main house, as well as Walt's colorful ranch stories. Ask him about the time his father came home with a Gila monster.

🏠 *1 1-bedroom cottage, 2 2-bedroom cottages, 1 3-bedroom cottage. Conference center, piano lounge, fireplace in 2 of the cottages. $95 for 2 guests in a cottage ($135 for 4 guests, $200 for 6 guests). Continental breakfast. No credit cards. Pets accepted in outdoor pen, corrals available for horses.*

School House Inn Bed & Breakfast

Box 32, 818 Tombstone Canyon, Bisbee 85603, tel. 520/432-2996 or 800/537-4333

The two-story brick Garfield School, in the Tombstone Canyon neighborhood on Bisbee's west side, was built in 1918 to educate children in grades 1 through 4. The original four large classrooms, one for each grade, were divided into apartments in the 1930s and used as a nursing home in the 1970s. Abandoned by 1981, the building was refurbished and converted to a B&B in 1989.

The innkeepers took the built-in schoolhouse theme and ran with it. Depending on how you feel about your school days, the guest rooms, all on the second floor, may strike horror into your heart or fill you with fond memories. Here's your chance to sleep, with impunity, in the Principal's Office, the Library, the Music Room, or the History Room, among others; just pick the subject you found the most soporific.

The spacious accommodations are country comfortable, with flowery quilted comforters, dark-wood furniture, lace curtains, and stenciled wall borders. Those at the front of the building provide views of upper Tombstone Canyon and the Mule Mountains.

🏠 *6 double rooms with baths, 3 2-bedroom suites. Library, barbecue, off-street parking. $50–$60 rooms, $70*

suites, full breakfast. AE, D, DC, MC, V. No smoking, no pets, no children.

Skywatcher's Inn

420 South Essex La., Tucson 85711 (directions to the inn, outside Benson, are complicated), tel. and fax 520/745-2390

Astronomers keep strange hours, not much different from those of rock stars. So don't be surprised if you learn that some of your fellow guests are taking late-afternoon naps when you check into this unique bed-and-breakfast, which has its own astronomical observatory. Or perhaps it's more accurate to say the Vega-Bray Observatory, just outside of Benson, has its own bed-and-breakfast: Dr. Ed Vega, a longtime amateur astronomer, built a stargazing facility that proved so popular that he ended up adding a place where visitors could bed down after a long night of looking into the skies.

Six professional telescopes, ranging 6–20 inches, are available to guests on two bases: Those sufficiently familiar with the equipment can rent it (except for the 20-incher) for $35. Others can pay $70 (per group) for basic instruction and guided viewing; more advanced supervision, including lessons in using the CCD imaging camera, can cost up to $150.

This is a great place for an educational family vacation. During the daytime, guests can browse a classroom with fossils, meteorites, and a variety of interactive projects; the room also includes an impressive science library. Those whose sights are not quite as high in the sky can sit out on one of two porches with impressive vistas and look at birds through mounted binoculars. And when Kartchner Caverns State Park opens nearby, there'll be a lot of attention paid to below-ground wonders.

The three guest rooms, two with private baths, one with a bath shared with observatory visitors (which means complete privacy in the morning, when there are no stargazers around) all offer comfortable contemporary furnishings in science-oriented settings. One room, with a domed ceiling, can function as a planetarium, another reveals the night sky above when you switch on a black light, and the third lets you turn on the lamps over your bed simply by touching the headboard.

For obvious reasons, breakfast tends to be served on the late side (between 9 and 10). However, a stocked refrigerator lets early risers prepare their own morning meals.

▦ *2 rooms with private bath, 1 room shares bath with observatory. Kitchenette in 1 room, full kitchen, 42″ TV and VCR with astronomy videos in living room/science studio, crib available. $75–$85, full breakfast. MC, V. No smoking indoors, pets accepted with advance permission.*

Tombstone Boarding House

108 N. Fourth St., Box 906, Tombstone 85638, tel. 520/457-3716

Those who like the intimacy of a B&B but feel a little odd about staying in someone's house will find the best of both worlds at the Tombstone Boarding House, in a quiet residential neighborhood. Shirley Villarin's two meticulously restored 1880s adobe houses sit side by side; both contain guest rooms with individual entrances, so if you like you can stay next door and then go over to the Villarin house to eat breakfast or watch TV.

The spotless rooms have refinished fir, maple, and oak floors and period furnishings collected from around Cochise County: for example, a cast-iron bed and a hand-carved wooden headboard from the 1880s. Breakfast, served in a cheerful, pretty, blue-and-white kitchen, usually includes bacon and eggs, fresh fruits

and juice, and Shirley's hot biscuits or muffins. Fresh-brewed coffee or tea is left in the guest parlor for early risers. Afternoon refreshments include crackers and cheese, cookies, and a variety of liquid refreshments. Those seeking romance should ask Shirley about her candlelight dinners, served in the inn's Blue Room.

▦ *9 double rooms with baths, 1 1880s miner's cabin. TV in guest parlor. $60–$80, full breakfast, afternoon refreshments. MC, V. No smoking indoors.*

Valle Verde Ranch Bed and Breakfast

Box 157, 2149 E. Frontage Rd., Tumacacori 85640, tel. and fax 520/398-2246

On the outskirts of Tubac, Arizona's first European settlement and now an artisans town, this B&B hearkens back to the days when wealthy Mexican-American ranchers ruled this part of the country. The central Spanish mission–style building was the main house of Valle Verde Ranch, built in 1937 out of adobe brick. Since the 1940s, the property has belonged to the family of the imperious Alexandra—she won't reveal her surname—and in 1994 she and her husband, Giorgio, who hails from Florence, Italy, opened it up to guests.

Filled with antique bibelots from the couple's various residences, the house is gorgeous—if not a bit museumlike. Most of the furnishings are European, but one item from America's not-so-gracious past stands out glaringly: the black lawn jockey that flanks the entryway.

Accommodations consist of three rooms in the main house, one with a private entrance and patio, and two separate casitas, both with kitchen facilities (including stocked refrigerators). All have TVs but only the large casita has a phone. Main house guests enjoy a Continental-plus breakfast.

🏠 *3 double rooms with bath, 2 casitas. Hot tub, refrigerators, TVs. $80–$95 rooms, Continental-plus breakfast; $100–$135 casitas. No credit cards. No smoking indoors, no pets, no children. Open last week of Oct.–last week of May, 2-night minimum in Feb. and Mar.*

Victoria's

Box 37, 211 Toughnut St., Tombstone 85638, tel. 520/457-3677 or 800/952-8216, fax 520/457-2450

Some say that spirits return after death to the place where they were happiest— which might explain the numerous reports of ghostly action at Victoria's, once a house of pleasure. The 1880 adobe structure was also host to a hanging judge and later served as a gaming establishment. You can't miss what is now a cheerful red-and-white bed-and-breakfast: It's right next door to the Tombstone Courthouse State Historic Park, and Zelda, a spiffily dressed life-size soft sculpture, is always out on the front porch to greet you.

Victoria's is still a house of pleasure, if not in the same sense as in the past. Hostess Victoria Collins knows how to make guests feel welcome, bringing out her fine china for such delicious breakfasts as chunky French toast made from home-baked bread and accompanied by fresh fruit. Other thoughtful touches include cookies in the rooms. The accommodations, though appropriately decorated in Victorian-era fashion, are not without modern comforts: Each has a TV as well as a bottled cold-water dispenser.

🏠 *3 double rooms with bath. TVs. $55–$75, full breakfast. MC, V. Smoking allowed in designated area, no pets, no children.*

The Vineyard Bed-and-Breakfast

92 Los Encinos Rd., Sonoita 85637, tel. 520/455-4749

The grape-growing region near Sonoita that's home to the Vineyard Bed-and-Breakfast is some of southern Arizona's prettiest country, its rolling desert grasslands flanked by several mountain ranges. And at an elevation of 5,100 feet, it offers sanctuary from the heat that sears more low-lying areas come summer.

Ron and Sue DeCosmo acquired their 20-acre property with its 1916 hacienda-style ranch house in 1994, and began welcoming guests in 1995. The grounds are shaded with ancient live oaks, and plum and peach trees overhanging the pool blossom profusely in the spring. A friendly burro, two dogs, and Fred, a chatty parrot, are among the inn's diversions, which also include hanging out in a hammock.

The three immaculate guest rooms in the antiques-filled main house have a cozy country feel; a separate casita is more southwestern in tone. All four units have private entrances. Breakfasts, served on a closed-in sunporch, are generous—sourdough pecan waffles, apple fritters, and puff pancakes are all possibilities. Fresh eggs come courtesy of the B&B's hens.

🏠 *3 rooms with private bath, 1 casita. Player piano, outdoor pool. $75 rooms, $85 casita, full breakfast. No credit cards. No smoking indoors, no pets, no children under 12.*

Yee Ha Ranch

Box 888, Sonoita 85637, tel. 520/455-9285

While out horseback riding in the open ranch country near Sonoita, Tucsonans Mary and Steve Harkin met and fell in love—with the area, as well as with each other. They vowed to return there and raise a family. Some two years later, they bought 120 acres of a 600-acre spread where cattle are run, and three years after that—in 1996—they opened a bed-and-breakfast on the property. Guests can't ride any of the five horses that the Harkins acquired (in addition to four cats and two dogs), but the couple is happy to arrange horseback excursions.

The updated Territorial ranch house–style lodging has three guest rooms, each with two private entrances: One opens onto a pretty interior patio, the other onto a porch; sunset-and bird-watching are major activities here. The major influences in the area, Mexican, Native American, and Western, are reflected in the individualized decor of the rooms, all of which have wood-burning stoves. Don't start thinking rustic, though. They also have TVs, VCRs, and bathtubs with jets.

🏨 *3 rooms with bath. Wood-burning stoves, TVs, VCRs. $85, Continental-plus breakfast. AE, MC, V. No smoking indoors, no pets, no children under 12.*

New Mexico

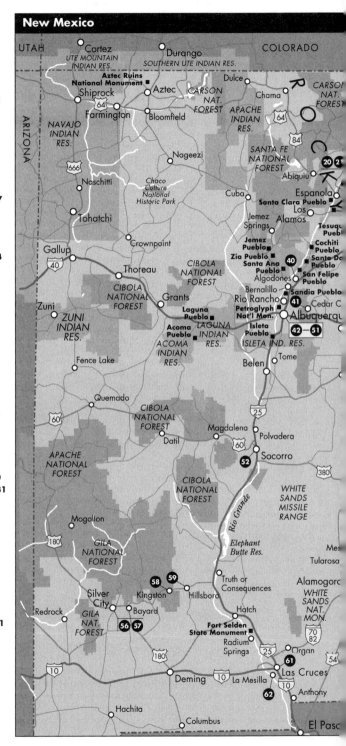

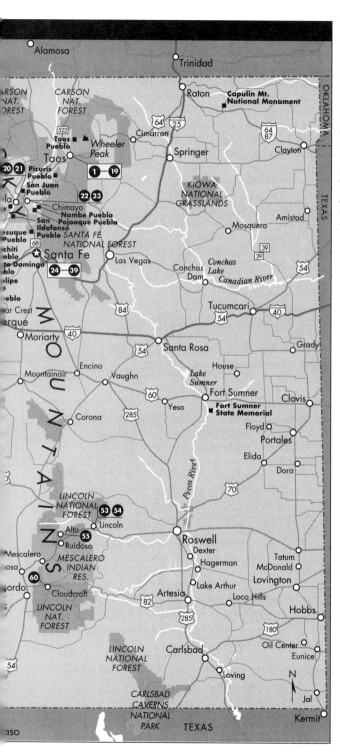

Santa Fe and Environs

Inn on the Alameda

Santa Fe is a beacon; the superstar attraction of the Southwest's burgeoning tourist boom. The City Different, as it is called, has become a favorite vacation retreat for New York publishers, Hollywood stars, and legions of other people who are drawn to its enchanting landscape, elegant hotels and fine restaurants, cultural scene, and long, colorful history; it is the oldest capital city in the United States.

And the City Different, with its crisp, clean air and bright, sunny weather, couldn't be more welcoming. Santa Fe stands proudly on a 7,000-foot-high plateau at the base of the Sangre de Cristo Mountains. It's surrounded by a 2,000-year-old Pueblo civilization and characterized by its nearly 400 years of Spanish/Hispanic inhabitation.

In this age of malls and urban sprawl, Santa Fe remains one of the few western cities that still radiates from its historic center, the town plaza, laid out in 1609. "Only three blocks from the Plaza," "one mile south of the Plaza," note restaurants, hotels, and bed-and-breakfasts in their advertising and brochures. Shops, galleries, and restaurants lining the Plaza pay high rents and high taxes, as any proprietor is quick to let you know in a casual, offhand moment.

Santa Fe is best characterized by its distinct Pueblo-style architecture, a predominance of adobe or pseudo-adobe that at times can be almost overpowering. But look closely and you'll see a mélange of architectural styles, including Victorian and American Craftsman, each reflecting the many cultures that have helped shape modern Santa Fe. Both ancient pueblos and the Hispanic villages, with their earthen tones and rounded, flowing lines, meld into the landscape. Here the earth still rules.

Be it the architecture, the light, the ambience, the lifestyle, or its novel residents, many visitors return here to live. So many, in fact, that real estate prices and taxes have soared and many of those born in the former Spanish Colonial capital can no longer afford to live in it.

Santa Fe is among the smallest state capitals in the country and is without a major airport, but visitors pour in year-round. The city's population, an estimated 62,000, swells to nearly triple that figure at Indian Market in August. Hotel rates are on a par with those of top hotels and resorts in popular spots all over the globe. Prices for contemporary artwork—Santa Fe is said to be the third major art center in the country, after New York and Los Angeles—are similarly high.

Rates in the city's numerous bed-and-breakfasts reflect this high pricing. Santa Fe bed-and-breakfasts also enjoy a standard of luxury uncommon to most parts of the country. Most inns will arrange dinner and airport transfer reservations, as well as entertainment tickets for their guests. Breakfasts, whether a full gourmet or Continental-plus presentation, tend to include a generous helping of regional specialties, fresh-baked breads and pastries, seasonal fruits and juices, and gourmet coffees and imported teas. By and large, no matter how high the cost, you won't feel shortchanged when you leave.

Places to Go, Sights to See

Art Galleries. Santa Fe's brilliant light, limpid skies, and timeless landscape of mountains and mesas have long hypnotized artists. The city has more than 125 galleries and no one knows how many full-time professional artists. The Santa Fe Convention and Visitors Bureau (*see* Tourist Information, *below*) has a broad listing of galleries, and the *Wingspread Collectors Guide to Santa Fe and Taos*, available at most city newsstands, bookstores, and hotels, is a good bet for those seriously interested in buying art in Santa Fe. Also helpful is the *Santa Fe Gallery Association* (Box 9245, tel. 505/982–1648). Standout galleries include *Nedra Matteucci's Fenn Gallery* (1075 Paseo de Peralta, tel. 505/982–4631); *Gerald Peters Gallery* (439 Camino del Monte Sol, tel. 505/988–8961); and *Cline LewAllen Galleries* (129 W. Palace Ave., tel. 505/988–8997).

Canyon Road. A symbol of Santa Fe, Canyon Road once served as an Indian trail. During the early part of the century, woodcutters with their loaded burros used El Camino de Cañon as their route into town, where they sold bundles of chopped wood door-to-door. The road's 2-mile stretch from the center of town is the historic center of Santa Fe's art colony and today is lined with many of the city's finest art galleries, shops, and restaurants.

Cathedral of St. Francis (213 Cathedral Pl., tel. 505/982–5619). Founded by Jean Baptiste Lamy, Santa Fe's first archbishop, this handsome French Romanesque-style cathedral was built by Italian stonemasons in 1869. A small adobe chapel on the northeast side of the cathedral houses *Nuestra Señora de la Paz* (Our Lady of Peace), the oldest representation of the Madonna in the United States.

Chimayo. Peaceful little Chimayo, 25 miles north of Santa Fe in the Sangre de Cristo mountains, is famous for its weaving, regional food, and the *Santuario de Chimayo*, sometimes called the "Lourdes of the Southwest." Many miracles are believed to have occurred in the small, colonial-style adobe church, and mud from the *pozito* (small well) inside the chapel is reputed to have healing properties. The Santuario draws a steady stream of worshipers all year long, but over Good Friday and Holy Week, as many as 50,000 people visit.

Indian Vendors. Under the shaded *portales* (a porch or large, covered area) of the Palace of the Governors on the north side of the Santa Fe Plaza, local Native American artisans display and sell their pottery and jewelry. All of the more than 500 vendors who are registered to sell under the portales are members of New Mexico pueblos or tribes.

Loretto Chapel (207 E. Santa Fe Trail, tel. 505/982–0092). A French Romanesque structure begun in 1873 and modeled after the famous Parisian church Sainte-Chapelle, Loretto Chapel (now a private museum) is known for the "Miraculous Staircase": Many of the faithful believe that it was built by St. Joseph, who, disguised, came to the aid of the church sisters.

Los Alamos. Some 45 minutes north of Santa Fe, west of U.S. 84/285 on NM 502, the birthplace of the atomic bomb spreads over fingerlike mesas at an altitude of 7,300 feet. Research continues at Los Alamos National (in areas such as nuclear weaponry, lasers, nuclear energy, and superconductivity). The town itself is relatively colorless but has a number of good restaurants, hotels, and museums, including the *Bradbury Science Museum* (15th and Central, tel. 505/672–3861) and *Los Alamos Historical Museum* (1921 Juniper St., tel. 505/662–4493).

Museums. The Pueblo-style *Palace of the Governors* on the north side of the Plaza is the oldest public building in the United States. It houses New Mexico's *History Museum* (tel. 505/827–6483), whose exhibits chronicle more than 450 years of territorial and state history. Almost next door is the *Museum of Fine Arts* (tel. 505/827–4455), with an impressive 8,000-piece permanent collection emphasizing the work of regional artists. The *Georgia O'Keeffe Museum* (tel. 505/995–0785), new in 1997, houses a comprehensive collection of the artists' works. The museum of the *Institute of American Indian Arts* (Cathedral Place, tel. 505/988–6211) is housed in the renovated former Federal Post Office. About a mile from the Plaza along the Old Santa Fe Trail is the *Museum of International Folk Art* (706 Camino Lejo, tel. 505/827–6350), among the town's most popular attractions. Next to it are two more excellent collections of Native American arts and artifacts: the *Museum of Indian Arts and Culture* (710 Camino Lejo, tel. 505/827–6344) and the *Wheelwright Museum of the American Indian* (704 Camino Lejo, tel. 505/982–4636).

Pueblos. Nineteen Pueblo and one Apache Indian reservations are found in northern New Mexico, where descendants of the ancient Anasazi Indians preserve their customs today. Each pueblo has its own personality, history, and specialty in art and design; those nearest to Santa Fe are Cochiti, Nambe, Pojoaque, San Ildefonso, Santa Clara, and Tesuque. To help decide which ones you want to visit, stop at the striking Indian Pueblo Cultural Center in Albuquerque (*see* Albuquerque section *below* for details), or call the Eight Northern Indian Pueblo Council office (tel. 800/793–4955).

Santa Fe Opera (Box 2408, Santa Fe 87504, tel. 505/986–5900). Each July and August, some of the most acclaimed talents of Europe and the United States perform at the Santa Fe Opera's spectacular indoor-outdoor amphitheater, carved into a hillside 7 miles north of the city, amid the piñons of the Sangre de Cristo foothills.

Santa Fe Ski Area (tel. 505/982–4429). Only half an hour from the Plaza, but 3,000 feet higher, this ski area is noted for excellent snowfall and a variety of terrain for all abilities.

Santuario de Guadalupe (100 Guadalupe St., tel. 505/988–2027). At the terminus of El Camino Real, 3½ blocks southwest of the Plaza, is the oldest shrine to Our Lady of Guadalupe (patron saint of Mexico) in the United States. Built by Franciscan missionaries between 1776 and 1795, it is now the center of the Guadalupe Historic District; adjacent Guadalupe Street is filled with colorful shops and restaurants.

Ten Thousand Waves (Box 10200, Santa Fe 87504, tel. 505/988–1047). Japanese aesthetics were joined with Mexican building material to create this enchanting mountain spa. Among the services available are saunas, herbal wraps, East-Indian treatments, and facials; communal and private hot tubs are available too.

The deeply relaxing water massages known as *Watsu* are perhaps the most special, as are the brilliant stars that glow over the resort at night. Kimonos, sandals, towels, and lockers are provided; bathing suits are optional.

Restaurants

Santa Fe is perhaps best known for its excellent New Mexican cuisine, a tantalizing array of classic regional specialties adapted generations ago from local ingredients—green and red chilies, a variety of peppers, ground and whole blue and yellow corn, pork, pinto beans, honey, piñon nuts, apples, and other native fare. Among the outstanding restaurants are the **Pink Adobe** (tel. 505/983–7712), **Casa Sena** (tel. 505/988–9232), **La Tertulia** (tel. 505/988–2769), **The Shed** (tel. 505/982–9030), and **Tia Sofia's** (tel. 505/983–9880). For a change of pace, and price, there's Canyon Road's posh **Compound** (tel. 505/982–4353), one of few restaurants in New Mexico where men are required to wear a jacket and tie, and **Corn Dance** (tel. 505/982–1200), which features unusual and tasty American Indian cuisine. Also, don't miss Mark Miller's award-winning **Coyote Cafe** (tel. 505/983–1615). Among its innovative northern New Mexican dishes are lobster enchiladas and ravioli filled with wild boar and goat cheese sausage. **El Farol** (tel. 505/983–9912), Santa Fe's oldest restaurant and bar, draws a festive crowd with its live music and delicious Spanish cuisine.

Chimayo boasts one of the most classic New Mexican restaurants in the region, **Rancho de Chimayo** (tel. 505/984–2100), whose regional fare is made from centuries-old family recipes. The elegant dining room at **Rancho de San Juan** (*see below*) has perhaps the finest food, prepared by French chefs, of any restaurant in greater Santa Fe.

Tourist Information

Los Alamos Chamber of Commerce (2132 Central Ave., Los Alamos 87544, tel. 505/662–8105). **New Mexico Department of Tourism** (Lamy Bldg., 491 Old Santa Fe Trail, Santa Fe 87503, tel. 800/545–2040). **Santa Fe Chamber of Commerce** (510 De Vargas Center, N. Guadalupe St., Santa Fe 87501, tel. 505/988–3279). **Santa Fe Convention and Visitors Bureau** (201 W. Marcy St., Box 909, Santa Fe 87501, tel. 505/984–6760 or 800/777–2489).

Reservation Services

Bed and Breakfast of New Mexico (Box 2805, Santa Fe 87504, tel. 505/982–3332). **New Mexico Bed and Breakfast Association** (Box 2925, Santa Fe 87504, tel. 505/766–5380 or 800/661–6649).

Adobe Abode

202 Chapelle St., Santa Fe 87501, tel.
505/983–3133, fax 505/986–0972

Pat Harbour is an inveterate collector with a passion for primitive art. Mexican pottery and American folk art, including a collection of rare ship engine molds, are in evidence everywhere in her charming adobe compound, built circa 1907 three blocks from the Plaza. The main house, with viga beam ceilings, hardwood floors, and a living room with fireplace, adjoins casitas flanking a shaded courtyard.

Two rooms added in 1993 are based on themes—the Bronco has saddles, lariats, twig furniture, and old Western furnishings, including a wall of Western hats and a baby's cowboy boots; the high ceiling Cactus Room features Oaxacan textiles, pottery, and colorful hand-carved animals. One two-room suite has south of France decor. The other accommodations are totally eclectic, combining hand-painted furniture with pencil-post beds and other antiques.

A hearty gourmet breakfast is served on one of Pat's many sets of china, including colorful dishes commissioned and handmade by local potters.

🛏 *6 double rooms with baths. Cable TV, private phones, coffeemakers, custom toiletries, and terry cloth robes in all rooms. $110–$150, full gourmet breakfast, sherry and cookies always available. D, MC, V. No smoking in rooms, no pets.*

Alexander's Inn

529 E. Palace Ave., Santa Fe 87501, tel.
505/986–1431

Owner Carolyn Lee, the daughter of a foreign service diplomat, traveled all over the world while she was growing up. But when it came time to raise her son Alexander, she decided to settle in

Santa Fe and launch a B&B. Santa Fe is the richer for it, and Carolyn hasn't done badly either since opening in 1986. Her charming establishment, only six blocks from the Plaza on historic Palace Avenue, sees a lot of repeat business and is often booked solid.

Carolyn exudes a refreshing wholesomeness and youthful vitality, which she brings to the B&B. However, the addition of twins to her family means that Carolyn's hands are rather full these days, and she relies on staff help to entertain guests. So as not to leave Alexander alone in the B&B business without sibling support, the Nicolas and Madeleine buildings are being added two blocks up the road.

The Craftsman-style two-story residence, built in 1903, is fronted by a deep veranda and covered with wooden shingles. Its spacious rooms are furnished with American country-style furniture. Fine woodworking is found throughout, as is pretty floral-patterned wallpaper. Three upstairs rooms feature walk-in size dormer windows that flood the rooms with light and produce odd and delightful nooks, crannies, and angles. The Lilac Room downstairs has a brick fireplace and original stained-glass windows, as well as a four-poster bed with a blue down comforter and feather pillows.

Across a small backyard, which bursts in summer with flower gardens under the shade of some immense old trees, are two cottages. The front unit has a loft-style bedroom up a spiral staircase, a complete kitchen, a fireplace, and a two-person hot tub. The rear unit has a raised kiva fireplace and Saltillo-tile floors.

In keeping with her healthful lifestyle, Carolyn's homemade granola, muffins, yogurt, sumptuous fruit salads, coffee, juice, and tea make for a hearty and delicious start for the day. In warm weather you can eat out on the rear deck; in spring an apricot tree bends its fragrant boughs over your table.

🏠 *3 double rooms with baths, 2 doubles share bath, 2 cottages. TV in cottages and in common room, fresh flowers, hot tub, health club membership and mountain bikes available free of charge. $75–$140, cottages $85–$160, Continental-plus breakfast, afternoon snacks. MC, V. No smoking, some pets allowed.*

Casa del Rio

Box 702, Abiquiu 87510 (19946 U.S. 84), tel. 505/753-2035, fax 505/753-9490

The setting is spectacular—12 acres of pastureland flanked by mountains, with the Chama River gurgling by, all in the heart of Georgia O'Keeffe country: Casa del Rio is 13 miles from Abiquiu and 27 miles from Ghost Ranch, both former homes of the artist. Eileen and Mel Vigil opened this small B&B with two separate casitas in 1988, and they are still at work on it. Past projects have included the addition of patio walls, an outdoor swimming pool, a water garden, and a meditation room.

The Vigils raise purebred Arabian horses on the property (guests who want to ride are invited to bring their own horses), and racks above the door frames display part of Mel's gun collection, including a prize Winchester. The public rooms in the main house are furnished with a combination of European antiques and regional pieces—tile floors, viga ceilings, and an antique curved-glass cabinet displaying Indian jewelry (it's for sale). The guest rooms feature hand-crafted Spanish Colonial-style furniture created by local carver Tim Roybal, whose work has been featured at the Smithsonian Institution.

🏠 *1 double room with bath, 1 casita. Fireplaces in both rooms, wake-up tray, fresh flowers, outdoor pool, water garden. $85–$115, full breakfast. No credit cards. No smoking indoors, no pets.*

Casa Escondida

Box 142, off NM 76 at Road Marker 0100, Chimayo 87522, tel. 505/351-4805 or 800/643-7201

An intimate and serene adobe with pitched tin roof, Casa Escondida is set on 6 fertile acres in the sleepy village of Chimayo, famous for its Hispanic weavers. The Sangre de Cristos tower lies to the east, with the Truchas Peaks and Santa Fe Baldy poking above the red and brown hills. Its rural setting has made it very popular with hikers and mountain bikers. Equally inspiring is owner Irenka Taurek, who speaks several languages.

The house is decorated with American Arts and Crafts furniture, lamps, and pottery. A large hot tub is hidden in a grove behind wild berry bushes. The main house has five rooms, all with private baths. Some rooms have kiva fireplaces and packed earthen floors. Others have private patios and decks—such as the airy, attractive upstairs Vista Room with a wrought-iron bed. Also upstairs, the Kiva Room has a perched beam ceiling, kiva fireplace, and an oversize tub. The Sun Room, large and bright with a private patio, has viga ceilings and a brick floor. The separate one-bedroom Casita Escondida also has a kiva fireplace and viga ceilings, along with Saltillo-tile floors, a lovely sitting area, and a kitchenette.

Manager Matthew Higgi serves breakfast in the dining room, which looks out onto a lawn with trees. An art studio with a pottery wheel, watercolors, oil paints, and sketching materials is scheduled to open to guests in 1998.

🏠 *5 double rooms with baths, 1 1-bedroom cottage. Full kitchen with microwave in casita, wildflower gardens, hot tub. $75–$130, cottage $150, full breakfast and port or sherry in evenings. AE, MC, V. No smoking, no pets.*

The Don Gaspar Compound Inn

623 Don Gaspar, Santa Fe 87501, tel. 505/986–8664 or 888/986–8664, fax 505/986–0696

Despite its proximity to Santa Fe's center, the Don Gaspar Compound feels worlds removed from urban life. Six spacious accommodations and a beautifully landscaped courtyard pamper guests within the property's adobe walls. Try to visit between May and October, when colorful flowers bloom along unhurried brick paths that weave between aspen, cottonwood, and fruit trees.

All guest rooms are individually decorated and have private entrances with pretty courtyard views, beds with down comforters, and kitchenettes.

The Southwest Suite, bathed in deep crimsons and sand colors, has a living room with a kiva fireplace and impressionist landscape prints on the walls. There's a separate room with a king bed and a fruitwood wardrobe. The Courtyard Casita, with a private garden, can sleep up to four. Like the inn's other casitas, it has French doors and a gas fireplace.

For even larger parties, the Mission-style Main House, built in 1912 and listed on the State Historical Register, has two bedrooms, a dining room, living room, and full kitchen. There's another two-bedroom adobe home about 2 miles from the Compound in a quiet residential area.

As sleepy eyes give way to morning hunger, guests may enjoy a gourmet Continental breakfast in their rooms, in the dining room, or in the sun. Opting for the courtyard, water trickles gently down a tiered fountain while fresh fruits and homemade breads, cereals, and regional specialties are laid out. Following breakfast, guests can easily walk to the Plaza where Santa Fe's best shops and sights await.

🏨 *5 double rooms with baths, Main House accommodates up to 6 people. TV, phone, microwave, refrigerator in all rooms. $85–$220, Continental-plus breakfast. AE, MC, V. No smoking, no pets.*

Dos Casas Viejas

610 Agua Fria St., Santa Fe 87501, tel. 505/983–1636, fax 505/983–1749

On historic Agua Fria Street, once part of the ancient Camino Real and right next door to the Guadalupe Inn (*see below*), is a half-acre walled compound containing Dos Casas Viejas (Two Old Houses). Dating back to 1860, they were last restored and revamped in 1990 to include such modern amenities as a 40-foot lap pool. Parts of the original portale still exist, as do the viga ceilings and Mexican-tile floors.

This a delightful place with some of the nicest rooms of any Santa Fe B&B. New Yorkers Susan and Michael Strijek took over the property in 1996, leaving Wall Street to pursue their dream of owning a B&B.

Beautifully furnished guest rooms and suites are in two separate adobes. The Southwestern decor might include Native American art, Mexican antiques, coved viga ceilings, Saltillo-tile floors, skylights, willow beds, and *latilla* (twig) doors. Suites have separate sitting rooms with stereos and minibars.

Breakfast, served in the dining room or by the pool, includes coffee, tea, squeezed orange juice, and fresh-baked breads and muffins.

🏨 *5 double rooms with baths, 2 minisuites, 1 suite. Cable TV, ceiling fan, mini-refrigerator, private entrance and patio, cotton robes, and raised fireplace in all rooms, lap pool. $165–$245, Continental-plus breakfast. MC, V. No smoking, no pets.*

Dunshee's

986 Acequia Madre, Santa Fe 87501, tel. 505/982–0988

Dunshee's is so pretty and romantic that former *Chicago Tribune* travel editor Al Borcover was married on the patio here on his fourth visit. A great buy for Santa Fe, this B&B offers two reasonable lodging options in the quiet, historic eastside neighborhood only a mile from the Plaza and just off Canyon Road. Don't be fazed by the dirt lanes; this is as upscale as Santa Fe gets.

The first option is in the restored adobe home of proprietor-artist Susan Dunshee: a large suite that includes a living room with a cozy seating area and a bedroom with a queen bed and Mexican-tile bath; a gourmet breakfast is served to guests of this room. The other choice is a two-bedroom adobe casita with a patio, living room, and a full kitchen with a dishwasher and a refrigerator amply stocked for do-it-yourself breakfasts. Both the suite and the casita have viga ceilings, kiva fireplaces, decorative linens, and folk art, and both have private entrances. In the casita's entrance hall, over an antique country table, hangs a striking fiber bas-relief made by Susan.

The backyard offers a shady portale, terraced gardens, wisteria vines, and fruit and aspen trees.

🏠 *1 2-bedroom casita, 1 1-bedroom suite. TV, stereo CD/tape player, microwave in suite, fresh flowers. $110–$120, full breakfast with suite, Continental-plus in casita. MC, V. No smoking, no pets.*

El Paradero

220 W. Manhattan Ave., Santa Fe 87501, tel. 505/988–1177

El Paradero, set on a street five blocks south of the Plaza, was built as a Spanish farmhouse between 1800 and 1820. Its Territorial-style details were added in the 1880s, its Victorian doors and windows appended in 1912. Ouida MacGregor and Thom Allen acquired the property in 1982 and added conveniences and the second-story rooms, while retaining the adobe's essential character, best described as funky or "down-home."

In the main sitting room, you'll find a piano, fireplace with alcove seating, oversize wooden chairs, *santos* (saints) carvings, and Indian kachina dolls. Nine of the guest rooms are on the ground level around the small courtyard and three are upstairs in the main house. The latter, flooded with sunlight, are the more luxurious and spacious, with Saltillo-tile floors, Talavera-tile baths, and handwoven textiles. Such tangy Southwestern entrées as *huevos rancheros*, blue-corn pancakes, and breakfast burritos are served in the sunny breakfast room.

🏠 *8 double rooms with baths, 4 doubles share 2 baths, 2 suites. Cable TV in suites, color TV in sitting room, 2 fireplaces in public areas. $65–$110, suites $135, full breakfast. MC, V. No smoking, pets allowed in some rooms.*

Grant Corner Inn

122 Grant Ave., Santa Fe 87501, tel. 505/ 983–6678

The only colonial style bed-and-breakfast in town, this is the place that innkeepers talk about when they get together over potluck dinners. It's one of the best run and most successful in the state. Owner Louise Stewart, daughter of Jack Stewart who founded the renowned Camelback Inn in Scottsdale, studied at the Cornell hotel school and worked as an interior designer before opening the Grant Corner Inn—and what a production it is.

Located only two blocks from the Plaza in a small tree-filled lot, surrounded by a veranda and garden, the house originally belonged to the Winsor family, wealthy New Mexican ranchers. The rooms and public areas are filled with antiques and treasures collected from around the world by Louise. Hand-stitched quilts, brass and four-poster beds, armoires, and artwork make each room unique. The undisputed star is Room No. 8, a visual treat with its white brass bed, love seat, quilted bedspread, Oriental rugs, and Old World touches. The downstairs public rooms also hearken back to grander days, with lace curtains, antique oak tables, ceiling fans, crystal chandeliers, and a legion of bunnies.

The breakfast menu includes such treats as banana waffles, eggs Florentine, and green-chili-laden New Mexican soufflé, all accompanied by fresh-ground European coffee, fresh-squeezed juice, fruit, and homemade rolls and jellies. Small wonder the public comes clamoring on weekends when the dining room is open to one and all. Meals are served in front of a crackling fire in the dining room or, in summer, on the veranda. Guests get a complimentary glass of wine in the evening. Elaborately prepared picnic baskets are available, too.

The Grant Corner Inn also operates the Grant Corner Inn Hacienda, a southwestern-style condominium six blocks away; it's available for parties of up to four. Rates ($215–$255 per night) include breakfast at the inn.

⊞ *7 double rooms with baths, 2 doubles share bath, 1 single. Cable TV and phones in all rooms, in-house massages available, lounge with dining nook, microwave, and refrigerator, privileges at nearby tennis club. $70–$155, full breakfast. MC, V. No smoking, no pets.*

The Guadalupe Inn

604 Agua Fria St., Santa Fe 87501, tel. 505/989-7422, fax 505/989-7422

Two sisters and a brother are the proud owners of this northern New Mexico–flavored B&B, which opened in 1992.

One of them, Dolores Myers, was born on the property, the site of her grandfather's grocery store. She speaks with authority about the many colorful characters who have resided in this historic area along the route of the Camino Real.

The breakfast area and living room are what you see when you enter the inn. With coved viga ceilings, lots of light, comfortable couches, Saltillo-tile floors, and fireplace, the space is very inviting. And just around a corner is a large indoor hot tub that looks out over a small garden where raspberries thrive in summer. People can choose their breakfast entrées—perhaps huevos rancheros, breakfast burritos, pancakes, or a western omelette.

Distinctive rooms feature handmade beds by renowned craftsman David C. de Baca, tin light fixtures, latilla ceilings, fanciful bathroom tile, and gas fireplaces. Popular with honeymooners is the Celebration Room, with its immense contemporary claw-foot tub surrounded by mirrors opening onto the bedroom. Number 9, great for singles traveling together, has two twin beds with copper headboards.

⊞ *11 double rooms with baths, 1 suite. Cable TV, phones and queen beds in all but 1 room, whirlpool tubs in 4 rooms, gas fireplaces in some rooms, covered parking. $125–$150, suite $175, full breakfast. AE, D, MC, V. No smoking, no pets.*

Inn of the Animal Tracks

707 Paseo de Peralta, Santa Fe 87504, tel. 505/988-1546

Three blocks east of the Plaza is this enchanting 90-year-old restored Pueblo-style house (it's actually brick beneath the plaster) with beamed ceilings, hardwood floors, and handcrafted furniture. The Inn of the Animal Tracks is one of the most popular B&Bs in town—people come just for the delicious afternoon repast, open to nonguests by reservation—when owner Myrna Wheeler sets out anything from a dip of frijoles, black olives, and green chili to tasty pastries and hot chocolate, coffee, or tea.

Playing off its animal theme, rooms have names like Eagle, Wolf, or Otter carefully selected to match their characters. Otter has the only tub, and Eagle the only fireplace. Rabbit, which must be entered through the kitchen, is full of stuffed and terra-cotta rabbits, rabbit books, rabbit paintings, and tucked under the bed are bunny-rabbit slippers. "I've always had a great love for animals," says Myrna, who allows no pets, although a mutt and two cats roam freely about the premises. The beds are all queen-size Swedish platform style, with down comforters and pillows, and feather mattresses. In the warmer months, a landscaped patio shaded by pear, apple, peach, and apricot trees is a pleasant place to relax.

🛏 *5 double rooms with baths. Air-conditioning, cable TV in guest rooms, fireplace in 1 guest room and in common room. $90–$130, full breakfast, afternoon tea. AE, MC, V. No smoking indoors, no pets.*

Inn on the Alameda

303 E. Alameda, Santa Fe 87501, tel. 505/984–2121 or 800/289–2122, fax 505/986–8325

Alameda means "tree-lined lane," befitting its location alongside the Santa Fe River, which gurgles virtually through the center of town. This setting, between the historic Santa Fe Plaza and gallery-filled Canyon Road, is both tranquil and convenient: Even without a car, guests have easy access to shopping, museums, and restaurants.

Opened in 1986, this lodging was originally intended to be a bed-and-breakfast with resident managers. However, it

soon blossomed into one of Santa Fe's most prestigious small hotels, combining the relaxed atmosphere of a New Mexico country inn with the amenities of a world-class hotel.

Rooms, in a contemporary adobe complex with a network of enclosed courtyards and portales are decorated in Southwestern colors, down to the accessories, beds, wall hangings, and wood-frame mirrors. Many rooms have handmade armoires, oversize chairs, headboards, and colorful tiles exemplifying the best of local craftsmanship. Deluxe rooms contain private patios or balconies and refrigerators. Prints and posters by Amado Peña, R. C. Gorman, and other renowned local artists grace the walls. The inn's individually designed suites are appealing, some more opulent than others. Room 140, for example, features two kiva fireplaces, two TV sets, two phones, and a minibar. Here and there you'll find a bleached cattle skull mounted on the wall or over a door.

Although the inn has no full-service dining room, its complimentary breakfast buffet includes homemade muffins, bagels, creamy pastries, cinnamon rolls, fruit and fresh-squeezed fruit juices, teas, and coffee. Guests may eat at tables in the lobby's spacious library or in the Agoyo Room lounge; room service is also an option. A number of fine restaurants are nearby. The inn helps with tickets and reservations for evening entertainment and has a number of attractive package arrangements with spas, tours, and ski resorts.

🛏 *58 double rooms with baths, 9 suites. Cable TV with HBO and robes in all rooms, massage room, exercise center, guest laundry, 2 outdoor hot tubs, full bar. $140–$215, suites $200–$350, Continental-plus breakfast. AE, D, DC, MC, V. Pets welcome.*

Inn on the Paseo

*630 Paseo de Peralta, Santa Fe 87501,
tel. 505/984–8200 or 800/457–9045, fax
505/989–3979*

In 1991 owners Nancy and Mick Arseneault won the Santa Fe Mayor's Award of Excellence for the restoration of their bed-and-breakfast, actually two former brick houses connected by a pitched roof reception building. Since then they've continued to refine and spruce up the turn-of-the-century Inn on the Paseo, four blocks from the Plaza and four from Canyon Road.

This southwestern B&B is tastefully decorated with homey and modern touches like handmade quilts and contemporary artwork. Guest rooms, some with private entrances and fireplaces, are furnished with four-poster beds or beds with hand-carved washed-pine headboards, local artwork, and handmade quilts. The upstairs suite, with a cathedral ceiling and open floor plan, has a whirlpool large enough for two; it's a wonderful spot for gazing out at Santa Fe's fabulous sunsets. It also has an excellent view of the historic Cross of the Martyrs. The rooms facing busy Paseo de Peralta may be noisy. A copious Continental breakfast buffet is served fireside in winter and on the patio or deck during the warmer months. It usually includes a tasty hot dish. The B&B also has a small, light-filled reading room adorned in soft pastels in which to relax.

▦ *18 double rooms with baths, 1 2-bedroom suite. Air-conditioning, cable TV, phones in rooms, fax service, off-street parking. $80–$175, Continental breakfast. AE, DC, MC, V. No smoking, no pets.*

La Posada de Chimayo

279 County Rd. 0101, Box 463, Chimayo 87522, tel. and fax 505/351–4605

New Mexico's first bed-and-breakfast, the rustic and peaceful La Posada de

Chimayo opened to guests in June 1981. It is tucked away in a valley 30 miles north of Santa Fe in one of the prettiest areas of northern New Mexico—a stunning hilly region on the High Road to Taos studded with orchards and picturesque villages, where the sky explodes into a shower of stars each night.

The inn is composed of two adobe guest houses. One, built in 1981, contains two separate suites, each with a sitting room, small bedroom, and bath. The room to the west has great views. Both are warmed by fireplaces, a Trombe wall, and backup electric heaters. Breakfast is served a minute's stroll down the dirt road at the other facility—a renovated farmhouse with double adobe walls built in the 1890s. A shady portale with porch swings wraps around two sides, and the building houses a pleasant dining area and living room, as well as two bedrooms.

Rooms in both guest houses are tastefully appointed with Mexican rugs, handwoven bedspreads, comfortable regional furniture, and some good books to read. The Lizard, in the farmhouse, is light-filled and cheerful, with a freestanding Mexican terra-cotta fireplace and packed earth floor.

Owner Sue Farrington, an expert on Mexico and Mexican cooking, offers a full breakfast in a variety of south-of-the-border flavors.

▦ *2 double rooms with baths, 2 suites. Fireplaces in all rooms, spacious grounds, walking trails. $80–$125, full breakfast, afternoon wine. MC, V. No smoking indoors, pets by arrangement, no children.*

La Tienda

445 W. San Francisco St., Santa Fe 87501, tel. 505/989–8259 or 800/889–7611, fax 505/820–6931

Built as a *tienda*, or general store, in the 1930s, this salmon-color adobe with turquoise trim is now a B&B; the building has been placed on the state historical register. Black-and-white photos of the Santa Fe community, taken at the turn of the century, line the walls of the old store common room where overnighters now take afternoon tea.

Three rooms occupy the main house, with another four in the adjacent, territorial-style brick house. The Trujillo Room has Saltillo-tile floors and Southwest pine furniture with teal, peach, and apricot glazes. Romero has hardwood floors, a sunporch great for summer breakfasts, and reproduction Gustave Baumann works of Old Santa Fe. The Montoya and Mascarell rooms can be combined to make a two-bedroom suite. As there is no dining room, owners Leighton and Barbara Watson deliver a Continental breakfast directly to guests' rooms in the morning, with homemade pastries and warm breads, Blue Lake ranch jams and fresh fruit.

🏠 *7 double rooms with baths. Cable TV, phones, private entrances, 3 rooms with fireplaces, 6 with mini-refrigerators. $90–$160, Continental-plus breakfast, afternoon tea. MC, V. No smoking indoors, no pets.*

Preston House

106 Faithway St., Santa Fe 87501, tel. and fax 505/982–3465

This 1886 blue-and-white Queen Anne Victorian house, the only one of its kind in Santa Fe and with all of its angles and turrets intact, is the elegant restoration of noted artist-designer Signe Bergman, who moved from Santa Barbara to Santa Fe in 1974 to pursue a painting career. It wasn't until she was commissioned to do a large hotel mural in 1978 that she began to think of opening an inn of her own. She purchased Preston House that year and set about restoring it, later adding an adobe guest house and two Queen Anne–style garden cottages to the property.

Preston House is tucked away in a quiet garden a few blocks from the Plaza. Its guest house is just across the street and the cottages are in the back. The main house is on the National Register of Historic Places.

The public rooms are open and sunny; fruit bowls, original, fantastically futuristic stained glass, lace curtains, and fresh-cut flowers add to the appeal. Books in the well-stocked library shed light on some of Preston House's former owners, among them three colorful characters: land speculator George Preston, who operated with a band of other charlatans in divvying up the Southwest territories after the Civil War; a man who exposed the gigantic Peralta-Reavis land-grant fraud; and a cure-all doctor.

Guest rooms in the main house are furnished in ornate late-19th-century fashion. Some have Edwardian fireplaces, ceiling fans, stained-glass windows, brass beds, Queen Anne chairs, and fringed lace tablecloths. Room 1, off the dining room, is for early risers. Rooms in the adobe guest house, in contrast, are done in the traditional Southwestern mode. Room 15, with a king and sofa bed, fireplace, and sitting room, has its own entrance opening up to an ivy-covered courtyard. The Queen Anne–style garden cottages, with floral prints, queen beds, single-size window seats, and fireplaces, couldn't be cozier.

An elaborate Continental breakfast is served in both the main house and adobe guest house. Full afternoon tea and dessert are offered as well. The owner's paintings, which hang in galleries and private collections all over the country, are displayed throughout the house and may be purchased.

🏠 *4 double rooms with baths, 2 doubles share bath in main house, 7 double rooms with baths in adobe guest house, 2 garden cottages. TV and phones in rooms. $75–$160, Continental-plus breakfast, afternoon tea. AE, MC, V. No smoking, no children.*

Pueblo Bonito

138 W. Manhattan Ave., Santa Fe 87501, tel. 505/984–8001, fax 505/984–3155

Secluded behind thick adobe walls, Pueblo Bonito was built in 1873 in traditional pueblo style. Laid out in a series of charming but aging suites connected by private courtyards and archways, the property was once a private estate with its own stable and landscaped grounds. Owners Herb and Amy Behm acquired this National Historic Landmark in 1985.

Each suite is named for an area Native American tribe and is furnished with regional treasures like Navajo rugs, baskets, Native American sand paintings, Pueblo and Mexican pottery, carved wooden santos, and other Spanish antiques. Most have traditional viga ceilings, and many have full kitchens and sofa beds; floors range from flagstone or brick to maple, oak, and pine.

The daily breakfast buffet, served in the dining room before a winter fire, includes seasonal fruits, juices, Danishes, muffins, croissants, cereal, fresh-brewed coffee, and an assortment of teas.

🏨 *11 double rooms with baths, 7 suites. Cable TV, fireplace in all rooms, outdoor hot tub, off-street parking. $95–$140, Continental-plus breakfast, afternoon refreshments. MC, V. No smoking, no pets.*

Rancho de San Juan

Box 4140, Espanola 87533, tel. 800/726–7121

Mountains, mesas, and the Ojo Caliente River valley make up the stunning vista from Rancho de San Juan, set beneath the petroglyph-dotted Black Mesa, 35 miles north of Santa Fe. Out in the middle of nowhere exists a stunning silence under a huge sky and this incredibly elegant Pueblo-style inn.

Conceived, owned, and run by David Heath and John Johnson, this enchanting B&B is their dream come true. David, formerly in real estate and retail—at Saks Fifth Avenue, among other fine stores—and John, a registered architect who worked extensively in the Far East, spent 10 years planning this career move. Searching for the perfect location, they stumbled upon this isolated valley and immediately knew they had found it. They bought a 225-acre tract.

When you enter the main building, an eye-dazzling painting of Navajo *yeis* (gods) greets you. To your left is the refined but relaxing living room, its 14-foot-high ceiling spanned by hand-peeled vigas centered by an immense fireplace. Oriental rugs, tile floors, wonderful Southwestern and Native American art and artifacts, carved-wood corbels, and antique doors are indicative of meticulous attention to detail and finely honed design sensibilities.

To your right is the 16-seat dining room, open to the public Wednesday through Saturday nights, and to guests any night of the week with prior notice. Limoges china, silver, and linen create a graceful impression, highlighted by the antique wooden fireplace mantel. Here John serves up full breakfasts to guests and exquisite dinner delicacies, focusing on northern Italian and French cuisine, or local specialties. A more intimate dining room, seating up to 12, is off to one side.

The nine accommodations cluster around a pretty courtyard. Each room has a different theme but all are as finely finished and have Frette robes, oversize towels, and beds decked out in all-cotton linens that starched and ironed. The San Juan room has a Victorian motif with a crocheted lace bedspread and plantation shutters. The Sierra Negra suite is located separately on the property, with a two-person spa, king-size bed, large sitting area, and kiva fireplace. The Black Mesa room contains a Territorial-style fireplace, a faux canopy bed, and a small flower garden. All rooms have ceiling fans.

Just a short walk from the inn is a series of sandstone caves created long ago by rushing waters. One of the caves has been carved into a shrine of vaulted ceilings, Gothic arches, and shell designs by artist Ra Paulette. Be sure to go take a look.

🏠 *4 double rooms with baths, 5 suites. Restaurant, outdoor patio dining with fountain, outdoor hot tub, facials and herbal wraps by appointment, hiking paths. $175–$250, full breakfast. AE, MC, V. No smoking, no pets, no children under 12.*

Territorial Inn

215 Washington Ave., Santa Fe 87501, tel. 505/989–7737, fax 505/986–9212

The last of the private homes along tree-lined Washington Avenue in the heart of downtown Santa Fe—just off the Plaza—the Territorial Inn was built in the 1890s by Philadelphian George Shoch. A stylish blend of New Mexican stone-and-adobe architecture, this pitched-roof structure is surrounded by large cottonwoods, a front lawn, and a private rose garden.

In recent years, the building was occupied by a law firm. Legal secretary Lela McFerrin acquired the property in 1989, and she preserved or restored much of the century-old building. Now the inn has the gracious feel of the days when it was home to Levi A. Hughes, a well-known Santa Fe merchant who, with his wife, graciously entertained high society and visiting celebrities of the day.

The reception area and living room are large and comfortable, with overstuffed couches and chairs, fireplaces, a large bowl of candies, and a set of encyclopedias. An eye-catching turn-of-the-century brick stairway leads to the upstairs guest rooms.

The 10 bedrooms range from large and luxurious to cozy and quaint; all are individually furnished with period pieces; canopy, brass, or four-poster beds; handmade quilts; ceiling fans; and down comforters. Many of the ceilings have canopy linings, traditionally found in early adobe homes with viga beams. (They originally helped to keep dirt, twigs, and insects from falling into the soup; here, they cover the fluorescent lighting fixtures used in the legal offices of the former occupants.) The best rooms are No. 9, with its four-poster canopy bed and Victorian fireplace; spacious No. 10., with a brass bed, pine armoire, and ceramic pedestal sink; and No. 3, with a private patio.

Breakfast—fresh pastries, strawberries and cream or other fresh fruit, juice, and coffee—is delivered to the bedrooms or, in summer, served in the rose garden. There's afternoon tea or lemonade and cheese, and brandy turndowns with chocolates at night.

🏠 *8 double rooms with baths, 2 doubles share bath. Air-conditioning, cable TV in all rooms, fireplace in 2 rooms, gazebo-enclosed hot tub, off-street parking, laundry service available. $80–$160, Continental-plus breakfast. AE, DC, MC, V. No smoking, no pets, no children under 10.*

Water Street Inn

427 Water St., Santa Fe 87501, tel. 505/984–1193

This inn, part of an award-winning adobe restoration, is just four blocks from the Plaza. The large to very spacious rooms all reveal a talented interior designer at work, from reed shutters and pine antique beds to hand-stenciled paintings, claw-foot tubs, beveled glass mirrors, and a mixture of Native American, Hispanic, and Cowboy Western artifacts. Daring color schemes, lots of light, and the novel furnishings make for a playful, yet very tasteful environment. Three suites have brick floors, daybeds, over-stuffed chairs, and indoor-outdoor patios with fountains.

Breakfast, served in your room, in a dining area, or on an outdoor sundeck, includes oven-fresh pastries, fruit bowls, cereals, juices, and coffees. Every evening local wines and hot hors d'oeu-vres are served in the inn's living room, which features a large fireplace and hand-glazed adobe walls.

🏨 *11 double rooms with baths. Cable TV, VCR, fireplace, and voice mail in all rooms, outdoor hot tub. $125–$195, Continental breakfast, evening wine and snacks. AE, D, MC, V. No smoking.*

Taos

Mabel Dodge Luhan House

Mysterious, spiritual, ageless Taos is an enchanted town of soft lines and delineations. Romantic courtyards, stately elms and cottonwoods, narrow, tangled streets, and a profusion of adobe all add to its timeless appeal.

Taos is 65 miles north of Santa Fe on a rolling mesa at the base of the rugged Sangre de Cristo Mountains, where lofty Wheeler Peak, the state's highest mountain, rises 13,161 feet. Fabulous ski slopes beckon in winter, while summer brings a flood of tourists who just want to soak in the scenery and breathe the good air.

Taos is actually three towns in one: Taos village (the center of Taos), Taos Pueblo, and Ranchos de Taos. Many people compare Taos village to the Santa Fe of yesteryear, before all the glitz and glamour arrived. In fact, Taos enjoys much of Santa Fe's charm while rejecting its commercialization. Taos Pueblo, 2 miles north of the commercial center of Taos and home of the Taos-Tiwa Indians, embodies an apartment-style pueblo dwelling that's one of the oldest continually inhabited communities in the United States. Ranchos de Taos, an adobe-house farming and ranching community 4 miles south of town was settled by the Spanish centuries ago and is best known for its San Francisco de Asis Church. These three distinct Taos faces merge at the place where the sky meets the mountains, in a magnificent 6,950-foot-high plateau setting.

With a combined population of some 4,500, Taos, the Taos Pueblo, and Ranchos de Taos offer a unique blend of history and culture. The town's appeal draws largely from its remarkable literary and artistic heritage. Taos has attracted artists and writers for almost forever, but none has had a more profound impact on the community than Briton D. H. Lawrence, who's become something of a cottage industry: Entrepreneurs have scrambled to create inns and restaurants in places that the author and his wife frequented.

Like Santa Fe, Taos has received its share of accolades of late. In 1992, the United Nations designated Taos Pueblo a World Heritage Site—one of only 17 in the United States and the second in New Mexico (the other is Chaco Canyon). The news delights opponents of the long-discussed, hotly disputed plan to build a commercial airport in Taos. Jets landing and taking off in the proximity of the Taos Pueblo would surely rattle its fragile adobe walls into rubble.

Bed-and-breakfasts in Taos, like those in Santa Fe, were built in the graceful, ground-hugging pueblo style common to both areas. However, because Taos is far less developed than Santa Fe, its B&Bs tend to be more secluded, making the best use possible of the mountain-rimmed, wide-open spaces surrounding them. Two are National Historic Landmarks: the Taos Hacienda Inn, set in a building that dates back to the 1800s with adobe walls that once formed part of the town's original La Loma Plaza fortification; and the Mabel Dodge Luhan House, a huge, rambling adobe built by the famed art patron.

Places to Go, Sights to See

D. H. Lawrence Ranch and **D. H. Lawrence Memorial** (along NM 522, about 15 miles north of town, tel. 505/776–2245). When Lawrence and his wife, Frieda, arrived in Taos, heiress Mabel Dodge Luhan offered them Kiowa Ranch, on 160 acres in the mountains north of Taos, as a place to stay. The property, now owned by the University of New Mexico, became known as the D. H. Lawrence Ranch, although it never actually belonged to the writer. The house is closed to the public, but the nearby memorial containing Lawrence's ashes may be visited.

Kit Carson Home and Museum (Kit Carson Rd., tel. 505/758–4741) is the former home of the famous mountain man and scout who left an indelible mark on the history of Taos. Carson purchased the 12-room adobe home in 1843 as a wedding gift for his bride, Josefa Jaramillo, who was 14 at the time. Carson is buried across town, four blocks northeast of the Plaza, in the wooded, 20-acre Kit Carson Park; Mabel Dodge Luhan is buried in the same small graveyard.

La Hacienda de Don Antonio Severino Martínez (4 miles west of Ranchos de Taos, tel. 505/758–1000) is one of the only fully restored Spanish Colonial adobe haciendas open to the public in New Mexico. The fortlike building on the banks of the Rio Pueblo served as the Martínez family's home and a community refuge against Comanche and Apache raids. The restored period rooms illustrate the lifestyle of the Spanish Colonial era, when supplies, other than what could be produced locally, came to Taos by oxcart on the Camino Real. The surrounding landscape, dotted with farms and grazing horses, tall cottonwood trees, and wooden fences, hints strongly of early settlement days.

Millicent Rogers Museum (4 miles northwest of the Plaza, tel. 505/758–2462) is the museum you should visit in Taos if you have time for only one. Representing the core of Standard Oil heiress Millicent Rogers's private collection, it contains more than 5,000 pieces of Native American and Hispanic art.

San Francisco de Asis Church (tel. 505/758–2754). The centerpiece of Ranchos de Taos, this monumental adobe mission church was built in the 18th century as a spiritual and physical refuge from raiding Apaches, Utes, and Comanches; its massive, buttressed adobe walls and graceful twin belfries have inspired generations of painters and photographers, including Georgia O'Keeffe, Paul Strand, and Ansel Adams. In the parish hall nearby, a 15-minute video explains the history and 1979 restoration of the church; the famous mystery painting, *Shadow of the Cross*, may be seen throughout the day.

Taos Plaza, lined with shops, galleries, and restaurants, bears only a hint of the grace, dignity, and stateliness of the Plaza in Santa Fe, although its history is drawn with the same pen. At the center of the Plaza, the U.S. flag flies night and day, as authorized by a special act of Congress in recognition of Kit Carson's heroic stand against Confederate sympathizers during the Civil War. Next to a covered gazebo, donated by Mabel Dodge Luhan, is an antique carousel that delights youngsters during special summer festivals.

Taos Pueblo (tel. 505/758–8626). For nearly 1,000 years, the Taos-Tiwa Indians have lived at or near the present pueblo site, the largest existing multistory pueblo structure in the United States and Taos's most popular tourist attraction. The pueblo today, without running water or electricity, appears much as it did when the first Spanish explorers arrived in New Mexico in 1540. Parking fees and camera permits are new, of course.

Walking Tours. Roberta Meyers, a native of Taos, leads historical walking tours through town. Meyers educates and entertains with character vignettes, in which she assumes the identities of famous figures like Georgia O'Keeffe, whom Meyers knew personally. The tours last about two hours and can be scheduled at your convenience. Contact Roberta Meyers (tel. 505/776–2562).

Restaurants

For a city with a population of fewer than 5,000, Taos has an extraordinary number of fine restaurants. **Casa Cordova** (tel. 505/776–2500), **Doc Martin's** (tel. 505/758–2121), and the **Trading Post Café** (tel. 505/758–5089) are upscale yet reasonably priced restaurants serving traditional Northern New Mexican and international dishes. A bit more casual in both price and atmosphere are the **Apple Tree** (tel. 505/758–1900), with a stylish, eclectic menu including mango chicken and shrimp quesadillas; **Ogelvie's** (tel. 505/758–8866), which serves prime Angus beef, seafood, and traditional Southwestern dishes in an often rowdy atmosphere; and the current Taos hot spot, **Fred's Place** (tel.505/758–0514), which serves Mexican food. **Lambert's** (tel. 505/758–1009) offers an imaginative menu with American fare, and **Joseph's Table** (tel. 505/751–4512) serves Italian and Mediterranean food in an intimate dining room.

Tourist Information

New Mexico Department of Tourism (Lamy Bldg., 491 Old Santa Fe Trail, Santa Fe 87503, tel. 800/545–2040). **Taos County Chamber of Commerce** (1139 Paseo del Pueblo Sur, Drawer I, Taos 87571, tel. 505/758–3873 or 800/732–8267).

Reservation Services

Bed and Breakfast of New Mexico (Box 2805, Santa Fe 87504, tel. 505/982–3332). **New Mexico Bed and Breakfast Association** (Box 2925, Santa Fe 87504, tel. 505/766–5380 or 800/661–6649). **Taos Bed and Breakfast Association** (Box 2772, Taos 87571, tel. 800/876–7857). **Traditional Taos Inns** (137 Kit Carson Rd., Taos 87571, tel. 505/776–8840 or 800/939–2215).

Adobe & Pines

U.S. 68 and Llano Quemado, Box 837, Ranchos de Taos 87557, tel. 505/751–0947 or 800/723–8267, fax 505/758–8423

With its 80-foot-long portale stretching the entire expanse of the main entryway, this 165-year-old adobe home surrounded by pine and fruit trees couldn't be more impressive. Set against the backdrop of the Taos Mountains in a beautiful pastoral setting, the property has its own stream with an old stone bridge that continues to inspire local poets. Owners Chuck and Charil Fulkerson traveled the world before settling in Taos, opening Adobe & Pines in the summer of 1991 after extensive renovations.

Four guest rooms in the main house have queen-size beds with fluffy goose-down comforters and pillows, hand-painted Mexican-tile baths, and fireplaces. The Puerta Rosa Room has a sauna, a deep soaking tub, and a bathroom fireplace. A separate cottage has a canopy bed, jet whirlpool bath, two fireplaces, and a kitchen. Each houses a large sitting area with a leather sofa and wet bar, separate bedroom, two-person jetted tub, two fireplaces, and French doors opening onto a private portale. Breakfasts such as banana pecan soufflée pancakes are presented in the glass-enclosed sunroom and dining area.

🏠 *4 double rooms with baths, 3 casitas. Jet tub in 1 room and all casitas, fireplaces in all rooms and casitas. $95–$150, full breakfast. MC, V. No smoking indoors, no pets.*

American Gallery Artists House

132 Frontier Rd., Box 584, Taos 87571, tel. 505/758–4446 or 800/532–2041, fax 505/758–0497

The 7-foot-tall, flat, black iron sculpture in front of the American Artists Gallery House isn't Kokopelli, whose flute-bearing image can be seen in every gift shop between San Diego and Santa Fe, but the *God of Bed and Breakfasts*, a special creation of artist Pozzi Franzetti. And it's not for sale—perhaps the only piece among the 500 or so works of art here that doesn't have a price tag. Although almost all B&Bs in northern New Mexico sell works by regional and nationally known artists—"It's a way to get paintings to hang on your walls without paying for them," says one wry innkeeper—this establishment is serious about its artistic endeavors. Owners LeAn and Charles Clamurro, who purchased the B&B in July 1994, have a passion for art, particularly that created by local artists. Charles especially is happy to discuss the array of art found in every room. The B&B frequently hosts art openings for featured artists; at other times, artists are invited to breakfast with the guests. Still, the B&B retains a relaxed atmosphere and, as Charles says, guests should "feel free to put their feet up on anything."

Another passion of the owners is their fine lodging. Charles is a graduate of the Cornell hotel program, and his experience includes a five-year stint running La Fonda Hotel in Santa Fe; LeAn has a similarly impressive background in hotel management and currently heads the Taos Bed & Breakfast Association's marketing committee. The inn is adjacent to a field where the Taos July 4th fireworks and the October Hot Air Balloon Festival take place, providing ringside seats for both.

Its seven rooms are spread throughout the adobe compound: three in the main house, two in an adjacent guest house, and the others in separate garden cottages. The relatively secluded Piñon Gallery Suite, or "honeymoon cottage," is decorated and furnished in Southwestern style with an abundance of local art on display. All rooms have Carmen Velarde kiva fireplaces, colorful Mexican tiles in the bathrooms, Native American rugs covering tile or wooden floors, leather drum tables, and carved furniture. There are also three Jacuzzi suites in adobes with vega ceilings and Saltillo-tile floors.

Breakfast is served promptly at 8 AM around a large table in a glass-enclosed greenhouse-style dining area. One of 10 or so standard breakfast entrées—chili egg frittata, blue-corn pancakes with fresh blackberries, pecan-stuffed French toast—is accompanied by fresh fruits, home-baked breads, and fresh-brewed coffee or a variety of teas.

🏨 *7 double rooms with baths, 2 min-isuites, 3 2-person Jacuzzi suites, out-door hot tub. $75–$150, full breakfast, afternoon beverages and hors d'oeuvres. AE, MC, V. No smoking, no pets.*

The Blue Door

64 La Morada Rd., Box 2953, Taos 87571, tel. 505/758-8360 or 800/824-3667

This 100-year-old adobe farmhouse stands in the foothills between Taos and Ranchos de Taos, near the famous San Francisco de Asis Church and sur-rounded by appealing shops. Here you'll find rural Taos at its finest in a pic-turesque setting amid orchards, flower gardens, lawns, and patios.

The Blue Door is owned by Bruce Allen, who makes and markets traditional Taos drums, crafted from carved tree trunks and covered with tautly stretched leather. His wares are everywhere to be seen at the B&B—coffee tables, decora-tive wall displays, end tables, book racks. Each of the two bedrooms is decorated in Southwestern style, with viga ceil-ings, wood floors, and, as you might ex-pect, Indian-drum end tables. Come morning, Bruce serves a Continental breakfast in a sunny breakfast nook.

🏨 *2 double rooms with baths. Cable TV in both rooms. $75–$85, Continental breakfast. AE, MC, V. No smoking, no pets.*

Brooks Street Inn

119 Brooks St., Box 4954, Taos 87571, tel. 505/758-1489 or 800/758-1489

This homey B&B with a circular drive and adjacent guest house was built in 1956 as an art gallery by local artist Rose Wodell. Later, Southwest writer Frank Waters married Rose and wrote part of the *Book of the Hopi* here. The house, built in the traditional pueblo style, in-corporates adobe bricks made on the property, beamed ceilings, polished wood floors, and a large stone fireplace. An elaborately carved corbel arch, the hand-iwork of Japanese carpenter Yaichikido, spans the entryway, and alongside the house is a shaded, walled garden with a hammock for two.

In the large living room, guests can enjoy locally famous coffee creations, like Taos Magic Mocha, while viewing paintings by local artists and listening to soothing Indian music. Southwestern-style guest rooms—three in the main house, three in the guest house—show great attention to detail, with fresh-cut flowers, hand-quilted duvets, hardwood floors, and vega ceilings. In the guest house, the Juniper Room displays local and primitive artwork, a table from the 1700s, a pinewood bed under a skylit ceil-ing, and a kiva fireplace. The Willow fea-tures a hand-painted Mexican screen and a willow latilla headboard.

A full breakfast features family recipes, including blue-corn pancakes with pineapple sauce, stuffed French toast with apricot glaze, and other home-baked delights. The owners, Carol Frank and Randy Hed, are great conversa-tionalists, and the mood at the Inn is very relaxed. Brooks, a Golden Re-triever, and Gracie, a Black Lab, con-tribute to the hospitality.

🏨 *6 double rooms with baths. Kiva fireplaces, espresso machine. $80–$105, full breakfast, afternoon snacks. AE, MC, V. No smoking indoors, no pets.*

Casa Europa

840 Upper Ranchitos Rd., Los Cardovas Route, HC 68, Box 3F, Taos 87571, tel. 505/758–9798 or 888/758–9798

There's a marvelous, ornate, 200-year-old brass bed in the French Room at the Casa Europa that must take an army of maids weeks to keep polished. But gleaming and polished it is, and you'll feel a little like Louis XIV or Catherine the Great as you drift off to sleep with sounds of crickets and field frogs wafting through the partially opened French windows above the courtyard of this 200-year-old hacienda. Casa Europa is run with care and precision by Marcia and Rudi Zwicker, the owner and chef of the popular Greenbriar Restaurant in Boulder, Colorado, for 16 years.

When they restored the inn in 1983, the couple left all its adobe bricks and wood viga ceiling beams intact. Among Casa Europa's many artistic treasures is the oldest door in Taos, discovered years ago in the basement of the Guadalupe Church and now decorating one of the B&B's hallways. The dining room, with its three foot-thick white adobe walls and hand-carved Spanish moldings, is also part of the original building, which dates back 200 years.

An Austrian crystal chandelier hangs over the beautiful curved staircase that leads to the guest rooms. These rooms, whose whitewashed walls are splashed with sunlight, have been furnished with an eclectic collection of European antique and traditional southwestern pieces. Paintings, arranged gallery style, feature Native American and other contemporary artists; there are also three signed etchings by Salvador Dalí. Each of the rooms is based on a theme. The Spa Suite on the first floor has stained-glass windows; a steam shower and bath; and a skylit two-person jetted tub.

The astounding summer pastry selection includes chocolate mousse cake, truffles, fresh fruit tarts, and Black Forest tortes. Steaming coffee is served in individual decanters.

🏠 *5 double rooms with baths, 2 suites. Phone, marble bath in all rooms, fireplace in 6 rooms, cable TV in public rooms, Swedish sauna, hot tub. $80–$135, full breakfast, afternoon pastries in summer, hors d'oeuvres in ski season. MC, V. No smoking, no pets.*

Casa de las Chimeneas

405 Cordoba Rd., Box 5303, Taos 87571, tel. 505/758–4777, fax 505/758–3976

Casa de las Chimeneas, 2½ blocks from the Plaza and secluded behind thick adobe walls, boasts cool, formal gardens and a stately entryway that wouldn't be out of place in a Loire Valley château. The interior of this Spanish-style hacienda, built in 1912 and renovated in the late 1980s, shows New Mexican luxury at its most refined, with tiled hearths, lush rugs, carved doors and posts, regional art, and vigas.

Chosen by *Ski* magazine as one of the top rooms in ski country, the Library Suite features a private entrance off the courtyard; a sitting room–library with beamed ceilings, wood floor, kiva fireplace, and bentwood rocker; and a bedroom with another fireplace and white-pine antique furniture. The other three accommodations are also stunners: The Willow has Mexican carved furniture, a pewter chandelier, and a skylight in the bath. A whitewashed antique headboard and dresser, two leather chairs, and an ornate handcrafted tin mirror decorate the Blue Room. The Garden Room has a deep tub, kiva fireplace, and a brilliant view of the garden framed by the boles of two massive cottonwood trees.

New Mexican breakfasts are served at a large table in the Main House dining room. Delicious selections include a Southwestern strata, blue-corn pancakes, and breakfast enchiladas.

🏠 *3 rooms with baths, 1 suite. Cable TV, phone, bar, mini-refrigerator in all rooms, hot tub. $125–$150, full breakfast, afternoon hors d'oeuvres. AE, MC, V. No smoking indoors, no pets.*

Casa de Milagros

321 Kit Carson Rd., Box 2983, Taos 87571, tel. 505/758–8001 or 800/243–9334, fax 505/758–0127

A single-story, turn-of-the-century adobe house, ½-mile east of the Taos Plaza, Casa de Milagros (House of Miracles) has the texture and flavor of the Taos of long ago, with all the conveniences of today. This unique Taos hideaway has everything—ambience, location, a hot tub, cable television, fireplaces, gourmet breakfasts, and a friendly, helpful staff.

Actually two buildings connected by a portale (where the hot tub is located), the inn is furnished throughout in a combination of regional styles and talents. Southwestern style predominates—viga ceilings, Mexican-tile bathrooms, custom cabinets, and lots of pottery, tapestry, and weavings. Works by Taos Pueblo artist Jonathan Warm Day and other Native American artists hang on the walls. Breakfast might include Häagen-Dazs vanilla French toast, eggs Milagros with a chili enchilada sauce, and fresh coffee.

🏠 *6 double rooms with baths, 1 2-bedroom suite. Cable TV in all rooms, wood-burning fireplaces in most rooms, kitchenette in 1 room, full kitchen in suite, hot tub, courtyard garden. $70–$180, full breakfast. AE, MC, V. No smoking, no pets.*

Cottonwood Inn

2 State Road 230, HCR 74, Box 24609, El Prado-Taos 87529, tel. 505/776–5826 or 800/324–7120

On the way to Taos Ski Valley, the two-story adobe Cottonwood Inn sits at the base of the Sangre de Christo Mountains. The location is perfect for skiers, and in summer, outdoor-enthusiast owners Bill and Kit Owen will help you on your way to biking, fishing, white-water rafting, horseback riding, or hiking in the beautiful surrounding area.

Guest rooms, decorated with New Mexican or Western themes, have down pillows and quilts, private baths, and panoramic views of the Taos mountains. The upstairs Garden Room with vega ceilings, a white kiva fireplace, and a jetted tub and shower overlooks Cottonwood's seasonal garden. Mesa Vista, the inn's most luxurious room, has an antique oak bed and sitting area, as well as a full-size hot tub set in a skylit rotunda open to the room.

Breakfast—including fresh baked breads and muffins and a meat dish—is served in the country-style dining room, while evening hors d'oeuvres are enjoyed by a crackling winter fire or in the summertime garden.

🏠 *7 double rooms with baths, some with balconies, steam showers, jetted baths, and fireplaces. $85–$160, full breakfast. MC, V. No smoking indoors, no pets.*

El Rincón

114 Kit Carson Rd., Taos 87571, tel. 505/758–4874, fax 505/758–4541

If you're looking for something unique, you've found it here. With its maze of rooms and hallways upstairs and down and its kitchens and courtyards, El Rincón looks like a cross between a set for a melodrama and a Western museum. Up front is the oldest trading post in Taos, still flourishing. Piled high with Western artifacts, feathered Indian headdresses, Navajo rugs, beads, drums, *santos* (saints) carvings, buckles, and pots, it has a one-room museum whose prized possession is a pair of Kit Carson's leather pants.

It's difficult to tell where the store and museum end and the bed-and-breakfast begins. Nina Meyers, daughter of Ralph Meyers, an old-time Taos resident, artist, and trader, has followed in her father's footsteps. Her own work and photographs, paintings, and other art, both contemporary and historic, fill the walls of the B&B.

El Rincón has the look of an organic building that's grown over the century, and now that Taos real estate prices have skyrocketed, the B&B has begun to grow up, instead of out. At press time, Paul "Paco" Castillo, who owns the B&B along with his mother, Nina, was installing a rooftop deck with hot tub, barbecue, and picnic table above the already luxurious Rainbow Room (it also has a full kitchen, washer and dryer, and dining area). The decor in the Santiago Room evokes images of Old World Spain, and it is only when you open a cabinet to find a TV and VCR or locate the Jacuzzi bathtub that you realize it's better appointed than most any room found in times past. Unit 12 has a canopied bed with a handmade wedding-ring quilt, heavily embellished with Spanish lace; there's a tiled floor-to-ceiling mural of the Garden of Eden in the bath. Unit 8, which has beautiful old corbels, murals, and woodwork created by local artisans, also has a kitchenette, hot tub, fireplace, stereo, and TV/VCR. Peek through the lace curtains on the windows and you'll see Kit Carson's house across the street.

The B&B is in the heart of bustling Taos, just a quarter-block from the plaza, and the thick adobe walls provide respite from noise and light. Guests who tire of roaming the plaza or skiing the mountains can retire to the cool depths, choose a movie from an extensive video library, and watch it in their room. They might also wander through the house and get Paco to take a break from his continual building projects and recount a bit about the building's history, such as why there is an old stone well sunk in the floor adjoining the kitchen (it is, of course, grated so you needn't worry if you have intrepid children).

🏠 *13 double rooms with baths, 3 suites. Refrigerators, whirlpool tubs, TV, VCR, stereo in all rooms, kitchens and hot tubs in 3 suites, video library. $59–$125, Continental-plus breakfast. AE, D, MC, V. Pets $5 per night.*

Hacienda del Sol

109 Mabel Dodge La., Box 177, Taos 87571, tel. 505/758–0287, fax 505/751–0319

The Hacienda del Sol, which borders 95,000 acres of Pueblo land and overlooks some of the most spectacular scenery in northern New Mexico, was acquired in the 1920s by art patron Mabel Dodge Luhan. She and her fourth husband, Tony Luhan, a Taos Pueblo Indian, lived here while building their main house, Las Palomas de Taos, now the Mabel Dodge Luhan House (*see below*). They kept the Hacienda del Sol as a private retreat and a guest house.

Although it's only about a mile from the Plaza and just off a main roadway, the inn remains secluded. Innkeepers John and Marcine Landon, who bought the property in 1991, make sure everything runs like clockwork. The house, a model of adobe construction built in 1810, has viga ceilings, arched doorways with *ristras* (string of dried chili peppers) hanging from them, and large, quiet rooms.

Author Frank Waters was living in the Tony Luhan Room when he saw a young Taos Indian being arraigned by three police officials for killing a deer; the incident was the inspiration for his classic novel of Pueblo life, *The Man Who Killed the Deer*. Containing a kiva fireplace, sheepskin rug, and a bench under the window shaded by what's believed to be the oldest cottonwood tree in Taos, the room has undoubtedly changed little. The more contemporary Los Amantes Room (The Honeymoon Suite) adjoins a private room with a double-size black Jacuzzi on a mahogany platform, amid a jungle of potted plants; there's a skylight above, and the attached bathroom is a celebration of decadence with its jet-black sink, tub, shower, and toilet, all with gleaming silver hardware. In the bedroom bookcase are *Edge of Taos Desert, Taos, A Memory,* and *Winter in Taos,* all by Mabel Dodge Luhan, and, of course, *The Man Who Killed the Deer.* Most of the rooms feature kiva fireplaces, Spanish antiques, Southwestern-style handcrafted furniture, and original artwork, much of it for sale. There's also an adobe casita with three guest rooms, two baths, and fireplaces, which can be rented as a suite.

Breakfast is served in front of the dining room fireplace or, weather permitting, on the patio. Entrées might include a blintz soufflé or blue-corn pancakes with blueberry sauce, complemented by a robust house-blend coffee.

🏠 *7 double rooms with baths, 2 doubles with separate bath, 1 suite. Cable TV in public room, outdoor hot tub, gift shop. $70–$120, suite $130, full breakfast, afternoon snacks. MC, V. No smoking, no pets.*

Inn on La Loma Plaza

315 Ranchitos, Box 4159, Taos 87571, tel. 505/758–1717 or 800/530–3040, fax 505/751–0155

This upscale, historic inn is easily one of Taos's nicest. A beautifully restored estate with viga and latilla ceilings and thick adobe walls, some dating back to the 1800s, it's only three blocks from the Plaza in a quiet setting of trees, fountains, and mountains. Owners Peggy and Jerry Davis were married in their inn in 1992. She was the mayor of Vail, while he was mayor of Avon, Colorado.

The light-filled sunroom, decorated with plants and a gurgling fountain, is used for breakfasts and afternoon snacks. Next door, the sitting room is cozy with original artwork, a fireplace, overstuffed chairs and couches, and a book collection. The house was formerly owned by artist Carey Moore, whose studio is now

the inn's premier suite. Also outstanding is the Happy Trails Room, complete with a bridle, chaps, and spurs, a horse-collar mirror, and an antique wooden rocking horse. All rooms are furnished with handcrafted pieces, pottery lamps, and Indian rugs.

🏠 *5 double rooms with baths, 2 4-person studios. Cable TVs, phones in all rooms, fireplaces, kitchenettes, robes, and hot tubs in studios, outdoor hot tub. $95–$195, full breakfast, afternoon refreshments. AE, MC, V. No smoking, no pets.*

La Posada de Taos

309 Juanita La., Box 1118, Taos 87571, tel. 505/758–8164 or 800/645–4803, fax 505/751–3294

The first B&B in Taos, La Posada opened in 1984 in a quiet, yet centrally located neighborhood. It's a pueblo-style adobe in the Historic District, built circa 1900 with beamed ceilings, a portale, and a surrounding latilla fence. The house opens up to a small courtyard in which there's a *ramada,* or "shaded place," where guests can sit with a book and enjoy the quiet afternoon. Fifty percent of La Posada's clientele are repeat visitors or referrals.

Innkeepers Bill and Nancy Brooks-Swan have endeared the common areas of their B&B with 18th- and 19th-century antiques and a collection of Blue Willow plates. Five of the six elegant guest rooms are in the main house, decorated with country antiques collected from around the world. All accommodations have tiled baths, private patios, and views of either the mountains or the flowered courtyards. All but the Taos Room have wood-burning stoves or kiva fireplaces, yet the latter compensates with a small sitting area, a library, and a window that frames Taos Mountain.

The Beutler Room has a king-size bed, chaise longue, and a whirlpool bath. The Lino contains an old English church pew and a queen bed. El Solecito, formerly the owner's quarters, has been opened up to create a spacious room with a private patio, Mexican trastero (combination closet and bench), cornerside kiva fireplace, willow chairs, Southwestern basketry, and a jetted bath. Across the adobe-walled courtyard, the cozy La Casa de la Luna de Miel (Honeymoon House) features a skylighted queen bed with roped vega posters and a sitting room with a raised kiva fireplace.

Come dawn, Bill and Nancy are hard at work preparing a full, hearty breakfast, which they serve in the high-vaulted dining room at 8 AM. Savory dishes may include traditional ham and country eggs or spicy Mexican burritos. After breakfast, guests can walk to Taos Plaza, only 2 ½ blocks away.

🏠 *5 double rooms with baths, 1 cottage. Library, TV in common room. $85–$120, full breakfast. No credit cards. No smoking, no pets, no children.*

Little Tree

226 Honda Seco Rd., Box 960, El Prado 87529, tel. 505/776–8467 or 800/334–8467

On a gentle road outside Taos stands a little tree silhouetted against the Sangre de Cristo Mountains, welcoming guests to a charming bed-and-breakfast inn of the same name. Built in 1991 in the traditional Southwestern adobe style, the Little Tree is owned by Kay Giddens and her husband, Charles, a former attorney: "I'd rather clean toilets than be a lawyer," he says, explaining his change in careers. The inn's proximity to the Taos Ski Valley makes it popular with the ski set, and it's also close to the famed Taos Pueblo.

All rooms have viga ceilings and are furnished Southwestern style, with carved wooden headboards and corn husks on the door. The mud adobe and Saltillo-tile floors are radiant heated. The Piñon and Juniper Rooms have kiva fireplaces and TVs with VCRs, and for families the Juniper and Spruce rooms can be rented together as a two-bath suite.

Breakfast is served in the library, as are refreshments in the late afternoon, when guests are invited to join their hosts for meeting and greeting. Three resident cats keep guard over the colorful property.

🏠 *4 double rooms with baths. Clock radio, down comforters, cookies, and fruit in all rooms, TV with VCR in 3 guest rooms, library. $80–$95, Continental-plus breakfast, afternoon refreshments. D, MC, V; checks preferred. No smoking, no pets.*

Mabel Dodge Luhan House

240 Morada La., Box 558, Taos 87571, tel. 505/751–9686 or 800/846–2235, fax 505/737–0365

This classic, rambling, pueblo-style structure, formerly the home of heiress Mabel Dodge Luhan and classified as a National Historic Landmark in 1991, has been a combined B&B and conference center for the past 15 years. Previously owned by actor Dennis Hopper, who stayed here while editing his film *Easy Rider*, the Luhan House today is owned by Robert and Linda Attiyeh from California. They have nine guest rooms in the main house, parts of which are more than 200 years old; eight more rooms are in a separate guest house built in the same pueblo style in 1989. A family-size gatehouse suite has two more bedrooms, a sitting room, kitchen, and three fireplaces.

Luhan bought the house in 1915, and she and her husband, Tony Luhan, spent the next seven years enlarging and remodeling it. The three original rooms grew to 17; the main part of the house rose from one story to three. Upon its completion in 1922, Mabel Dodge Luhan took the lead in promoting the Southwest as a utopia, offering her literary and artistic friends an antidote to civilization. Her guests here included D. H. Lawrence, Georgia O'Keeffe, Willa Cather, Mary Austin, and John Marin.

The creative spirit nurtured so lovingly by Luhan, who died in the house in 1962 at the age of 83, still exists today. The inn is frequently used for literary workshops, educational conferences, and yoga retreats.

A living room, sitting room, and separate library are at the center of the main house, joined by a string of bedrooms furnished with turn-of-the-century pieces. The master suite on the second floor still contains Luhan's magnificently carved double bed, as well as a kiva fireplace and entrance from the patio. And in the bathroom is a mural painted on the window glass by D. H. Lawrence, who was shocked that the bathroom had no curtains and anyone could see in when Mabel bathed. In the separate guest house, all the rooms are decorated in Southwestern style, with carved, hand-painted furnishings.

If you crave crisp service and a lot of pampering, don't look for them here. The floors creak, and you have to be part mountain goat to maneuver the loftlike stairs leading to the Solarium bedroom at the top of the house. But if you're an adventurous spirit and want to soak up the magic days of the past that made Taos what it is today, this is the place to come.

▦ *14 double rooms with baths, 2 doubles share bath, 1 suite. Extensive grounds, conference facilities. $75–$200, full breakfast. AE, MC, V. No smoking, no pets.*

Old Taos Guesthouse

1028 Witt Rd., Box 6552, Taos 87571, tel. 505/758–5448 or 800/758–5448

Nestled in a wooded grove on a rise 2 miles west of Taos, this casual and moderately priced adobe inn was built as a trapper's cabin in 1860. Expanded con-

siderably over the years, Old Taos Guesthouse is set on 7½ acres of pasture and alfalfa fields. The portale in front looks like it could be from the set of *Gunsmoke*. A straw-bale *tapia*, or arched gateway, has been added to the house.

The guest rooms, each with a private courtyard entrance, feature New Mexico–style furnishings, many of them made by owners Tim and Leslie Reeves, self-confessed ski bums and outdoor enthusiasts. There are Western decorative touches throughout—local artwork, Mexican pottery, and antique farm tools. The Taos Suite boasts a raised platform bed and a sofa bed, a bleached cattle skull over a kiva fireplace, and a kitchen. At breakfast, Tim and Leslie serve up an expanded Continental breakfast, including stewed, home-grown apples, home-baked honey bread, and lemon-nut muffins. The B&B draws many from the young, blue-jean generation, and guests enjoy soaking themselves in the outdoor hot tub under the starlit nights.

▦ *7 double rooms with baths, 2 suites. Cable TV in common room, hot tub. $70–$115, Continental-plus breakfast. MC, V. No smoking, no pets.*

Orinda Bed and Breakfast

461 Valverde, Box 4451, Taos 87571, tel. 505/758–8581 or 800/847–1837

Orinda is a dramatic adobe estate, built in 1947 and surrounded by towering elm and cottonwood trees. The drive is flanked by pastures where the Pratts keep two llamas. Indoors the B&B is populated by the dogs, Sadie and Kiva, and Melvin the cat. Owners since September 1992, George and Cary Pratt have updated, remodeled, and enlarged the original structure, which is within walking distance of the Taos Plaza.

Guests gather in the house's comfortable common room with a large TV, a video library, and a selection of board games, as well as a fireplace and a huge picture window that frames the Taos Mountains. Orinda's spacious rooms, two of which can be combined into a suite, have kiva fireplaces, traditional viga ceilings, Mexican-tile baths, and separate entrances. Thick adobe walls ensure peace and quiet.

Breakfast is served in the two-story sun atrium amid a gallery of artwork, all crafted by local artists and all for sale. But don't even think about touching the antique Navajo blankets!

🏨 *4 double rooms with baths. 42" cable TV in common room, video library, kiva fireplaces. $70–$88, suite $170 for 4 people, full breakfast, afternoon refreshments. AE, D, MC, V. No smoking, no pets.*

The Ruby Slipper

416 La Lomita Rd., Box 2069, Taos 87571, tel. 505/758-0613

Diane Fichtelberg and Beth Goldman, who consider Taos a mythical land, turned to Oz for the name of their inn; the guest rooms, too, allude to characters who accompanied Dorothy on her voyage. Now in its seventh year, the Ruby Slipper is ecoconscious with spiritualist overtones; only all-natural foods are served and *ochos de Dios* (God's eye) symbols are used for do-not-disturb signs. The inn draws an eclectic clientele and welcomes a mixed gay and straight crowd.

One of the few adobe B&Bs in Taos with a gabled roof, the central 1930s farmhouse has three guest rooms; two adjoining adobe buildings have two rooms each. All the rooms have private entrances and include either kiva fireplaces or gas stoves, Mexican-tile baths, and locally crafted furniture—simple and practical, handmade, and hand painted in the bright colors of the Santa Fe school. The full breakfasts served each morning range from hot apple cheddar omelettes and whole wheat banana pancakes to

homemade granola with fresh fruit; guests can always choose between two options.

🏨 *7 double rooms with baths. Outdoor hot tub. $79–$114, full breakfast, in-room coffee and snacks. AE, D, MC, V. No smoking, no pets.*

Salsa del Salto

Hwy. 150, Box 1468, El Prado 87529, tel. 505/776-2422 or 800/530-3097

A combination ski lodge and ranch-style home, Salsa del Salto sits on the mesa at the foothills of the Sangre de Cristo Mountains, in a rural area crisscrossed with ancient *acequias* (irrigation ditches) developed by the Indians and early Spanish settlers. Visitors to the famed Taos Ski Valley, only 10 miles east, love this clubby hideaway, designed for owners Mary Hockett and Dadou Mayer by architect Antoine Predock. In the winter, Mayer, a renowned French chef, doubles as a ski instructor; Hockett, a native-born New Mexican, is also an avid skier. The two outdoor enthusiasts added a tennis court and swimming pool outside, and will set guests up with hiking, mountain biking, and skiing trips.

All the guest rooms are furnished with handcrafted New Mexico furniture and have king-size beds with goose-down comforters and tiled baths, as well as spectacular views of the nearby mountains. The Honeymoon Suite features a fireplace with copper detailing. A full gourmet breakfast, highlighted by jellies, jams, and fresh-baked croissants, is served each morning in the sunny two-story-high common room with a huge fireplace and an antique stove that's used as a buffet counter.

🏨 *10 double rooms with baths. Outdoor heated pool, hot tub, tennis court. $85–$160, full breakfast. MC, V. No smoking indoors, no pets.*

Taos Country Inn at Rancho Rio Pueblo

Box 2331, Upper Ranchitos and Karavas Rds., Taos 87571, tel. 505/758-4900 or 800/866-6548, fax 505/758-0331

Yolanda Deveaux opened the Taos Country Inn after her children left for college, and in many ways the inn still feels like a family home. Yolanda resembles a hummingbird as she flits through spacious and well-lit rooms ensuring that guests' needs are met and adding thoughtful touches along the way, such as preparing fires in the rooms of guests returning from a day of skiing. In the morning, the aroma of strong coffee and good things cooking wafts through the rooms and hallways of this sprawling Spanish hacienda, parts of it built nearly two centuries ago. Yolanda is from an old-line Taos family that acquired the hacienda 20 years ago. Her father, Dr. Reynaldo Deveaux, "delivered half the people in Taos," she says.

The inn is on 22 acres of pastureland and cultivated orchards and gardens, 1 mile north of town adjoining the Rio Pueblo. Guests can wander about in the fields, marveling at the distant mountain horizons, still snowcapped in the spring; chat with a field hand burning off sections of grass; and photograph the horses and sheep in a neighbor's farmyard. In summer, local artists often set up their easels in the gardens.

The house reflects the talents of skilled local craftsmen—doors by Leroy Mondragon and Roberto Lavadi, abstract paintings in huge swatches of shocking red by James Mack, and fireplaces by Carmen Velarde, the Leonardo of fireplace makers. The public rooms, whose large windows bring the outdoors in, are filled with handcrafted furnishings, couches upholstered in textured desert tones, and glass-topped saguaro or cholla cactus-rib tables.

The guest rooms are spacious and sunny. All have stuccoed fireplaces, sitting areas, leather sofas, Native American artifacts, Southwestern artwork, and king- or queen-size beds with fluffy down comforters and a mountain of pillows.

At breakfast—served at natural wood tables, one long and formidable, others smaller and more intimate—Yolanda unsuccessfully urges a second plate of Belgian waffles, piled high with whipped cream and strawberries, on a guest who could hardly manage the first. Her entrées might include cream cheese and salmon omelets or *huevos rancheros* or other regional specialties, all accompanied by a buffet of fruit dishes, yogurt, pastries, and breads. A small refrigerator contains juices and other soft drinks to which guests may help themselves at any time.

🏠 *9 suites. Phones, fireplaces, and cable TV in rooms, VCR units on request, massage available. $110–$150, full breakfast, afternoon refreshments. MC, V. No smoking indoors, no pets, no children.*

Albuquerque

Casas de Sueños

The only major city in northern New Mexico (Santa Fe is tiny by comparison), Albuquerque wields its fair share of magic. Visitors can ascend a breathtaking 2.7 miles to Sandia Peak on one of the longest aerial tramways in the world or watch the sky fill with color each October as 500-plus balloons take to the clouds in the world's largest hot-air-balloon festival.

Time travel is simple here, too. Picturesque Old Town Plaza hearkens back to 1706, when 15 families petitioned King Philip of Spain for permission to settle at a bend in the Rio Grande. Along legendary Route 66, now called Central Avenue, outbursts of neon celebrate America's mid-century romance with the automobile. One hour's drive and a thousand years away, Acoma Pueblo looks much as it did in 1540, when Spanish conquistadors first sighted the Native American village atop a towering mesa.

With half a million people, or close to one-third of New Mexico's population, Albuquerque is the largest metropolis in the state. It lies at the intersection of I-25 and I-40, New Mexico's two most important freeways, and is home to the state's largest airport, its largest university, many of its major cultural institutions, and most of its high-tech industry.

Despite its size, Albuquerque retains a small-town feel. Central Avenue and the railroad tracks divide the city into quadrants—SW, NW, SE, and NE—which are then broken down into smaller enclaves. New Mexico is typically referred to as a land of three cultures—Native American, Hispanic, and Anglo—but in fact a much greater variety of cultures have long spiced the city's social stew.

The terrain of this vast, sprawling city is also diverse. From an elevation of around 4,800 feet in the north and south Rio Grande valleys, the land rises slowly in the east until it reaches 6,500 feet in the foothills of the Sandias, the dramatic peaks that dominate the city. On the west side, a 1,700-foot-high mesa topped by extinct volcanoes emerges abruptly from the valley floor. Temperatures can vary as much as 10°F in Albuquerque, with the sun brightly shining on one side of town and snow falling on the other.

Albuquerque's bed-and-breakfasts are as colorful as the city itself. You'll find everything here, from an ancient adobe farmhouse built on the ruins of a Pueblo Indian village, to a former bordello, to a modern hacienda designed by a stockbroker on the lam. You can stay in the center of Old Town's activities or in a secluded rural setting just 15 minutes away—and pay rates much lower than those in the smaller, more trendy towns to the north. You can generally find exactly the room you want—except during the balloon fiesta (see below), when the town is filled to its vigas with hot-air enthusiasts.

Places to Go, Sights to See

Acoma (40 mi west of Albuquerque, Box 309, Acoma 87034, tel. 800/747–0181). Set atop a 357-foot mesa that rises sharply from the floor of a dry valley, Acoma Pueblo was built more than 1,000 years before the conquistadors discovered it in 1540. It is thought to be among the longest continually inhabited locales in North America. It is a "traditional" pueblo, without electricity or running water.

Highlights of a visit, allowed by guided tour only, include the mission church of San Esteban del Rey, built between 1621 and 1641, and the fine, thin-walled pottery of the Acoma Indians.

Albuquerque International Balloon Fiesta (8309 Washington Pl. NE, Albuquerque 87113, tel. 505/821–1000). An estimated 1.1 million folks converge on the city for this nine-day event, held the second weekend of October. Among the highlights are a "rodeo" of specially shaped balloons; parachute jumps; stunt flying; and the sight of hundreds of brightly hued balloons rising at dawn in the clear skies over town.

Biological Park (903 10th St. SW, tel. 505/764–6200). This new environmental museum comprises the Rio Grand Botanic Garden and the city aquarium. The latter displays an artificial coral reef with extensive marine life, a moray-eel tunnel, and a shark tank. Next door, the botanic garden has two wings; one showcasing desert plants and the other housing greenery from Mediterranean climates.

Indian Pueblo Cultural Center (2401 12th St. NW, tel. 505/843–7270 or 800/766–4405). Boasting the largest collection of Native American arts and crafts in the Southwest, the center's lower-level exhibits trace the history of the Pueblo Indians; upstairs, ceramics, jewelry, rugs, and other authentic items from the various Pueblos are on sale. Ceremonial dances are performed here on weekends, during the summer, and on special holidays.

Old Town. The site of the original Spanish settlement in 1706, this tree-shaded, four-block square remains a cultural and commercial hub. Most of the old adobe homes were converted into shops, galleries, and restaurants, but the *San Felipe de Neri Church* (2005 Plaza NW, tel. 505/243–4628), built the year Albuquerque was established, still stands facing the Plaza. Adjacent to Old Town, the *Albuquerque Museum of Art and History* (2000 Mountain Rd. NW, tel. 505/242–4600) is home to the largest collection of Spanish Colonial artifacts in the nation; it also has a good collection of contemporary New Mexican art. Just across the street, the *New Mexico Museum of Natural History* (1801 Mountain Rd. NW, tel. 505/841–2800) has interactive exhibits that include an active volcano, dinosaurs, and an ice cave, along with a Dynamax theater. Most kids will also love the small *American International Rattlesnake Museum* (202 San Felipe NW, tel. 505/242–6569) in the heart of Old Town, which houses the largest collection of live rattlesnakes in the country. The *Old Town Information Center* (tel. 505/243–3215) is across the street from the San Felipe de Neri Church.

Petroglyph National Monument (6900 Unser Blvd. NW, tel. 505/839–4429), 8 miles west of Albuquerque at the site of five extinct volcanoes, contains nearly 15,000 ancient Native American rock carvings, or petroglyphs. They are believed to have been inscribed on the lava formations of the 17-mile-long West Mesa escarpment between AD 1100 and 1600.

Rio Grand Nature Center State Park (2901 Candeleria Rd. NW, tel. 505/344–7240), on the east bank of the Rio Grande in a cottonwood forest, is home to all manner of birds and migratory fowl. Its unique visitor center is constructed half above and half below ground.

Sandia Peak Ski and Tramway (10 Tramway Loop NE, tel. 505/856–7325 for tram and ski information). A modern Swiss-built tramway lofts visitors to Sandia Crest, the 10,678-foot summit of the Sandia Mountains at the outskirts of Albuquerque. From the sky-top observation deck, you can see as far as Santa Fe to the northeast and Los Alamos to the northwest—a 360-degree panorama spanning 11,000 square miles. Twenty-five downhill runs, a ski school, and a rental shop operate on the mountain from mid-December through mid-March. From Memorial Day through October, the trails are given over to mountain bikers; call 505/242–9052 for information about facilities and bike and ski rentals. Year-round, the sky-high *High Finance Restaurant* (tel. 505/243–9742) has good food along with great views.

The **University of New Mexico** (east of I-25 on Central Ave., tel. 505/277–0111 for general information) has many outstanding galleries and museums that are open to the public, free of charge. The *Maxwell Museum of Anthropology* (tel. 505/277–4404) chronicles human history in general and the history of the Southwest in particular; a gift shop offers a wide selection of traditional and contemporary crafts. The largest fine art collection in the state, including works by Georgia O'Keeffe and an outstanding photography collection, may be viewed at the *University Art Museum* (tel. 505/277–4440). Lithography is the focus of the *Tamarind Institute* (tel. 505/277–3901), where prints by professionals are displayed alongside those of the school's students. Two blocks south of the campus, the *Ernie Pyle Memorial Library* (900 Girard Blvd. SE, tel. 505/256–2065) is in the memorabilia-filled home of the Pulitzer Prize–winning war correspondent.

Restaurants

Albuquerque's restaurants, as diverse as the city's neighborhoods, tend to be neither very expensive nor very formal. At the upper end are the **Monte Vista Fire Station** (tel. 505/255–2424), serving New American cuisine in a bright, chic setting; the **Artichoke Cafe** (tel. 505/243–0200), with an eclectic Continental menu and a two-level dining room; **Maria Teresa** (tel. 505/242–3900), offering New Mexican specialties in an 1840 Old Town adobe; and, the most formal of them, the **Rancher's Club** (tel. 505/884–2500), a masculine room with white-glove service and fine prime rib and seafood. The four casual and colorful **Garduño's** restaurants (tel. 505/298–5000, 505/821–3030, 505/880–0055, or 505/898–2772) serve good New Mexican food and margaritas to lively mariachi music. Other moderately priced places include **Scalo** (tel. 505/255–8781), a spirited Northern Italian spot featuring fresh pasta, and **Seagull Street** (tel. 505/821–0020), a seafood restaurant where Cape Cod meets the mesquite grill. Another notable downtown eatery is the **Rio Bravo Brewpub** (tel. 505/242–6800), with a hot mesquite grill and beers—such as the tasty High Desert Pale Ale–created on the premises. **Stephens** (tel. 505/842–1773), serving Continental dishes in a former warehouse, is close to Old Town. In Corrales, **Casa Vieja** (tel. 505/898–7489) offers northern Italian and French food in an old Spanish house.

Tourist Information

Albuquerque Convention and Visitors Bureau (20 First Plaza, Suite 601, Albuquerque 87102, tel. 505/842–9918 or 800/284–2282). **Albuquerque Hispanic Chamber of Commerce** (202 Central SE, Suite 300, Albuquerque 87102, tel. 505/ 842–9003 or 800/754–4620). **Greater Albuquerque Chamber of Commerce** (401 2nd St. NW, Albuquerque 87102, tel. 505/764–3700).

Reservation Services

Albuquerque Bed & Breakfast Association (Box 10598, Albuquerque 87194, tel. 800/916–3322). **Bed and Breakfast of New Mexico** (Box 2805, Santa Fe 87504, tel. 505/982–3332). **New Mexico Bed and Breakfast Association** (Box 2925, Santa Fe 87504, tel. 505/766–5380 or 800/661–6649). **New Mexico Central Reservations** (121 Tijeras Ave. NE, Albuquerque 87125, tel. 800/466–7829).

Adobe and Roses

1011 Ortega Rd. NW, Albuquerque 87114, tel. 505/898-0654

A blue mailbox marked "1011" is the only indication that you've arrived at Dorothy Morse's place in Albuquerque's North Valley, a rural enclave 15 minutes from downtown; there's literally no sign of a commercial establishment on gravel-lined Ortega Street. And the sense that you're visiting a friend—one who respects your privacy and has unusually attractive guest quarters—lasts throughout a stay at Adobe and Roses.

Dorothy originally rented out an extra suite in her home as a onetime favor to an overbooked innkeeper but later decided, with her daughters off in college, that running an inn might not be a bad idea. In 1988, she began building a separate two-unit guest cottage, laying the floors and tile herself. After more than three decades on the premises, she has a lovely and comfortable establishment.

The pueblo-style main house and guest cottage are indeed made of adobe, and, yes, there are roses everywhere, but they don't dominate among the wildly colorful blossoms on the 2-acre grounds. Most outstanding, maybe, are the rich purple irises that grow along the banks of a tranquil fishpond in May. At sunset, all colors are transformed as the clouds behind the Sandias, off to the east, turn brilliant shades of pink.

The guest rooms fulfill every Southwest fantasy, terra-cotta pottery, equipale (pigskin) chairs, tinwork mirrors, wood-beam ceilings, Saltillo-tile floors, exposed brick walls, and kiva fireplaces. All are light, airy, and large—the suite in the main house easily fits an upright piano in the sitting room—with individual cooling and heating units. Down comforters also help keep things cozy at night, when the 5,000-foot altitude can send the mercury dipping.

You can choose to eat breakfast in the dining room, on the portale, or in your room. Freshly ground coffee, homemade breads, muffins, and coffee cakes are staples; for those who like hot meals, Dorothy will prepare such specialties as a grits, chili, cheese, and asparagus casserole made with eggs laid by the chickens that wander the grounds. Best of all, because you're not *really* at a friend's house, you don't have to offer to do the dishes (the bad news, of course, is that you'll be receiving a bill).

🏨 *1 double room with bath, 2 suites. TV, kitchenette, kiva fireplaces in all rooms, private entrances, laundry facilities available, barbecue grill, horse boarding. $55–$85, full breakfast. No credit cards. No smoking, pets allowed, 2-night minimum.*

Adobe Garden

641 Chavez NW, Albuquerque 87107, tel. 505/345-1954

Set on 3 acres in a quiet neighborhood of Albuquerque, owners Lee and Tricia Smith opened this bed-and-breakfast in 1993. The common areas of the main house reflect the owners' worldwide travels, from the Bolivian and Lebanese artifacts in the hallways to the Korean rice chest, Chinese wall screen, and Japanese hibachi that decorate the sitting room.

There are three bedrooms in the main house; two have fireplaces. The upstairs room has a queen-size brass bed as well as a daybed, white wicker furniture, a wood-burning stove, and an impressive evening view of the city's lights. Next to the main house, a three-bedroom bunkhouse sleeps up to eight. This spacious building isn't glamorous (it was a stable in the 1940s), but families or large parties will appreciate the separate sitting room with an old woodstove, full kitchen with washer and dryer, phone, and television.

Each morning, fresh fruits, yogurts, breakfast breads, and cheeses are served in the main house. The dining room opens up to a portale, and in the courtyard you'll see tall cottonwood trees, a grape arbor, and a refreshing swimming pool.

🏨 *3 double rooms with baths, 8-person bunkhouse. Outdoor pool. $89–$150, Continental-plus breakfast. No credit cards. No smoking indoors, no pets, no children under 10.*

Bottgër Mansion

110 San Felipe NW, Albuquerque 87104, tel. and fax 505/243–3639 or 800/758–3639

This elegant, light blue Victorian-style B&B, built in 1912 by German-born Charles Bottgër, was once called "The Pride of Old Town." Under owners Patsy and Vince Garcia, who took control in 1992, it is returning to its former glory. With Old Town right out the door, the Albuquerque Country Club just a few blocks away, and the downtown area a 15-minute walk, one of the most appealing aspects of this B&B is its location.

Another is the character of the residence. Professional fixer-uppers, the Garcias acquired a real gem in this National Historic Landmark. Many interesting people have passed through its gate, among them Machine Gun Kelly and his cohorts. This and many other stories tumble from cheerful Patsy, who grew up in the area. Vince's family was one of the 12 families that founded Old Town in 1706, so the Garcias really know this intriguing section of Albuquerque.

All the rooms are named after family members. The Sofia Room has an ornate, delicately imprinted pressed-tin ceiling, a brass bed, and an adjoining sunroom with twin beds, tea table, and view of the courtyard. The Mercedes Room has a black marble jetted tub, wood shutters, and pink marble floors. Lola has a mural painted by one of the residence's former owners (George Gallegos), a ceiling frieze, a bathtub and shower flanked by marble columns, and a separate sitting room. Miquela, on the second floor, is decorated in ruby colors and has a four-poster mahogany bed with satin fabrics and lace drapes.

The living room has a striking marble fireplace, crystal chandelier, Tiffany-style lamps, and antique chairs and couches with ornately worked wood trim. Breakfast burritos smothered in green chili, Russian crepes, stuffed French toast, or whatever's for breakfast is served in your room, outdoors in the courtyard, or in the sunny dining room with white wrought-iron tables and chairs. A refrigerator is well stocked with refreshments, and guests are welcome to it day or night.

🏨 *5 double rooms with baths, 1 quad, 1 suite. Ceiling fans and radios in all rooms, mobile phone, TV in living room. $89–$139, full breakfast, afternoon snacks. AE, D, DC, MC, V. No smoking, no pets.*

Britannia and W. E. Mauger Estate

701 Roma Ave. NW, Albuquerque 87102, tel. 505/242–8755, fax 505/842–8835

The residential neighborhoods surrounding Albuquerque's downtown business district have been revitalized in recent years, and the eye-popping restoration of the Britannia and W. E. Mauger Estate in 1984 helped pioneer this effort. You'd never suspect now that the dignified redbrick Queen Anne, built in 1897 and on the National Register of Historic Places, was once a boarding-house.

Victoriana reigns in this antiques-filled B&B, from the dark-blue flowered wallpaper, lace antimacassars, and reproduction Victrola in the common room, to various period bureaus, desks, and beds in the guest rooms. All the accommodations are tastefully furnished, but they lack bathtubs (showers only). A three-course breakfast, which might include breakfast burritos or cheese frittatas, is served on the tiny sunporch or in the indoor dining room.

Its location, smack against downtown, has proven popular with business people, but Martin Sheen and Linda Ronstadt have also stayed here.

🏨 *7 double rooms, 1 single, all with baths. TVs, coffeemakers, hair dryers, irons, and clock radios in all rooms, refrigerators in most rooms, balcony in 1 room, fireplace and TV in sitting room, sunporch, patio, off-street parking. $75–$130, full breakfast, snacks, evening wine and cheese. AE, D, DC, MC, V. No smoking, children and pets by prior arrangement.*

Casa del Granjero

414 C de Baca La. NW, Albuquerque 87114, tel. and fax 505/897-4144

Casa del Granjero means the "farmer's house," but don't start thinking rustic. It's the rare field hand who hangs his hat in a place that has a glass-enclosed hot tub building and 52-inch stereo TV, business office with copier and fax, and plush white terry guest robes. Some mighty sophisticated folks have stayed here, among them, actor Mickey Rourke.

There *is* a rural quality to the inn's 3-acre North Valley property. But the B&B's Spanish appellation plays on the name of owners Butch and Victoria Farmer, who bought the Territorial-style adobe in 1987. More than 100 years old, the house was in rather sad shape when they acquired it. Butch, a contractor, converted the courtyard to a great room and added three baths, three sitting rooms, a portale, and an outbuilding.

The Farmers hadn't intended to operate a B&B, but when friends began urging them to open up their lovely home to guests, they decided to give it a go. It was such a success that Butch added a gazebo, bathhouse, hot tub, waterfall,

built-in barbecue, and four more guest rooms in a separate ranch-style home across the street: the Bunk House.

Butch's construction skills can also be seen in many of the touches in the seven guest rooms: Santa Fe-style pine beds, carved wood corbels and beams, bright Mexican tiles inset into the kiva fireplaces. Victoria combs yard sales and auctions for treasures, coming up with an antique trastero or perhaps one of the colorful kilims or Navajo rugs scattered throughout the house. Even Butch's mother contributes to the cause, stitching pretty quilts for the rooms. The enormous Corte Grande Suite has a queen-size canopy willow bed with artificial ivy intertwined in the wood, two daybeds tucked in the adjacent room, and Tiffany-style lamps. Of all the accommodations, the Allegre Suite, with its lace-curtained canopy bed, is the most romantic.

Victoria, known as one of the best cooks in the community, prepares a serious breakfast feast—everything from Italian to New Mexican specialties; one morning you might be served a breakfast burrito with avocado, fresh fruit, and flan. You can indulge, with peer support, at the long dark-wood table in the huge central dining room, or out on the portale with its willow patio furniture.

🏨 *3 double rooms with baths, 4 suites. Desks and kiva fireplaces in all but 1 room, private entrances onto portale in suites, VCR and video library in common room. $89–$149, full breakfast. MC, V. No smoking, pets boarded nearby.*

Casas de Sueños

310 Rio Grande SW, Albuquerque 87104, tel. 505/247-4560 or 800/242-8987, fax 505/842-8493

Houses rarely determine their own fate, but that's just one of the many ways in which Casas de Sueños (Houses of Dreams) is exceptional. In 1979, lawyer Robert Hanna commissioned Albuquerque architect Bart Prince to design an office above the entry to his low-slung adobe complex. So many people came by to gape at the result (the office looks like an enormous snail) that Hanna spent half his time inviting them in to look around. In 1990 he decided to turn this pleasant but distracting activity into a business—and thus a B&B was born.

The artistic inclinations of this inn, one block from Old Town, aren't limited to its recent addition. Casas de Sueños was designed as an artists' community in the 1930s by painter J. R. Willis; at the perimeter of his house and studio he built a group of rental cottages, which now house guests. Little inspirational paths and niches, some with bubbling streams, abound in the complex, and a profusion of blossoms climbs up walls and spills out onto a lush lawn. There are more than 50 rosebushes and a dozen varieties of grapevines on the acre of grounds.

In addition, the inn's dining room, where a gourmet hot and cold buffet is set out each morning, doubles as a gallery for local artists. With its French doors, lace tablecloths, viga ceilings, and kiva fireplace, the room is warm and cheerful. On nice days, you can head out to the lovely adjoining patio.

The guest rooms—or casitas—with private entrances to the courtyard, are decorated in different styles, each more attractive than the last. Most have fresh flowers and luxurious bedding; many have kitchens, fireplaces, Oriental rugs, and ornate wood furnishings acquired from the estate of a Spanish nobleman. The La Cascada suite lets out onto its own private waterfall; the Porter features a Willis mural and private patio with outdoor hot tub; Secret Garden has a four-person hot tub and a private massage room. If it's space you need, La Mirada is a two-bedroom suite with an enormous living room, vega ceilings, kiva fireplace, and Oriental artwork.

🏨 *15 1-bedroom casitas with baths, 4 2-bedroom casitas with baths. TVs, phones, fireplaces, mini-refrigerators, and hot tubs in many rooms, library, off-street parking. $85–$215, full breakfast, evening hors d'oeuvres. AE, D, DC, MC, V. No smoking, no pets.*

Casita Chamisa

850 Chamisal Rd. NW, Albuquerque 87107, tel. 505/897-4644

The first B&B in Albuquerque, Casita Chamisa is also historic in other ways. Originally an adobe farmhouse dating back to 1850, it sits atop the ruins of five successive Pueblo and pre-Pueblo village sites, the oldest dating from around 720 BC! Jack Schaefer, previous owner of the home and author of *Shane*, used to find pottery shards from time to time (Shaefer used the present living room as his writing studio). The mother lode was hit when current owners Kit and Arnold Sargeant began construction of the B&B's 30-foot pool. Kit, an author and archaeologist, enlisted the help of the University of New Mexico to conduct a thorough excavation. More than 150,000 pottery shards and artifacts were eventually recovered. Some remain on view at the home in the basement.

Set in the pastoral North Valley, which was settled in the 1600s by the Spanish colonialists, this B&B has everything you associate with the region. It is shaded by massive river cottonwoods, which keep the place cool on even the hottest days. Chickens, roosters, beehives, herb and vegetable gardens, horses (not for riding), cats, fruit trees, and winding *acequias* (irrigation ditches) retain the former farm's character.

There are only two accommodations, so tranquility is the order of the day. The six-person ivy-covered guest house has a small sitting room with a corner kiva fireplace, a queen bed, a private patio, and a greenhouse where you can sit and read or write. The kitchenette and a separate bedroom with twin beds covered with French knot bedspreads make this an ideal place for a small family. Animals, a sandbox, swing set, green house, and pool are real attractions for kids. The charming bedroom in the main house comes with a Mexican tin mirror and a hand-carved Mexican headboard; it also has a kiva fireplace and private entrance near the indoor pool and hot tub. Rich hibiscus and other tropical plants surround the pool.

The home contains a great library and a baby grand piano and is filled with wonderful arts and crafts from around the world, including a basket collection, Mexican textiles, and odds and ends gathered by Arnold during his worldwide travels with the U.S. Army.

A country Continental breakfast is served on a plant-filled, enclosed, glass-covered patio, in the dining room before a small fireplace, or out on the portale. It includes fruit, juices, coffee and tea, as well as coffee cakes and muffins, or another slice of history: some of Arnold's fresh sourdough bread, made from a 200-year-old Basque starter.

🏠 *1 double room with bath, 1 2-bedroom casita. Fireplaces in both rooms, library, enclosed pool, hot tub, greenhouse, gardens, sundeck. $95, Continental breakfast. AE, D, MC, V. No smoking indoors, pets and children welcome.*

Elaine's

Box 444, 72 Snowline Estates, Cedar Crest 87008, tel. 505/281-2467 or 800/821-3092

It might be hard to decide which you like better, Elaine O'Neil or her house, but then the two are inextricably intertwined. One of the nicest building contractors you're ever likely to meet, Elaine supervised the construction of her rough-hewn stone-and-log cabin down to the last interesting detail—for example,

the ornate iron braces that anchor the joints of the ceiling beams, which are at once decorative and functional.

A winding dirt road leads up to Elaine's, set in the heart of the Sandia Mountains in Cedar Crest, 15 miles east of Albuquerque on the historic Turquoise Trail to Santa Fe. But the bed-and-breakfast's rustic setting and structure belie its elegant interior. If the Victorians had slalomed, they doubtless would have headed to just such a retreat for après-ski sherries.

Although there are fine antiques all around the house, this is a cheerful, unpretentious place. Light from huge windows in the two-story-high cathedral ceiling streams into an upstairs common area, where an enormous stone fireplace is fronted by comfortable couches. Guests often just flop down on the plush hunter-green carpet and play one of the board games stocked in the rooms, read, or stare into the flames.

One of the second-level rooms has a whirlpool tub, while the third-level room has dramatic views of mountains and plains in three directions. Fresh flowers and soft, downy bedding help make all three accommodations, which mix sturdy wood furnishings and more delicate antiques, very appealing. One disadvantage: Because the romantic top-floor bedroom was built loft style, its occupants can overhear late-night revelers on the lower level—but it is still Elaine's most popular room.

Breakfast here, served in an airy, plant-filled breakfast room, is simple but hearty; large helpings of fresh fruit, pancakes or waffles, and sausage are standard, but guests can get pretty much what they like. Afterward, many find that the crisp mountain air inspires them to take a long walk. Charlie, a fat golden retriever who likes to laze on "his" front porch bench, will happily accompany guests on a hike through the Cibola National Forest, abutting the inn's 4 acres.

Eliot, part wolf, part German shepherd, disdains Charlie's friendly doggie ways but always condescends to come along for the exercise.

🏠 *3 double rooms with baths. Private balcony in top room, books in rooms, wraparound deck, hiking trails on property, skiing and horseback riding nearby. $85–$99, full breakfast. AE, D, MC, V. No smoking, no pets.*

Hacienda Vargas

1431 El Camino Real, Box 307, Algodones 87001, tel. 505/867–9115 or 800/261–0006

In 1990, when Jule and Pablo Vargas came to tiny Algodones, about 20 miles north of Albuquerque, they bought a sprawling hacienda that had changed a lot in the past 200 years—in a town that had changed very little. Hacienda Vargas, now a repository of New Mexico history and culture, was a group of small adobe units and a stagecoach stop in the mid- to late-1800s. In the early 1900s, the house, by then a single structure, was used as an Indian trading post.

The Vargases did a lot of renovating, but the house still retains much of its original flavor, due in no small part to the mature cottonwoods and small Spanish chapel on the 2-acre grounds. The seven guest rooms successfully blend antique furnishings with contemporary-Southwest bedspreads and art; the romantic Kiva Room has its own skylit Jacuzzi tub and a separate sitting area, as do two newer rooms, San Felipe and Santa Ana. A particularly tasty breakfast dish served here is "Kika's scramble"—spicy eggs topped with toasted nuts.

🏠 *7 double rooms with baths. 5 kiva fireplaces throughout house, library, art gallery portale, barbecue, "romance" packages with champagne. $79–$139, full breakfast. MC, V. No smoking, no pets.*

Old Town Bed & Breakfast

707 17th St. NW, Albuquerque 87104, tel. 505/764–9144 or 888/900–9144

Owner Nancy Hoffman's welcome—a basket of fruit and homemade cookies—is simple but very appealing, and so is her B&B. It's on a tree-shrouded, quiet street just two blocks from charming Old Town, the city's major museums, and an attractive park, and was built in 1940 by Albuquerque architect Leon Watson—a pioneer in the use of adobe in modern home design.

The bright, spacious downstairs suite with a latilla ceiling, kiva fireplace, and Saltillo-tile floor embraces Southwestern design. The adjoining sitting room and library provide additional sleeping space if needed. A beautiful skylit bath with whirlpool tub is adjacent to the suite and shared with the owner. The cheerful, small upstairs room has great views of the mountains and the surrounding flowering trees.

When it's nice out, fresh-squeezed juice, coffee, and homemade breads, muffins, or cobblers are served on the pretty patio; on chilly mornings, a woodstove in the living room warms the adjacent dining area.

🏠 *1 double room with shower, 1 suite. Off-street parking. $65–$80, Continental breakfast. No credit cards. No smoking, no pets.*

Sarabande

5637 Rio Grande Blvd. NW, Albuquerque 87107, tel. 505/345–4923 or 888/506–4923, fax 505/345–9130

This tranquil lodging in the quiet Los Ranchos de Albuquerque section of town is a bit formal, in part because the Territorial-style home, built in 1987, still looks brand shiny new. A Japanese garden and fishpond at the side of the house, along with a profusion of well-trimmed flowers and trees surrounding the tiled courtyard fountain and all sides of the home, also add to the sense of orderliness here.

A common sitting room with contemporary Southwestern art and a kiva fireplace adjoins a country-style kitchen and dining room with a wood-burning stove and huge, old-fashioned butcher block; your favorite hot breakfast is served here. (The host will ask your breakfast wishes the night before—the Farmer's frittata remain a consistent favorite.) The romantic Rose Room houses a raised kiva fireplace, soaking tub, and wall-to-wall carpeting. The Iris Room, with a stained-glass representation of the flower, looks out onto real blooms in the courtyard and onto the B&B's heated, 50-foot lap pool and hot tub.

🏠 *3 double rooms with baths. Fireplace in sitting room, hot tub, pool, library, all-terrain bicycles. $85–$110, full breakfast. MC, V. No smoking, no pets, no children.*

Yours Truly

160 Paseo de Corrales, Box 2263, Corrales 87048, tel. 505/898-7027 or 800/942-7890, fax 505/898-9022

Opened in 1987 by Pat and James Montgomery (who call themselves "loonatics"—they have two hot air balloons!), this B&B exudes the owners' personal warmth and outgoing natures. Their adventurous side is also evident—from the sunrise hot-air balloon rides they pilot to the commodious hot tub on the large brick patio. Yours Truly has a bit of a party atmosphere, with hot air balloon friends coming and visiting Pat and James, who live in a room dubbed "Margaritaville." Perched on a hillside, the B&B overlooks the Rio Grande Valley, the lazy and charming village of Corrales, and the towering Sandias. It's a great place to watch the mountains turn pink at sunset or see a moonrise, and great bird-watching lies just a few steps out the front door.

The modern adobe's bedrooms are not large, but they are quite comfortable and attractive. One room features a king bed set in adobe; overhead glass brick blocks let in the afternoon light while a gas fireplace illuminates the night. Even the shower in this room's bathroom is fun: Dual heads provide water for two, so bring a friend! Also, every room hides a skeleton in the closet.

Pat pulls out the stops at the breakfast buffet, using her best crystal, sterling, and china to serve tasty, fresh-baked goods—say, praline French toast or jalapeño bread—fruit, and coffee. Every guest gets a personalized napkin with his or her name printed on it to keep as a souvenir.

🏠 *4 double rooms with baths. Guest robes, TVs, and radios in all rooms, kiva fireplaces in 2 rooms, clerestory windows, large music selection, fireplace in living room, hot-air balloon rides ($250 for 2 people). $80–$90, full breakfast, afternoon wine and snacks. AE, MC, V. No smoking in bedrooms.*

Southern New Mexico

The Lodge

Folks who fly into Albuquerque International Airport tend to flock north to chic Santa Fe and Taos—great news for those opting to explore equally beautiful, much less trafficked southern New Mexico. One might almost suspect residents of the region below I-40, casting a wary eye on rocketing real estate rates to the north, of spreading the word that the lower two-thirds of the state is entirely arid and flat.

Nothing could be further from the truth. In southwestern New Mexico alone, local roads lead to three national forests, a dozen mountain ranges, countless cascading streams, and myriad mineral hot springs. On NM 90 west from Silver City, for example, the road rises from the foothills of the Pinos Altos Mountains and winds up through the thick pines of Gila National Forest to Emory Pass, where, from a vantage point of 8,228 feet, the breathtaking Black Range Mountain valley spreads out as far as the eye can see.

The landscape of south-central New Mexico is equally dramatic. Between the towns of Las Cruces and Socorro, the Rio Grande widens out into Elephant Butte Lake and into the Bosque del Apache, a wintertime sanctuary for the endangered whooping crane. East of Las Cruces, the shifting gypsum sands of White Sands National Monument predict the snowy peaks of the Sacramento Mountains, set against the lush green of Lincoln National Forest. The more northerly route to Lincoln forest and the White Mountains from Socorro arrows past Valley of Fires State Park, 44 miles of gray-and-pink volcanic rock formed by one of the nation's best-preserved lava flows.

If the southeastern region seems to conform most to the stereotype of desert desolation, it provides a geological lesson in the value of looking below surfaces. Beneath miles of flat, scrubby terrain lies one of the most wondrous natural spectacles of all—Carlsbad Caverns National Monument— its huge, subterranean chambers a showcase for massive stalactites and stalagmites and delicate aragonite crystal sculptures.

The history of the West is painted in broad strokes on this richly textured natural canvas. Ancient pottery and dwellings of the Mimbres, Pueblo, and Gila peoples bear witness to some of the complex civilizations that existed here before Spanish conquistadors and priests put their mark on the area in the 17th century, while vast, open pits and abandoned cities such as Hillsboro and Kingston attest to the gold-, silver-, and copper-mining madness that literally had its impact 200 years later. On the heels of the rush for mineral riches rode Billy the Kid, whose legends were made and played out in such boomtowns as Silver City and Mesilla. Rough-and-tumble as those times may have been, it was all minor mayhem compared to the act that gave the region its sobering global significance: On July 16, 1945, the world's first atomic bomb was detonated at Trinity Site, in the Tularosa basin northwest of Alamogordo.

Outdoor activities abound in the area—fishing in Caballo Lake, say, or skiing in Cloudcroft or Ruidoso, where a world-class horse track draws those whose idea of exercise is filling out a racing form. Indeed, the region's surprising array of attractions tends to inspire many to stay longer than planned—which is not a problem. Laid-back southern New Mexico may not have the abundance of upscale accommodations that the north enjoys, but friendly, scenic, and often sophisticated inns are here for the finding, almost all at reasonable rates.

Places to Go, Sights to See

Carlsbad Caverns National Park (3225 National Parks Highway, Carlsbad 88220, tel. 505/785–2232), at the southeastern end of the state, is one of the largest and most impressive cave systems in the world. Touring it on the longer Natural Entrance Route, on foot, offers a truer experience of the cavern's depth, but the Big Room Route, which takes visitors down via high-speed elevator, is an easier way to view all the major formations. If you visit between late May and mid-October, be sure to come back at sunset to see tens of thousands of bats fly en masse out of the cavern.

Gila Cliff Dwellings National Monument (NM 15, 44 mi north of Silver City, Route 11, Box 100, Silver City 88061, tel. and fax 505/536–9461) is at the edge of the Gila Wilderness, surrounded by the Gila National Forest. A 1-mile loop trail leads to and through seven natural caves that hold 40 well-preserved rooms constructed of stone and mud mortar by the Pueblo Indians in the 13th century. Near the visitor center are the remains of a pit house used by the Mogollón Indians somewhere between AD 100 and AD 400.

Las Cruces and Mesilla. At the junction of two major highways, I-10 and I-25, Las Cruces and the adjacent town of Mesilla have long been transportation hubs: El Camino Real, the old Spanish trade route, ran through Las Cruces, and Mesilla was a major stop for the Butterfield Trail Overland stagecoach. Now the largest city in southern New Mexico and home to New Mexico State University, Las Cruces hosts a number of small museums and galleries; information on these and a self-guided walking tour of two historic districts are available at the convention and visitors bureau (*see* Tourist Information, *below*). The lovely plaza and surrounding buildings in the restored 19th-century town of Mesilla, where the Gadsen Purchase was ratified and Billy the Kid was tried and sentenced to death, now house small shops and businesses. Mementos of the adobe fort set up on the Rio Grande in 1865 to protect residents of Mesilla Valley from Apache attack may be viewed at *Fort Selden State Monument* (15 mi north of Las Cruces, tel. 505/526–8911).

Lincoln. Tiny Lincoln was most notoriously the site of the 1878 Lincoln County War, in which two opposing factions clashed over lucrative government contracts for one year. Billy the Kid, who took part in a number of the gun battles, spent the last four years of his life on a nearby ranch. Today, the town is a National Historic Landmark, its only street (Hwy. 380) lined with buildings dating from its tumultuous past, including the *Tunstall Store Museum* (tel. 505/653–4372) and the *Lincoln County Courthouse Museum* (tel. 505/653–4372). The *Historical Center* (tel. 505/653–4025) runs a 15-minute slide show introducing Lincoln's attractions.

Ruidoso. On the eastern slopes of the pine-covered Sacramento Mountains, Ruidoso is a sophisticated year-round resort that retains its rustic small-town charm. Each summer the town becomes the epicenter of American quarter horse racing, thanks to *Ruidoso Downs* (Hwy. 70, tel. 505/378–4431), a state-of-the-art track. Down the road, the 40,000-square-foot *Museum of the Horse* (Hwy. 70, tel. 505/378–4142 or 800/263–5929) has more than 10,000 equine items, including paintings, drawings, and bronzes. Bordering Ruidoso to the west is the *Mescalero Apache Indian Reservation*, which has a general store, a trading post, and a small museum. The real attractions here, however, are the Apache-owned and - operated *Inn of the Mountain Gods* (Carrizo Canyon Rd., Box 269, Mescalero 88340, tel. 505/257–5141 or 800/545–9011), a resort with a full-blown casino, and the *Ski Apache* area (NM 532, tel. 505/336–4357) on the nearby 11,400-foot Sierra Blanca, which has fine-powder skiing from Thanksgiving until Easter Sunday.

Silver City. One of many mining towns that mushroomed in the southwestern corner of the state in the latter half of the 19th century, Silver City, unlike others, survived the crash of the silver market in 1893. A number of self-guided walking tours are available from the chamber of commerce (*see* Tourist Information, *below*): One leads to the well-preserved Victorian downtown area. The *Western New Mexico University Museum* (Fleming Hall, tel. 505/538–6386) houses the largest display in the United States of prehistoric pottery by the Mimbres Indians, and the *Silver City Museum* (312 W. Broadway, tel. 505/538–5921), in an 1881 mansion, exhibits mining tools and household effects of early town inhabitants. Two open-pit copper mines close by display a harsh beauty: the *Phelps-Dodge mine*, at the end of town south on NM 90, and the *Santa Rita/Chino mine*, 15 miles east on NM 152.

Socorro. About 75 miles south of Albuquerque in the Rio Grande valley, this small city dates back to 1615, when Spanish Franciscan priests built Nuestra Senora del Socorro (Our Lady of Help) mission on what was then the land of the Pueblo peoples. Its rowdy heyday, however, was in the 1880s, when the advent of the railroad transformed this mining town into a major shipping center. A self-guided walking-tour brochure of the town's historic buildings, including the *San Miguel Mission*, built on the site of the original mission between 1819 and 1821, is available at the Socorro Chamber of Commerce (*see* Tourist Information, *below*). Also of interest is the *Mineral Museum* at the New Mexico Institute of Mining and Technology (tel. 505/835–5420), with samples of more than 10,000 minerals from around the world. In the winter, the 57,000-acre *Bosque del Apache National Wildlife Refuge* (18 mi south of Socorro, tel. 505/835–1828) is a must-see: From late November through early February, tens of thousands of Arctic-bred snow geese and ducks, along with sandhill cranes, bald eagles, and red-tailed hawks, rest here on their migratory route south.

Truth or Consequences. This slow-paced Western town doesn't seem to have changed much since 1950, when it changed its name from Hot Springs as part of a promotion for the 10th anniversary of a popular radio quiz show. A health resort at the turn of the century, T or C (as it's known locally) still retains a number of the mineral bathhouses that drew people in droves. *Geronimo Springs Museum* (325 Main St., tel. 505/894–6600), which explores the history of the area, devotes a wing to Ralph Edwards, host of the "Truth or Consequences" radio show (the town also holds an annual festival in his honor). Fishing and water sports are

popular at nearby *Elephant Butte Lake State Park* (tel. 505/744–5421), 7 mi to the
north, and *Caballo Lake State Park* (tel. 505/743–3942), 14 mi south.

White Sands National Monument (15 mi southwest of Alamogordo, Box 1086,
Holloman Air Force Base, NM 88330, tel. 505/479–6124). A scene out of *Lawrence
of Arabia*, with shifting sand dunes 60 feet high, White Sands encompasses
145,344 acres, the largest deposit of gypsum sand in the world; it's one of the few
landforms recognizable from space. There's a 16-mile loop trail from the visitor
center for those who want to explore the monument in a vehicle, and a mile-long,
self-guided nature trail for walkers.

Restaurants

Tiny Capitán, near Ruidoso, is home to **Hotel Chango** (tel. 505/354–4213), an
excellent restaurant with a surprisingly sophisticated Continental menu. In
Cloudcroft, **Rebecca's** at The Lodge (*see* review, *below*) serves fine Southwestern-
inspired dishes in a stunning mountain setting. Visitors to Hillsboro's **Sweetwood
BBQ** (tel. 505/895–5642) can enjoy tender brisket of beef smoked with sweet
applewood; seating is outside in an apple orchard or in a rough-cut cedar barn;
keep in mind that this closes at nightfall. In Mesilla, the informal **Little Nellie's**
(tel. 505/523–9911) dishes up good Mexican fare and has a patio and bar; **Mesón de
Mesilla** (*see* review, *below*), with its fine Continental fare, is the more upscale
dining choice in town. **La Lorraine** (tel. 505/257–2954), in Ruidoso, serves classic
French cuisine in cozy country-French surroundings. At Silver City's low-key,
family-run **Jalisco Restaurant** (tel. 505/388–2060), you can't go wrong ordering
anything with green chili in it. In Socorro, the casual-clubby **Val Verde Steak
House** (203 Manzanitas St., tel. 505/835–3380) is great for ribs and sirloin, and the
stuffed sopaipillas at **Frank & Lupe's El Sombrero** (210 Mesquite, tel. 505/835–
3945), a colorful, down-home eatery, can't be beat.

Tourist Information

Las Cruces Convention and Visitors Bureau (211 N. Water St., Las Cruces
88001, tel. 505/524–8521 or 800/343–7827). **Lincoln Hospitality Group** (Box 27,
Lincoln 88338, tel. 505/653–4676). **Ruidoso Valley Convention and Visitors
Bureau** (720 Sudderth Dr., Box 698, Ruidoso 88345, tel. 505/257–7395 or 800/253–
2255). **Silver City Chamber of Commerce** (1103 N. Hudson St., Silver City
88061, tel. 505/538–3785 or 800/548–9378). **Socorro Chamber of Commerce** (Box
743, Socorro 87801, tel. 505/835–0424). **Truth or Consequences Chamber of
Commerce** (Drawer 31, Truth or Consequences 87901, tel. 505/894–3536 or 800/
831–9487).

Reservation Services

Bed & Breakfast of New Mexico (Box 2805, Santa Fe 87504, tel. 505/982–3332).
New Mexico Bed and Breakfast Association (Box 2925, Santa Fe 87504, tel.
505/766–5380 or 800/661–6649).

Bear Mountain Guest Ranch

Box 1163, Silver City 88062, tel. 505/538-2538

Myra McCormick, the crusty proprietor of the Bear Mountain Guest Ranch, has a firm house rule: Her guests must take their assigned places at the table, introduce themselves at the beginning of dinner, and refrain from interrupting when another person is speaking. She also urges visitors to enjoy the outdoors; bird-watching is especially encouraged and, in truth, this is really a place for avid bird-watchers. If it all feels a bit like summer camp for grown-ups, it's hard to resist the lovely setting, the camaraderie, or Myra herself, who's been running the place since 1959 and clearly has her guests' best interests at heart.

The two-story, white Territorial-style ranch house was built in 1928, and Myra runs it as you would a rugged lodge in that era. As she says, "This isn't a wine and cheese place" (although guests may bring their own). The ranch sits on 160 acres abutting the Gila National Forest on the outskirts of Silver City and is an ideal base for hiking and bird-watching. Nights are often chilly, but guests can warm themselves at a stone fireplace in the high-ceiling, wood-beamed main room. Accommodations are spartan, with what looks to be 1950s- or '60s-era furnishings.

🏨 *11 double rooms with baths, 2 3-room suites, 1 2-person cottage, 1 4-person cottage. Electric blankets, kitchenettes in 2 cottages, outdoor ramada, sunporch, nature classes available. $95–$105, breakfast, sack lunch, and small dinner included, weekly and "lodge & learn" rates available. No credit cards. No smoking in indoor common rooms, well-behaved pets only.*

The Black Range Lodge

Star Rte. 2, Box 119, Kingston 88042, tel. 505/895-5652, fax 505/895-3326

If you've taken the mountain road from Silver City to Kingston (population 30, down from 7,000 in 1880), nestled in the Gila National Forest, chances are you're not looking to drive anywhere else very soon. And the Black Range Lodge, a rustic three-story brick, stone, and strawbale building, will only strengthen your urge to stay put. Here people come to learn about making efficient use of energy with mud, bamboo, and strawbale. You'll find that projects are constantly underway out back. Accomplishments include a greenhouse with 300 types of plants, a cob-constructed igloo used to house tools, and an eagle-shape bench of mud.

Los Angeles filmmaker Catherine Wanek and Pete Fust (who holds a Guinness World Record for Frisbee throwing) have created a fun, relaxed environment. The first floor of the lodge has a wall of free video games, Foosball, and a pool table, and the surrounding area offers extensive hiking, mountain biking, and bird-watching. Expect to do a fair amount of cooking in the spacious, sun-filled kitchen, as the nearest restaurant lies in neighboring Hillsboro and isn't open for dinner. Guest rooms are furnished in an eclectic but pleasing blend of Victorian and Southwestern styles, antiques and Oriental rugs counterpointing terra-cotta and turquoise doors, wood floors, and, in some cases, wagon-wheel chandeliers.

🏨 *4 double rooms with baths, 3 suites. Private balcony in 2 rooms, piano, TV/VCR room, video library patio, Ping-Pong, Foosball, pool, greenhouse. $60 first night, $45 each additional night (except holidays), full Continental breakfast. D, MC, V. Smoking outside or on balconies only.*

The Carter House

101 N. Cooper St., Silver City 88061, tel. 505/388-5485

The lovely Colonial Revival-style Carter House, set on a rise next to Silver City's old county courthouse, was built in 1906 by the owner of the nearby Tyrone Copper Mine. In 1989, Lucy Dilworth restored the residence, which was a medical clinic in the 1930s. A B&B occupies most of the building; the former X-ray rooms in the basement are now an immaculate youth hostel (B&Bers can use the facility's washer/dryer and kitchen).

The five first-floor guest rooms are not overly large, but all are light-filled and decorated in a cheerful Southwestern and country-French combination of earth-tone floral bedspreads, pine or wicker headboards, light-wood furniture, and tasteful art prints. In the evening, you'll make the morning's breakfast selections on a form; a copious cold spread supplements the hot dishes, cooked when you arrive at the table. Please note that this property was for sale at press time; call ahead to check for any changes.

⊞ *4 double rooms with baths, 1 suite. Clock radios, ceiling fans in all rooms, free local calls, library, TV room, off-street parking. $60–$71, full breakfast. MC, V. No smoking, no pets.*

Casa de Patrón

Box 27, Lincoln 88338, tel. 505/653-4676 or 800/524-5202, fax 505/653-4671

Billy the Kid stayed here against his will in 1879, when the Territorial-style adobe house belonged to Lincoln County clerk Juan Patrón. These days folks come voluntarily to see this historic Old West town, perhaps the best preserved in the Southwest.

Many come to this spotless B&B for the warm hospitality and attention to de-

tail—handmade soaps and night-lights in the baths—provided by hosts Jeremy and Cleis Jordan. Conversations with the Jordans in the viga-beamed sitting room can go on into the wee hours. The talk often continues over breakfast, a hearty country-style repast that might include citrus-pecan waffles or *huevos heraldo* (eggs sautéed with sharp cheese, onions and bell peppers). Billy the Kid is believed to have been detained in what is now the dining room. After breakfast, Cleis, an accomplished musician, sometimes plays from the grand piano or pipe organ, located in the sitting room.

In the main house, dating back to 1860, you'll find three guest rooms with wood floors and area rugs, high vega ceilings, Western-style antiques and collectibles, expensive washboards, and lace curtains that set a genteel tone. Directly behind the main house is the Old Trail House, which houses two spacious suites that overlook a courtyard with Chinese-elm and Juniper trees, flower beds, and vegetable gardens. Both suites have sitting rooms with fireplaces, wet bars, and refrigerators; the Eastburn Room has a two-person whirlpool tub.

A few minutes' walk from the main house are two adobe guest casitas decorated in contemporary style with a New Mexican flavor. The romantic Casa Bonita has a half-loft bedroom, cathedral ceiling, and downstairs living area. Surrounded by grama wild grass, many animals come to visit the casitas—deer herds are common late-night visitors. Hiking trails lead right from the Casa de Patron into the surrounding hills.

⊞ *3 double rooms with baths (1 adjoining), 2 luxury suites, 1 1-bedroom casita, 1 2-bedroom casita. Kitchenette in 1 casita, coffeemaker and refrigerator in other, clocks in rooms, fireplace, pipe organ, and piano in common areas, patio, portale, off-street parking. $79–$107, full breakfast in rooms, Continental breakfast in casitas. MC, V. No smoking indoors, no pets.*

Eaton House

403 Eaton Ave., Socorro 87801, tel. 505/ 835–1067 or 800/383–CRANE, fax 505/ 835–3527

Unlike other adventurers who headed west to seek their fortune and built houses in familiar East Coast style when they arrived, Colonel E. W. Eaton— Civil War hero and founder of a smelter—constructed a thick-walled Territorial adobe for his young New Mexican bride in 1881. Yet the wealthy Eatons did indulge in some "civilized" Eastern touches: lead-glass windows and a built-in classical-revival colonnade bookcase grace their elegant home, which remained in family hands for nearly 100 years.

Innkeepers Anna Appleby and Tom Harper have retained the original blend of New Mexican and Victorian styles. Their seven guest rooms—all with private entrances off a shaded brick portale—are decorated with impeccable taste. The Vigilante Room features a Santa Fe–style bed and trastero crafted by a local artisan, as well as a colorful Mexican-tile sink. Matching carved wooden beds built for twin girls 80 years ago are set in Daughters' Room, which also boasts a fluted-glass light fixture original to the house. The Colonel Eaton Room has a queen-size pencil-post bed so high you need a stool to climb in, lowered imported Dutch tile in the bath, and delicate English lace curtains. The Piro Room, named after Indians who originally inhabited the area, celebrates Native American history and culture with an Alamo rug on the wall, Navajo kachinas atop the kiva fireplace, and baskets decorating the room.

This B&B is an extremely popular spot for bird-watchers, largely because it's near the Bosque del Apache, a wildlife refuge on the banks of the Rio Grande. In fact, five biological life zones surround Eaton House, including the Sevilleta National Wildlife Refuge and Cibola National Forest. Both Tom and Anna are avid bird-watchers, and Anna will prepare a light "Early Birder" breakfast basket for guests who want to set off first thing in the morning. After birding, guests will return to a Continental breakfast with plenty of fresh fruits, breakfast breads, and coffee cakes. Also, Anna and Tom serve coffee all morning in the sitting room, which has a spotting scope available to guests.

🛏 *1 single room with bath, 6 double rooms with baths. Phones, ceiling fans in rooms, library, fireplace, binoculars and field guides available. $75–$120, Continental breakfast, afternoon refreshments. AE, MC, V. No smoking, no pets, no children under 14.*

The Ellis Store & Co. Country Inn

Hwy. 380, mile marker 98, Box 15, Lincoln 88338, tel. 505/653–4609 or 800/653–6460, fax 505/653–4610

This lodging's history dates back to 1850, when it was a modest, two-room adobe in territory where the Mescalero Indians still posed a threat to settlers. During the Lincoln County War, the building's thick walls provided refuge for members of the McSween faction, and Billy the Kid was kept here pending his trial. Today, the house looks out on a peaceful lawn where deer graze in the evening.

In 1993 David and Jinny Vigil ended their 10-year search for a B&B with this one. David, a former engineer whose family has been in New Mexico for nearly 300 years, has done a lot of work on the building, adding bathrooms and meticulously restoring the front portale to include its historic sag. Guests sit under it in the quiet of the morning while enjoying Jinny's gourmet cooking. In the evenings, her culinary skills draw people from as far away as Carlsbad. They come to enjoy such delicacies as rack of antelope or venison loin as part of a six-course meal served in the spacious depths of a dining room glowing with light from the fireplace.

Three of the guest rooms in the main house have wood-burning stoves and each is named for a former resident of the house (though Billy the Kid only needed to stay a few days to get one named after him). Rooms, decorated with antiques, range from Old West style to Victorian. Dr. James room attracts honeymooners with its king canopied bed, lace curtains, and fresh flowers. Behind the building sits the Mill House, which contains four more rooms sharing baths and a large gathering room with sofas and easy chairs.

However, it would be hard to imagine a guest staying indoors when there is so much to see in the surrounding area. David offers horseback hunting trips for ruggedly inclined guests, and there is fishing in the creek that runs through the property. Guests also have the option of hiking or taking a historical tour of Lincoln.

🏠 *3 double rooms with baths in main house, 1 double with bath and 3 doubles sharing 2 baths in Mill House. Wood-burning stove or fireplace in 3 rooms, fishing, hunting, hiking. $79–$99, full gourmet breakfast; 6-course dinner served by reservation. D, DC, MC, V. No smoking indoors, no pets, no children under 12.*

The Enchanted Villa

Box 456, Hillsboro 88042, tel. 505/895–5686

This white Territorial-style adobe, built on the main street of tiny Hillsboro in 1941, once served as a mountain retreat for a British nobleman, Sir Victor Sassoon. It was designed by the great-aunt of the current innkeeper, Maree Westland, who returned from Alaska to buy the home she'd played in as a child.

Family pictures line the staircase walls of this airy, light-filled lodging, which has the welcoming, casual warmth of a family home. This is not a showcase for period antiques or Southwestern arti-

facts: Furnishings tend toward the contemporary and nondescript. The Santa Fe Room, perfect for families, features a king bed and separate sleeping alcove with a twin bed. The turquoises and pinks of the guest rooms—all of which have king-size beds, dressing rooms with sinks—may be a bit bright for some tastes. But the two outdoor patios are lovely, and Maree is a knowledgeable, genial hostess. She'll send you off to explore historic Hillsboro with a full, delicious morning meal: fancy egg dishes, soufflés, or casseroles with fruit, home-baked muffins, coffee cake, or biscuits, and juice and fresh-ground coffee.

🏠 *5 double rooms with baths. Fireplace, TV/VCR room, video library, dog run. $70, full breakfast. No credit cards. No smoking in guest rooms.*

The Lodge

1 Corona Pl., Box 497, Cloudcroft 88317, tel. 505/682–2566 or 800/395–6343, fax 505/682–2715

Cloudcroft's Lodge embodies the yin and yang of late-Victorian design in a singularly appealing fashion. Built in 1899 by the Alamogordo and Sacramento Mountain railway to house its workers, this ornate but imposing structure has a lobby where any hunter would be proud to rest a gun: A stuffed bear stands snarling in the corner, and a long-horned eland stares down from over the copper fireplace at deep-maroon leather couches and chairs. But pink-floral carpets lead down the hallway to individually decorated rooms with chenille bedspreads, period antiques, pastel-flocked wallpaper, ceiling fans, and, in many cases, four-poster beds.

Some of the accommodations are rather small, but they're accordingly less expensive. And if you get one with a view, it'll open up the space immeasurably. If you don't, you can always climb up to the hotel's copper-covered bell tower, which Judy Garland visited with Clark Gable. On a clear day, you can see White

Sands National Monument in the distance. Those who really want to hide away with friends can rent the Retreat, a four-bedroom cottage with a kitchenette, located just across the front parking lot from the main building.

The pool on the lush back lawn is inviting in warm weather, but winter is as delightful as summer in this mountain retreat. A gently sloping, pine-shrouded golf course on the grounds becomes a playground for cross-country skiers; downhill runs at the Cloudcroft Ski Area are only 2 miles away; and snowmobiling and horse-drawn-sleigh rides can be arranged through the front desk.

Any time of year, it's a treat to visit Rebecca's, the Lodge's elegant American-Southwestern dining room, named after the putative resident ghost. A full American breakfast is included in room rates for those who stay at the Pavilion, a bed-and-breakfast about ½ mile to the south of the main building that's still considered part of the Lodge. This single-level B&B is rustic in style—rooms have beamed ceilings, knotty-pine walls, and, in some cases, enormous stone fireplaces.

🏠 *10 single rooms with baths, 30 doubles with baths, 7 suites in hotel, 11 doubles with baths in B&B, 1 4-bedroom cottage. Phone and cable TV in all rooms, sauna, spa, bar, gift shop, conference facilities. $65–$199, the Retreat cottage $269, full breakfast included for those in suites or at the Pavilion B&B. AE, D, DC, MC, V. No pets.*

Lundeen Inn of the Arts

618 S. Alameda Blvd., Las Cruces 88005, tel. 505/526–3326 or 888/526–3326, fax 505/647–1334

You'll think you've died and gone to Santa Fe when you wake up at this arty, upscale bed-and-breakfast, but you'll be paying Las Cruces prices for the experience. Owned and designed by architect Gerald Lundeen and his wife, Linda, whose impressionist art gallery is on premises, the inn is designed to nurture aesthetic impulses in its visitors.

Gerald seamlessly joined two 1895 adobe houses, one Mexican Colonial and the other Pueblo style, in order to create the B&B; what was once the patio between them became the 18-foot-high Marienda Room, where most of the inn's activity takes place. Guests attend art classes, conferences, and performances in this unusual space, which is decorated in an eclectic (and ecumenical) fashion: The ornate wood balustrade is from a synagogue in El Paso and the pressed-tin ceiling frieze is from a Methodist church in Lordsburg. Huge Palladian windows let in lots of light at breakfast, when guests enjoy elaborate meals here—at least one hot entrée as well as a tempting variety of baked goods.

Reading niches and comfortable sitting areas abound in both wings of the house. Guest rooms are named for Western artists such as Georgia O'Keeffe and Frederic Remington. The one dedicated to Native American painter R. C. Gorman has a kiva fireplace, viga beams, and a curved seating nook with built-in bookcases. The connection between artist and decor is occasionally mysterious—one wonders, for example, how cowboy painter Gordon Snidow might feel about being represented by a room with a bidet in it—but never mind: All the accommodations are beautifully furnished with a whimsical mix of antiques and newer, handcrafted pieces. And, naturally, the walls are decked with art prints and reproductions. A restored adobe in the back of the Inn adds three casitas with full baths to the rooms available. In fact, the Lundeen Inn offers long-term residence if you find you just can't separate yourself from Las Cruces.

The Inn offers courses in silversmithing, ceramics, coil pottery, and architecture, all of which are taught semiannually. Most of the classes last for five days, and people sign up months ahead for them, but guests can sign up for single classes. There is also a course on breadmaking, and to this end the Lundeens have installed an Indian *horno,* a lumpy adobe oven that can bake up to 18 loaves at a time.

🏨 *20 double rooms with baths, 6 suites. Phones, TV, fireplaces, balconies, kitchenettes in some rooms, off-street parking. $70, suites $85–$125, full breakfast. AE, D, DC, MC, V. No smoking, children and pets by advance arrangement.*

Mesón de Mesilla

1803 Avenida de Mesilla, Box 1212, Mesilla 88046, tel. 505/525–9212 or 800/ 732–6025, fax 505/527–4196

It'd be worth staying at this 1983 pueblostyle inn, 10 minutes from historic Mesilla Plaza, for its restaurant alone. Folks drive here from all over southern New Mexico to enjoy such well-prepared Continental dishes as seared sturgeon in pesto or chateaubriand for two. For inn guests only, a full gourmet breakfast is served in a lovely glass-enclosed atrium. If you're planning to explore the area and return for lunch or dinner, keep in mind that the restaurant's popularity makes parking tricky during peak hours.

The view from the inn's back patio and from the second-floor balcony is also a lure; it's easy to forget you're near Las Cruces, the second-largest city in the state, when you look out across rows of well-tended cotton fields to the towering Organ Mountains. Rooms are decorated in attractive Southwestern colors with light-wood furniture and a few antiques; all have TVs, clock radios, and ceiling fans. Lower-priced singles are a nice option for students or traveling businesspeople.

🏨 *2 single rooms and 7 double rooms with baths, 7 suites. In-room phones available, TVs in rooms, kiva fireplaces in king suites, pool, off-street parking,* *banquet room. $55–$135, full breakfast. D, DC, MC, V.*

Sierra Mesa Lodge

Fort Stanton Rd., Box 463, Alto 88312, tel. 505/336–4515

This elegant blue country French–style house, with a gray stone chimney and white trim, stands in colorful contrast to the deep-green pines of the Lincoln National Forest that surround it. After they decided to open an inn, graphic designer Larry Goodman and his wife, Lila, an accountant, spent 12 years researching the perfect place and architectural design for it. In 1987, they came up with a winner on both counts about 10 minutes from downtown Ruidoso.

Above all, the lodge is geared toward romance. There are no phones or TVs to disturb the quiet setting, and the only interruption you'll have is when breakfast arrives at your bedroom door. The five lovely theme rooms have ceiling fans, queen-size beds with fluffy down comforters and pillows, built-in window seats, and delicate porcelain dolls. The Victorian room is pretty in pink, with a satin settee, claw-foot tub, fringed lamp, and marble tables, while the Oriental is a stunning Japanese-inspired study in black and red. An elaborate breakfast—green chili soufflés, say, or croissant French toast—is presented on fine china. The soothing hot tub, set in its own redwood room looking out into the woods and lighted with strings of tiny bulbs after dark, contributes to the sense of romantic solitude.

🏨 *5 double rooms with baths. Clocks, kimonos in rooms, hot tub, hiking trails. $95–$100, full breakfast, afternoon tea. D, MC, V. No smoking indoors, no pets, no children.*

Texas

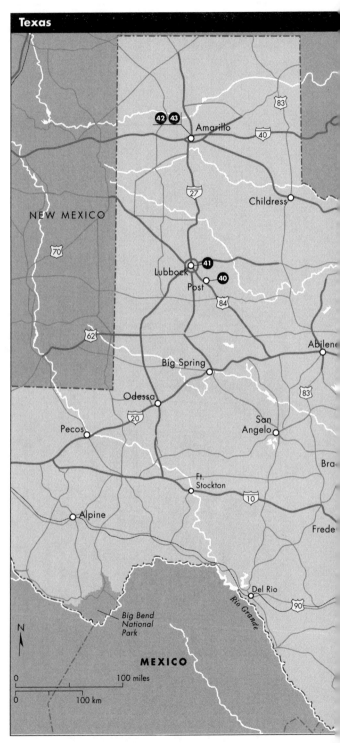

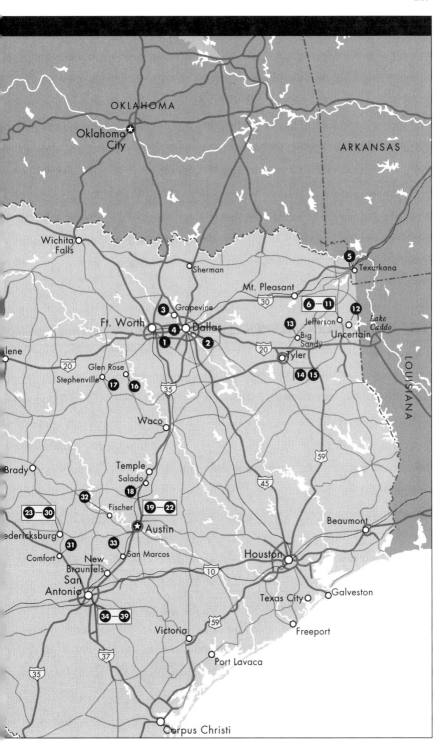

OKLAHOMA

Oklahoma City

ARKANSAS

Wichita Falls

Sherman

Mt. Pleasant

30

6—11

12

Grapevine

3

Ft. Worth

4

Dallas

1

2

20

13

Jefferson

Big Sandy

Uncertain

Lake Caddo

5

Texarkana

LOUISIANA

lene

20

Glen Rose

Stephenville

17

16

Tyler

14 15

35

Waco

Brady

Temple

Salado

18

32

Fischer

19—22

45

59

Beaumont

23—30

ederickburg

31

33

Austin

Comfort

New Braunfels

San Marcos

San Antonio

10

Houston

Texas City

Galveston

34—39

37

59

Victoria

Freeport

35

Port Lavaca

Corpus Christi

East Texas

Hotel St. Germain

Including Dallas and Fort Worth

*Bordered on the north by Ross Perot's hometown of Texarkana;
on the east by Texas's only natural lake, Caddo Lake; to the
west by onetime rollicking Fort Worth; and to the south by
historic Waxahachie and the first rumblings of the Hill
Country, east Texas is a land of piney woods, antiques shops,
hallowed century-old neighborhoods, and traditional stone-
faced Baptists proud of their roots and their property.*

*When railroad baron Jay Gould offered to run track through
the east Texas port town of Jefferson and was rebuffed more
than a century ago, local folklore has it that Gould angrily
scrawled in the register of the Excelsior House Hotel the
words, "The End of Jefferson." And indeed, Jefferson was
soon a port town no longer. The natural log dam on the
Red River broke, draining water from Cypress Bayou and
bringing an end to the city's steamboat commerce forever. The
city's population dwindled from 35,000 to 3,000. Ironically,
however, the historic town has returned to prominence in
recent years, not despite—but precisely because of—its*

*refusal to change with the times. The Excelsior House still
stands after about 140 years of continuous operation and is
surrounded by scores of well-preserved Greek Revival and
Victorian homes.*

*The preservation of things past is a theme that extends
throughout much of east Texas. As you travel west from
Shreveport, Louisiana, to Dallas on I-20, detour to Jefferson,
Gladewater, Pittsburg, and Mount Pleasant; you'll discover
that the woods lining the highway drape an antiques shopper's
paradise. Marshall, where potters have been mining clay from
east Texas's rolling hills for more than a century, turns out
more than a million pots each year. In Rusk, the Texas State
Railroad Historical Park's ancient steamers take visitors on a
19th-century train ride.*

*The region's identity changes abruptly, however, as the shiny,
sharply angled skyscrapers of Dallas come into view. Dallas
is defined by the progress of "bidness"—the forward march of
bankers, high-techsters, and oilmen—and the tearing down
of the old and the building of the new. Its critics say Dallas is
a city obsessed with appearances. And indeed, this metropolis
offers a beautiful skyline, a thriving nightlife inhabited
by bright young émigrés from parts north, a Super Bowl
champion football team, and a splashy, $157-million
symphony hall.*

*Yet, for all these attractions, visitors from around the world
still mostly come to Dallas to view the totems that recall the
city's greatest shame—the Texas School Book Depository, the
grassy knoll, the site on Commerce Street downtown where
President John F. Kennedy was fatally shot.*

*About 30 miles west of Dallas, the city of Fort Worth manages
to retain the flavor of its Wild West past while burgeoning
as a modern city. The former rip-roaring cowboy town,
known for its gunfights and cattle drives, has preserved its
roots both institutionally, through the maintenance of the
historic Stockyards, and culturally, through the down-to-earth*

approach to life that still permeates the city. But Fort Worth is no backwater; its cultural establishment is the envy of many larger cities, including Dallas. Some may sneeringly dismiss it as "Cowtown," but in many respects the city provides the best of what both tradition and progress have to offer.

Fort Worth, however, has only a handful of inns, largely because of zoning laws, and Dallas's offerings tend toward the unadorned host home, better suited for the business traveler than the tourist. There are a number of charming hideaways though that exist on the outskirts of the two major cities. On the other hand, Jefferson has gone B&B crazy—ever since the town's first bed-and-breakfast opened in 1983 as a response to the lengthening waiting list for lodging at the fabled Excelsior House, new places have popped up all over. There are about 60 such establishments in operation today.

Places to Go, Sights to See

Antiques. The main thoroughfare of tiny Gladewater, the region's self-styled "antiques capital," is lined by a seemingly endless parade of retailers peddling collectibles. But the town has become such a popular stop among travelers that it's difficult to find real bargains here. One might have better luck in other east Texas towns, from Pittsburg to Marshall, where antiques shops can be found in abundance. Jefferson, in particular, has nearly 40 such stores. In the Dallas–Fort Worth area, Arlington is home to eight antiques markets. The largest antiques event in the area, a flea market with as many as 5,000 vendors known as Trade Days, is held the Friday, Saturday, and Sunday preceding the first Monday of each month, in Canton.

Arlington. Largely because of its location between the population centers of Dallas and Fort Worth, this overgrown suburb of 284,000 has evolved into a kind of municipal amusement park. Arlington's many diversions include *Six Flags over Texas* (tel. 817/640–8900), *Six Flags Hurricane Harbor* (tel. 817/265–3356) water park, and *Texas Rangers baseball at The Ballpark in Arlington* (tel. 817/273–5222 ballpark information; 817/273–5100 ticket office). For grown-up fun, an entertainment district offers an increasing number of attractions including *Johnnie High's Country Music Revue* (tel. 817/226–4400 or 800/540–5127) and *Theatre Arlington* (tel. 817/275–7661).

Caddo Lake. Hung with Spanish moss and edged with bald cypresses, Caddo Lake is a fishing mecca straddling the Texas-Louisiana border. At various times it has been home to the beleaguered Caddo Indians, to bootleggers hiding out in its dense shore growth, to the great singer of spirituals Leadbelly (reared at

Swanson's Landing), to thriving steamboat traffic from New Orleans, and to all manner of legend. *Caddo Lake State Park* (Hwy. 43, tel. 903/679–3351), on the southern shore of the lake near Karnack, offers camping, cabins, fishing, swimming, and boating.

Glen Rose. A popular day trip for Dallas–Fort Worth urbanites, this beautiful town in the countryside 80 miles southwest of Dallas was once aptly known as "Glen of Roses." Its attractions include the *Fossil Rim Wildlife Center* (turnoff on U.S. 67, 3 mi southwest of town, tel. 817/897–2960), where you can see a wide variety of rare endangered species; *Dinosaur Valley State Park* (4 mi north of town on Park Rd. 59, tel. 817/897–4588), which displays fossil prints of prehistoric reptiles; the leisurely Paluxy River; and one of Texas's premier golf courses, *Squaw Valley* (on U.S. 67, ½ mi east of town, tel. 817/897–7956).

Grapevine. Just three minutes from DFW International Airport (one of the world's busiest) is a slice of small-town Texas. Grapevine's restored Historic District includes many old structures that now house shops and eateries. There are also some wineries in the area. The family-owned *La Buena Vida Vineyards* (tel. 817/481–9463), right in Grapevine's historic district, offers a taste of locally produced vintages. The most lavish operation is *Delaney Winery and Vineyards* (tel. 817/481–5668), a chateau-style winery with a 10-acre vineyard. *La Bodega Winery and Tasting Room* (tel. 817/329–3145) is the first winery in a major U.S airport; sample its product and other Texas wines in DFW's Terminal 2E (across from Gate 6). The city's newest attraction is *Grapevine Mills* (tel. 817/251–4013), the largest shopping and entertainment center in the Dallas–Fort Worth Metroplex with over 200 shops.

Jefferson. This town of 2,200 offers more than its share of quiet pleasures, particularly for those who love architecture and history. Museums include the *Texas Heritage Archives & Library* (202 Market St., tel. 903/665–1101), housing one of the finest collections of Texas historical material, including first-edition books by Davy Crockett. For information on horse-drawn-carriage and trolley tours of the town's historic homes, contact *Tour Headquarters* (tel. 903/665–1665). A fun time to visit Jefferson is during Pilgrimage Weekend, the first weekend in May, when residents dress in period garb, private historic homes open up for public tours, and a historic drama is performed at the Jefferson Playhouse.

Stockyards Historic District. This area near downtown Fort Worth recalls the prosperous days of 1902, when two major Chicago meatpackers, Armour and Swift, set up plants to ship meat across the country in refrigerator cars—an innovation. In the Livestock Exchange Building where cattle agents kept their offices, you'll find the *Stockyards Museum* (131 E. Exchange Ave., tel. 817/625–5087). Nearby, *Cowtown Coliseum* (121 E. Exchange Ave., tel. 817/625–1025) is the site of Saturday- night rodeos. Also here are what's left of a complex of cattle, goat, and sheep pens; horse and mule barns; and, of course, *Billy Bob's Texas* (2520 Rodeo Plaza, tel. 817/624–7117), billed as the "world's largest honky-tonk." Exchange Avenue is lined with restaurants, clubs, western-wear stores, and famous spots like the White Elephant Saloon and the Stockyards Hotel. The *Tarantula Excursion Train* (2318 8th Ave., tel. 817/763–8297) offers tours from the Stockyards to Grapevine.

West End Historic District. A gathering of brick warehouses built between 1900 and 1930, this corner of downtown Dallas had deteriorated badly before it was resurrected as an entertainment district in 1976. Now filled with restaurants, shops, and nightclubs, it is one of the city's biggest tourist draws. It is anchored by the *West End MarketPlace* (603 Munger Ave. at Market St., tel. 214/748–4801), once a candy and cracker factory and now a lively, five-story shopping and dining center built around an atrium. The West End is right around the corner from a considerably more somber Dallas tourist stop: The former *Texas School Book Depository*, from which Lee Harvey Oswald fired the shots that killed President Kennedy, houses the *Sixth Floor Exhibit* (tel. 214/653–6666)—displays on Kennedy's fateful 1963 Dallas visit.

Restaurants

In Jefferson, the chef-owned **Stillwater Inn** (tel. 903/665–8415) offers Continental cuisine, ranging from roast Cornish hen to tasty pork tenderloin, in a charming converted home (*see* review, *below*). For more casual dining, **Auntie Skinner's Riverboat Club** (tel. 903/665–7121) serves up home-style cooking and the restaurant's own bottled hot sauce. Zydeco and Cajun bands entertain on Saturday evenings.

For those who like their seafood with a Mexican accent, **La Calle Doce** (tel. 214/941–4304), in a remodeled house, serves the most mouthwatering mariscos (shellfish) in Dallas. Also moderately priced, **Jennivine** (tel. 214/528–6010) looks like an English pub and features a Continental menu that includes fine fish dishes and specialty salads; the sherry trifle alone is worth the trip. For real Texas-style barbecue, you can't top **Sonny Bryan's Smokehouse** (5 locations, call for addresses, tel. 214/357–7120), whose inexpensive menu includes thick-sliced smoked brisket, tasty sausage, and chicken.

In Fort Worth, **Joe T. Garcia's** (tel. 817/626–4356) serves up family-style Tex-Mex dinners, either indoors or in a sprawling open-air garden. Another moderately priced downtown restaurant, **Rodeo Steakhouse** (tel. 817/332–1288) has an Old West theme, hearty steaks, and a good salad bar.

Grapevine's **Dorris House Cafe** (tel. 817/421–1181) is in a 19th-century Victorian house. Here you can choose from dishes like roasted vegetable strudel and pan-seared salmon with white wine Buerre Blanc sauce.

Tourist Information

Arlington Convention and Visitors Bureau (Box A, Arlington 76004, tel. 817/640–0252 or 800/342–4305). **Dallas Convention and Visitors Bureau** (1201 Elm St., Suite 2000, Dallas 75270, tel. 214/746–6677). **Fort Worth Convention and Visitors Bureau** (415 Throckmorton, Fort Worth 76102, tel. 817/336–8791 or 800/433–5747). **Grapevine Convention and Visitors Bureau** (One Liberty Park Plaza, Grapevine 76051, tel. 800/457–6338). **Marion County Chamber of Commerce** (118 N. Vale, Jefferson 75657, tel. 903/665–2672). **Marshall Convention and**

Visitors Bureau (213 W. Austin St., Box 520, Marshall 75671, tel. 903/935–7868 or 800/953–7868). **Texarkana Chamber of Commerce** (Box 1468, Texarkana 75504, tel. 870/792–7191). **Tyler Area Convention and Visitors Bureau** (407 N. Broadway, Box 390, Tyler 75710, tel. 903/592–1661 or 800/235–5712).

Reservation Services

Bed and Breakfast Texas Style (4224 W. Red Bird La., Dallas 75237, tel. 972/298–8586 or 800/899–4538). **Book-A-Bed-Ahead** (Box 723, Jefferson 75657, tel. 903/665–3956 or 800/468–2627). **Jefferson Reservation Service** (Box A, Jefferson 75657, tel. 903/665–2592 or 800/833–6758).

Caddo Cottage

Rte. 2, Box 66, Uncertain 75661, tel. 903/789–3988 or 903/789–3297, fax 903/789–3916

Retirees Pete and Dorothy Grant went into the lodging business by accident. They moved to the cottage they owned on Taylor Island in moss-draped Caddo Lake for the peace and quiet, but the run-down place next door was such an eyesore that they were spurred to buy it and spruce it up. The result is Caddo Cottage, a homey, comfortable spot for those who want to enjoy a day or a weekend casting their lines into the best and biggest fishing hole in East Texas. Shoppers from nearby Jefferson also frequent the cottage, as do gamblers headed to the casino riverboats in Louisiana, 45 minutes away.

The Grants know that the lake, and its pleasures, are the main reason folks visit tiny Uncertain, and they have fashioned a bed-and-breakfast well suited to that purpose. Their functional two-story cottage includes a fully equipped kitchen, a laundry room, and a covered patio with a gas grill. The furniture is contemporary and comfortable—guests don't have to worry about breaking expensive antiques. The property also has a private pier with a deck and boathouse. A Continental breakfast might include pastries and croissants, fresh juice, and just-ground coffee.

🛏 *1 2-bedroom cabin. Air-conditioning, TV, full kitchen, boat house and dock. $85, Continental breakfast. No credit cards. No pets, 2-night minimum on weekends.*

Charnwood Hill

223 E. Charnwood St., Tyler 75701, tel. 903/597–3980, fax 903/592–6473

In the city that hosts the famed Texas Rose Festival, you can pay no greater compliment to a residence than to say that a Rose Queen lived there and that the Queen's Tea was held on the lawn. Tyler's Charnwood Hill, converted to a B&B in 1993, has housed not one but two queens: Margaret Hunt, daughter of the late oilman H. L. Hunt, was crowned in 1935; Jo Anne Miller received the honor in 1954.

As much as the yellow rose of Texas, the name Hunt is the stuff of Lone Star legend. And the Charnwood Hill estate, where the Hunt family lived before moving to Dallas in 1938, does not disappoint. Built in the 1860s by the headmaster of a school for girls, the three-story structure housed both a college and a hospital during the 19th century. The elegant, Greek Revival–influenced residence was bricked in 1901 by J. B. Mayfield, who raised a family here before selling the home to Hunt.

Hunt added his own touch to the home: a third-floor Art Deco suite constructed for daughters Margaret and Caroline. The suite's stark whites, barely-there pastels, and indirect lighting combine to stamp an indelible air of Great Gatsby–era privilege on the accommodation, and they contrast sharply with the frilly, floral guest bedrooms that dominate the first and second floors.

Male business travelers tend to favor the sprawling Millers' Trophy Room, named for H. C. Miller, who bought the house from Hunt. The blue-and-burgundy room has a full bar, gun cabinet, and bed that can be folded into the wall to make room for a small conference area.

Throughout the high-ceiling home, the furnishings are extravagant. The Walker family purchased the residence from the Millers in 1978, and in a four-year restoration, they have spared no expense to create a regal atmosphere, with crystal chandeliers, 100-year-old Oriental rugs, and antique pieces.

Common areas include a library and TV room, two second-floor balconies, and a screened swing porch. Guests enjoy a breakfast that might feature eggs Benedict or French toast in the formal dining room. And, more than 50 years after it served as the setting for Hunt's Queen's Tea, the west garden is as lovely as ever.

🏨 *5 double rooms with baths, 1 suite. TV/VCR in most rooms, phones in rooms, free airport transfers. $95–$175, suite $270, full breakfast, complimentary beverages. D, MC, V. No smoking indoors, no pets.*

The Excelsior House

211 W. Austin St., Jefferson 75657, tel. 903/665–2513

The Excelsior House is the remarkably restored centerpiece of Jefferson, a town sometimes called the "Williamsburg of Texas." Built in the 1850s by riverboat captain William Perry, the historic hotel has remained in continuous operation since then, although by the middle of this century, the brick-and-timber structure had slowly deteriorated and was largely forgotten.

Its rebirth began in 1954, when Estella Fonville Peters purchased the inn and undertook its renovation. Opening the building to public tours, filling the drawing room with the music of noted orchestras, and hosting elaborate balls, she revived interest in the hotel—and, in the process, sowed the seeds of Jefferson's commercial future. The Jessie Allen Wise Garden Club bought the hotel when Peters died in 1961 and has maintained and operated the facility with care ever since. The club has also made significant improvements, such as adding bathrooms and tearing down walls between the tiny rooms once consigned to traveling salesmen.

With iron columns and a lacy ironwork gallery that lend flourish to the simple rectangular edifice, the Excelsior House looks like it came to the Wild West by way of New Orleans. The ballroom features a French chandelier, Oriental rugs, antique marble mantles, and a pair of period pianos. The dining room includes

a glassed-in patio, where guests can enjoy a Plantation Breakfast of orange blossom muffins, country ham, scrambled eggs, and biscuits.

Each of the inn's 13 guest rooms and suites has a story to tell. Past guests have included William Vanderbilt and Oscar Wilde; both Ulysses S. Grant and Rutherford B. Hayes slept in what is now the Presidential Suite. Lady Bird Johnson was a frequent visitor and donated a good deal of the furniture in the room that bears her name. All the rooms are furnished with antiques, including marble-topped dressers, spool beds, and mahogany, cherry, and maple pieces.

Spurned railroad tycoon Jay Gould had predicted doom for Jefferson in the Excelsior House lobby in the 1870s, so it's fitting revenge that one of the hotel's most popular rooms is named after him. Across the street from the hotel, "Atlanta," Gould's decadently ornate private railroad car, is open to public tours.

🏨 *11 double rooms with baths, 2 suites. Air-conditioning, TV in all rooms. $65–$100, breakfast not included. No credit cards. No smoking, no pets.*

The Hotel St. Germain

2516 Maple Ave., Dallas 75201, tel. 214/871–2516 or 800/683–2516, fax 214/871–0740

In a city known for glitziness, the Hotel St. Germain is perhaps the definitive lodging. Nestled amid some of Dallas's most exclusive restaurants and shops, the boutique hotel, opened in 1991, gives visitors the chance to indulge in the high life of a different time and place: 19th-century France.

A Victorian prairie mansion built in 1906 for a prominent Dallas financier and home for many decades to a variety of commercial ventures, the inn was purchased in 1989 by Claire Heymann. She set out to reclaim the structure's noble origins while paying tribute to her own

French-Creole roots. You enter through a large entry hall embellished with crackle-back moldings and crystal chandeliers; from the moment you open the hotel's front doors, you're swept into a lavish, self-contained universe.

Heymann's secret is painstaking authenticity. A New Orleans native whose mother was an antiques dealer, she has been assembling French collectibles since her childhood. Her acquisitions are complemented by her knowledge of French design, developed through frequent trips abroad and study at the University of Paris.

The entry hall gives way to a pair of sitting rooms, a parlor, and a library, each housing its own treasures—such as the library's grand piano, bedecked with ancient, marbled candelabra. The dining room, which looks out onto a New Orleans–style walled courtyard with a fountain, is perhaps the most evocative of Gaul: The long table, draped in a burgundy damask tapestry, is topped by a rose-filled centerpiece that rests on a silver Alsatian platter; a mid-19th-century French basket chandelier hangs from the room's ceiling. Breakfast—which typically includes fresh fruit compote, croissants, quiche, and café au lait—is served on a rare, century-old set of Limoges china. Dinner, which could be lamb tenderloin or game hen, is served Friday and Saturday nights.

Upstairs, the seven spacious guest suites feature plush, canopied feather beds. All have wood-burning fireplaces, sitting rooms, and baths with soaking tubs or whirlpool baths. Although rates are prohibitive, and the hotel has a reputation for boarding the glitterati, Heymann promotes her inn as a place where common folk can come for that once-in-a-lifetime splurge.

🏨 *7 suites. Limited restaurant, air-conditioning in all rooms, cable TV, VCRs available, phones and mini-refrigerators in rooms, robes, room service, Crabtree and Evelyn soaps, concierge, valet parking, nightly turn-down service, privileges at nearby fitness club. $245–$600, Continental breakfast. AE, DC, MC, V. No smoking, no pets.*

House of the Seasons

Box 686, 409 S. Alley St., Jefferson 75657, tel. 903/665–1218 or 800/245–3889

One of East Texas's most intriguing architectural specimens, this 1872 house exemplifies the transitional period between Greek Revival and Victorian styles, with Italianate touches all its own. The most dazzling feature is the large dome that juts from the roof; the cupola's interior walls feature sunlit frescoes representing the four seasons, which can be viewed from the first floor.

The guest rooms are in a re-created carriage house on the estate, but visitors are welcome in the main house, where owners Kirby and Cindy Childress live. Breakfast is served in the antiques-laden dining room. The public pays for tours of the house, but the Childresses enjoy taking their B&B guests around at night and allowing them to climb into the cupola.

The exquisite 1870s period suites in the Carriage House are dominated by huge beds stacked with soft linens; all have baths with stained-glass windows. Personalized touches include a spinning wheel in one room and an antique pump organ in another.

🏨 *4 suites. Air-conditioning, cable TV, whirlpool bath in each room. $125–$135, full breakfast. MC, V. No smoking indoors, no pets.*

Inn on the River

205 S.W. Barnard St., Glen Rose 76043, tel. 972/424–7119 or 800/575–2101, fax 972/424–9766

Originally part of a popular spa and sanatorium run by Dr. George P. Snyder, a self-proclaimed "magnetic healer," the

Inn on the River remains a soothing resting place for the world-weary traveler. Nestled among 200-year-old trees on the banks of the Paluxy River, this is one of the largest country inns in Texas and is run as professionally as a fine hotel.

This B&B, 80 miles from Dallas, offers a package for small corporate groups, with single-occupancy accommodations, three meals, refreshment breaks, and use of the inn's top-notch conference center starting at $185 per person per day. Individual travelers are accepted on weekends only. Four-course gourmet dinners are also served on weekends for $30 per person.

Most rooms include queen beds and a combination of antiques and reproductions. An extraordinary breakfast may include hot berry cobbler in winter or a cold banana bisque in the summertime.

▥ *19 double rooms with baths, 3 suites. Air-conditioning in all rooms, heated outdoor pool. $115–$195, full breakfast. AE, D, MC, V. No smoking indoors, no pets, no children.*

Maison-Bayou

300 Bayou St., Jefferson 75657, tel. 903/ 665–7600, fax 903/665–7100

On moss-draped Big Cypress Bayou, just past downtown, lies Jefferson's most ambitious B&B. Jan and Pete Hochenedel's Maison-Bayou is set on 55 wooded acres and is patterned after an 1850s Louisiana antebellum plantation in Pete's family.

The main house is an authentic reproduction of a plantation overseer's home. Here the Hochenedels serve a full breakfast on weekends, with Southern entrées such as "swamp eggs," an oven-baked omelet filled with spinach, and brandied peaches.

But the most unique aspect of this B&B is the guest accommodations. Four cabins, modeled after slave quarters, offer primitive-style furnishings (but with the luxuries of full baths and central air and heat). Even the smallest details evoke authenticity: Mosquito netting hangs over one bed, sugarcane grows in front of the quarters, burlap curtains provide privacy. One dogtrot cabin features an open porch separating two accommodations. All the cabins overlook Beaver Pond, an oxbow lake that's popular with anglers. If you don't bring your fishing gear, the Hochenedels will supply cane poles.

▥ *10 double rooms with baths. Air-conditioning, kitchen in some rooms, games rooms, flat-bottom boat with 1 cabin, fishing, horseback riding, nature trails. $79–$135, full breakfast. MC, V. No smoking indoors, no pets.*

Mansion on Main

802 Main St., Texarkana 75501, tel. 870/ 792–1835 or 214/348–1929, fax 870/793– 0878

Tom and Peggy Taylor, who own Jefferson's McKay House (*see below*), chose a good spot to open their second B&B: Texarkana received lots of attention as the hometown of Ross Perot. Down the street from the Taylors' mansion, in fact, is the Perot Theatre, a performing arts center renovated with the billionaire's help.

The wood-frame, neoclassic Mansion on Main was built for the widow of a Confederate veteran in 1895; the structure's most striking external features—14 two-story cypress columns—were added later. The residence has been well preserved, retaining its original oak, walnut, and mahogany parquet floors, and a glamorous winding staircase. The Taylors added four bathrooms.

This inn follows the McKay House's strategy of blending elegance and fun, down to many of the same distinctive details such as the period hats, gowns, and nightshirts distributed to guests. All densely adorned with antiques, the guest rooms vary from the modest Butler's Garret to the elegant, two-chambered Governor's Suite.

▦ *5 double rooms with baths, 1 suite. Air-conditioning, telephones and cable TV in rooms. $60–$109, full breakfast. AE, MC, V. Smoking on balconies and veranda only, no pets.*

McKay House

306 Delta St., Jefferson 75657, tel. 903/665–7322 or 800/468–2627, fax 903/665–8551

In 1877, when Jefferson was a worldly river port, it was rocked by the brief visit of "Diamond Bessie"—the stage name of Annie Stone Moore Rothchild, a popular entertainer. While in town with her husband, a wealthy Cincinnati gambler named Abe Rothchild, the pair walked alone into a field. A gunshot was heard, and Abe returned alone, claiming his wife had shot herself by accident. After three trials over seven years, Rothchild was a free man, but the people of Jefferson never accepted the "not guilty" verdict.

One of the attorneys who successfully defended Rothchild was Hector McKay, the first of two generations of McKays who lived in this 1851 Greek Revival. In the early 1980s, the McKay House was purchased by Dallasites Tom and Peggy Taylor, who, through extensive renovations, transformed it into the city's most luxurious B&B.

The inn is furnished almost entirely with antiques, mostly Eastlake, many of them quite valuable. But this place is anything but stuffy. Innkeepers Joseph and Alma Anne Parker know how to break the ice, from the funny period hats distributed for visitors to wear at breakfast, to Victorian gowns and nightshirts provided in the rooms, and, in one room, his-and-hers claw-foot tubs that offer an opportunity for simultaneous scrub-downs. An ancient Packard pump organ is played to call guests to the hearty "Gentleman's Breakfast," which is served in period dress and may consist of honey-cured ham, cheese biscuits, and homemade pineapple zucchini bread and strawberry preserves. Afterward, guests can relax on the wide front porch, outfitted with a swing and white wicker chairs.

The guest rooms are individual in personality but uniform in elegance; each has such furnishings as a canopy bed and antique armoire. The two downstairs rooms have coal-burning fireplaces; the two upstairs suites feature a balcony, skylight, and his-and-hers tubs; and a downstairs suite includes two bedrooms, each with its own fireplace. But perhaps the most memorable rooms are the two set off from a central, dogtrot hall in the tin-roofed Victorian garden cottage located behind the main house. The Keeping Room, in particular, is amusingly authentic: A claw-foot tub sits exposed in a bay window, next to a transplanted outdoor privy, fully equipped with a lantern and a Sears Roebuck catalog.

▦ *4 double rooms with baths, 3 suites. Air-conditioning, cable TV, phones in all rooms. $85–$95, suites $125–$145, full breakfast. AE, MC, V. Smoking on porches only, no pets, 2-night minimum on holiday weekends.*

Miss Molly's Bed & Breakfast

109½ W. Exchange Ave., Fort Worth 76106, tel. 817/626–1522 or 800/99–MOLLY, fax 817/625–2723

As the drovers on the street below brought in herd after herd of longhorns, hitting every saloon and dance hall on the way to the stockyards, the guests in the second-floor walk-up gazed down, primly elevated from the fray. In the early 1900s, the eight rooms that now make up Fort Worth's best bed-and-breakfast housed the guests of Miss Amelia Eisner's Furnished Rooms, an oh-so-proper hotel.

By the 1930s, however, the wild ways of the stockyard district had had their influence; the hotel had become an infamous brothel named for its madam, Miss Josie. When Mark and Susan Hancock renovated and reopened the abandoned space as Miss Molly's in 1989, they decided to name adjacent rooms after Miss Josie and Miss Amelia—provoking guests to wonder whether either, or both, of the former proprietors might be turning in their graves.

Located over the Star Cafe steak house in the Fort Worth Stockyards Historic District, Miss Molly's may be the most mythically Texan of Texas's bed-and-breakfasts. The rooms, which form a circle around the registration desk at the top of the stairs, are chock-full of saddles, stirrups, cowboy hats, buckskin, and other Western paraphernalia. What keeps the whole thing from being hokey is that the artifacts are authentic: The rope that dangles from the wall mirror in one room, for example, is the actual one used to win the Fort Worth rodeo in 1928.

The rooms have been furnished to appear as they did in the 1920s: iron beds draped with colorful quilts; ceiling fans; a washstand with a bowl and pitcher. With the exception of Miss Josie's room, none of the rooms have private baths. Three bathrooms with pedestal sinks, claw-foot tubs, and pull-chain toilets stand side by side in one corner of the establishment.

Mark encourages folks to mingle; they say they measure success by the number of friends they and their visitors have made here. Guests are given custom-made blue-and-white ticking robes to wear to the copious Continental breakfast buffet, which typically features coffee cakes, muffins, biscuits and gravy, egg casserole, strawberry bread, and a fruit cup.

▦ *1 double room with bath, 7 doubles share 3 baths. Fans in all rooms. $95–$170, Continental breakfast. AE, D, DC, MC, V. No smoking, no pets.*

1934 Bed and Breakfast

322 College St., Grapevine 76051, tel. and fax 817/251–1934

While working on a reconstruction project at La Buena Vida Vineyards in Grapevine, Willie Livingston looked down the street and spied a Craftsman-style house for sale. For years, Willie, an engineer, and wife Wanda, a former home economist, had taken on home restoration projects for pleasure. Before they knew it, they were proud owners of the 1934 house and set about converting it into Grapevine's first bed-and-breakfast.

What attracted the Livingstons to this 3,500-square-foot house was that it had only had two previous owners. All the original fixtures and woodwork—and even rugs—were still in place. Built by the Lipscomb family as their first "city home" after years of farm living, the house was filled with extravagant features, from quarter-sawn oak floors to hand-beveled glass doors. Spiraled wood rods still hang over the windows. The living room, where guests often congregate in the evening hours, has a spectacular tile fireplace.

The Rose Room, with blushing rose-tinted walls, is the most flamboyant room. A pencil-post king-size bed looks out over a trompe l'oeil library. Down the hall, the Main Street Room, with a wallpaper border of an old main street scene, has the original cedar-lined closet, wood paneling, and a quilted bedcover. The two-room Sun Room Suite has a double bed and trundle, the larger room includes a fireplace. Glass pocket doors lead into a sitting area, which has a table and chairs that look like they're from an old-fashioned ice-cream fountain.

With its location just minutes from Dallas–Fort Worth International Airport, the 1934 House is popular with business travelers as well as couples looking for a leisurely getaway. The home is just steps from the La Buena Vida

Vineyards, where you can take a tour and enjoy tastings of the local product, and from the Dorris House, a favorite with locals for fine dining in an historic setting.

▦ *2 double rooms with baths, 1 suite. Air-conditioning, phones, TV in meeting room. $95–$115, full breakfast. AE, D, MC, V. No smoking, no pets, no children.*

Oxford House

563 N. Graham St., Stephenville 76401, tel. 254/965–6885, 254/968–8171, or 800/711–7283, fax 254/965–7555

The Oxford House of tiny Stephenville, just a few miles from Glen Rose, is one of the more squeaky-clean, professionally run B&Bs in Texas. It's also distinguished by the fact that it's been owned by the same family since 1898. It was built by Judge W. J. Oxford and is now in the hands of his grandson, Bill, and Bill's wife, Paula.

Guests are offered complimentary beverages when they arrive at the Oxfords' well-preserved Victorian home, painted pale blue with dark-blue-and-burgundy trim. Perhaps the home's most prized antique is the pump organ brought to Texas on covered wagon from Tennessee by Bill's great-grandparents. An 1890s sleigh bed, beveled-glass mirrors, antique armoires, marble-top dressers, and claw-foot tubs are among the home's other treasures.

Breakfast may include baked French toast with hot fruit topping, sausage biscuits, or German cinnamon rolls. The dining room can accommodate up to 40 guests for catered luncheons, birthday dinners, bridal showers, or business meetings.

▦ *4 double rooms with baths. Air-conditioning in all rooms, tearoom–gift shop. $75–$85, full breakfast, afternoon tea. MC, V. No smoking, no pets, no children under 6.*

Pride House

409 E. Broadway, Jefferson 75657, tel. 903/665–2675, fax 903/665–3901

The Pride House has the distinction of being the first B&B in Jefferson and, according to the owner, the oldest in Texas. A gabled mansion built from a mail-order blueprint in 1888, the house had been badly damaged by fire when Sandy and Ray Spalding purchased it in 1978. They meticulously restored the old home, and then—inspired by the spillover of customers at the Excelsior House—opened it to lodgers the next year. The Spaldings have since moved to Oregon, leaving managers Carol Abernathy and Christel Frederick to run the place. In addition to being personable, the innkeepers whip up a mean egg casserole.

The stick-style Victorian home (named after the Spaldings' son, Pride) is caramel colored with white gingerbread trim and stained-glass windows. The antiques found throughout come in a variety of styles, including Eastlake and country primitive. Behind the lodging's main house, which has six guest rooms, an expanded former servants' cottage offers four additional bedrooms, all with English country decor. Guests eat breakfast at comfortable tables in the main house.

▦ *10 double rooms with baths. Air-conditioning in all rooms. $65–$110, full breakfast. D, MC, V. No smoking, no pets, 2-night minimum on weekends.*

Sanford House

506 N. Center St., Arlington 76011, tel. 817/861–2129

Tucked on a quiet residential street just a short walk from Arlington's entertainment district, Sanford House gives adults a chance to enjoy a quiet getaway. Sanford House resembles a 19th-century French country structure but is actually a recent construction accurate in historic details down to a detached "carriage house."

Although it is located with a mile of the Ballpark at Arlington and a short drive from Arlington's theme parks, most visitors at Sanford House come for a quiet retreat. Tall shade trees drape over the expansive lawn where guests can relax in a gazebo, take a dip in the pool, or read a book on one of the many porches.

The tranquil atmosphere continues in guest rooms named for major composers. The antiques-filled Beethoven Room invites relaxation before its fireplace; the Brahms Room, with an intimate reading nook overlooking the front yard, tempts visitors to curl up and spend an afternoon. The quietest rooms are found in the carriage house, where the Bach and the Strauss rooms have balconies overlooking the lawn and gardens.

▦ *7 double rooms with private baths. Air-conditioning, TV in some rooms, swimming pool, massages available. $125–$175, full breakfast. MC, V. No smoking, no pets, no children.*

The Seasons

313 E. Charnwood, Tyler 75701, tel. 903/533–0803, fax 903/533–8870

Regardless of the season, the living is easy at The Seasons, an elegant 1911 home that invites guests to enjoy a romantic getaway. Lumberman Sam Littlejohn, the original owner, imbued his estate with the finest woods, from the tiger oak floors to the curly pine woodwork that frames doorways and the parlor fireplace.

Nestled between Tyler's historic and azalea districts, this home is the neighbor of the larger Charnwood Hill B&B (*see above*) and shares the same opulent atmosphere. The Seasons was converted into a B&B by Jim Brown, a petroleum engineer working in banking, and his wife, Myra, an artist who specializes in

wallscapes. Myra has transformed each of the four guest rooms into a representation of a season. The Summer Room comes alive with geraniums; the Fall Room is crisp with rag rolled walls done in an autumnal shade; and the Winter Room re-creates a Victorian ice-skating park, complete with small park benches and white sheepskin rugs in front of a fireplace, with a painted backdrop of skaters on an outdoor pond.

Cheeriest is the Spring Room. Sunny with corner windows, the room has a picket-fence bed, a painted arbor on the walls, light green carpet, and furnishings that carry on the Secret Garden theme. The rooms also contain memorabilia from Jim's family, such as photos and hatboxes.

▦ *4 double rooms with baths. Air-conditioning, ceiling fans in all rooms. $85–$125, full breakfast. AE, D, MC, V. No smoking, no pets, no children.*

Stillwater Inn

203 E. Broadway, Jefferson 75657, tel. 903/665–8415, fax 903/665–8416

The Stillwater Inn is Jefferson's best restaurant, and atop that restaurant is the town's most unusual B&B. Wishing to take advantage of the bed-and-breakfast craze in Jefferson but short on space, owners Bill and Sharon Stewart ingeniously built three guest rooms into the structure's gables. With their dramatically pitched ceilings, stained-glass windows, and sunny skylights, the rooms are bright and cheerful and well complemented by the simple, stripped-pine furnishings throughout.

Among the pines and magnolias on the Stewarts' estate, a private cottage behind the Stillwater Inn is also available to guests. It is adorned simply, with pine floors, vaulted ceilings, and wicker furnishings. Another outbuilding houses conference and party facilities for up to 48 guests.

All overnight guests enjoy a free breakfast at the inn's restaurant. You might notice something different about the black coffee table in the living area of the restaurant's adjoining parlor: It is actually an enormous, 8-foot-long bellows, once used for industrial purposes but not recommended for stoking the parlor's own fireplace.

▦ *3 double rooms with baths. Air-conditioning, cable TV and phones in all rooms, refrigerator in common area. $90–$100, full breakfast. AE, MC, V. No smoking, no pets.*

The Village Bed and Breakfast

Hwy. 155 N., Box 928, Big Sandy 75755, tel. 903/636–4355 or 800/BB–ANNIE, fax 903/636–4744

The Village—formerly called Annie's—is more than the only bed-and-breakfast in Big Sandy; it's an industry—and, for most people, the only reason to come to Big Sandy.

"Annie" is Annie Potter, whose multi-million-dollar mail-order needlecraft and pattern business, Annie's Attic, Inc., got started with a $100 investment in 1973. When mail-order customers began to trickle into Big Sandy (population 1,200), Annie would serve them tea but had no real means of entertaining them. So, about a decade ago, she began assembling the Victorian Village, a cluster of three brightly painted, converted Victorian homes. In addition to the B&B, the complex now includes a restaurant and tearoom and a needlecraft gallery and gift shop.

The bed-and-breakfast is a large, gray-and-white, seven-gabled house, which had only one story when it was constructed in 1901 for the former mayor and postmaster G. A. Tohill. Potter had a second floor and attic added and filled virtually every corner of every room with antique Victorian furnishings. They are often draped with quilts or other craft works, including many crocheted by Potter. Antique sewing machines are also on display throughout.

The 12 guest rooms are designed for two people, but many can sleep more because they include sitting areas with sofa beds. The best of them all, the Queen Anne Room, has a queen bed, a sofa bed, and a spiral staircase that leads to twin beds in a loft. And, like the Garret and Balcony rooms, it has a private balcony.

Needlecraft festivals, crochet seminars, and other events are often held on the village grounds.

Innkeepers Clifton and Kathy Shaw will organize a barbecue for your group, chat with you on the front porch—or leave you alone if you crave privacy. For those not interested in crochet and needlepoint, there are precious few attractions in Big Sandy itself. This is especially true on Saturday, when the town pretty much shuts down in deference to the Sabbath of the Worldwide Church of God, headquartered in the area. Still, given the quality of rooms and service, the Village is one of the B&B bargains in the region.

▦ *7 double rooms with baths, 5 doubles share 3 baths. Mini-refrigerators in all rooms, TV in some rooms. $50–$115, Continental breakfast. D, MC, V. No smoking, no pets.*

San Antonio, Austin, and the Hill Country

The Ogé House on the Riverwalk

The heart of Texas is a place of hills and valleys, of rivers and dust.

San Antonio is the home of the Alamo, where the famous defeat ultimately inspired the United States to annex Texas at Mexico's expense—and, ironically, to create the nation's most Mexican-American-powered metropolis.

Austin is the home of both the state capitol, where the legislature is known for its cowboy-hatted, hang-'em-high politicos, and the city's most laid-back liberal enclave, the University of Texas, whose tie-dyed student population inspired the 1992 cult film Slacker.

Hill Country is the home of hundreds of bed-and-breakfast establishments. Many of these are in Fredericksburg, a Teutonic town of fewer than 7,000 people, with a reputation for peace and quiet that has turned it into a busy tourist mecca.

All in all, San Antonio, Austin, and the Hill Country form Texas's most intriguing triangle, in terms the area's geography and its diverse mix of cultures and attractions.

*German settlers left a thick accent on Comfort and
Fredericksburg and New Braunfels, where the würstfests
are as common as the pink granite hills, blanketed with
cedars and live oaks that define the region. Native American,
Mexican, and Polish cultures have melded in Bandera, the
state's dude-ranch capital. A politician who started out along
the Pedernales River and ended up in the White House left a
mark on the Hill Country, too—in the town of Johnson City.*

*You should find a cure for whatever ails you somewhere in
these parts. Choose from the gently rolling hills and friendly
little towns of Hill Country; the cheering hubbub of San
Antonio's River Walk, or the beer gardens of Fredericksburg;
the soothing natural springs in San Marcos and Austin; or
rivers ripe for water sports, among them the Guadalupe,
Medina, Blanco, Pedernales, and Llano.*

*In the past few years, as demand among visitors has grown,
bed-and-breakfasts have blossomed like the wildflowers found
throughout the region. The styles range from Southern
plantation houses to German fachwerk (log-and-stone
cabin) homes, with nearly everything in-between. Most of
the bed-and-breakfasts in Fredericksburg are gästehauses,
or unattended guest houses; the morning meal is in the
refrigerator when visitors arrive. In the last few years, upscale
establishments, such as San Antonio's Ogé House, have
emerged on the scene, setting new standards of quality and
professionalism for bed-and-breakfasts throughout the region.*

Places to Go, Sights to See

The Alamo (Alamo Plaza, San Antonio, tel. 210/225–1391). At the heart of San Antonio, the Alamo stands as a repository of Texas history, a monument to the 189 volunteers who died here in 1836 during a 13-day siege by the Mexican dictator General Santa Anna. When the Alamo was finally breached, at a terrible cost to the Mexican Army, the slaughter that followed would be remembered as the catalyst of the Texas Revolution. Today, the Alamo is filled with guns and other paraphernalia belonging to William Travis, David Crockett, James Bowie, and the other martyrs. Nearby, at the 1859 Menger Hotel in Alamo Plaza, you can sample the mango ice cream so cherished by President Bill Clinton that he had hundreds of gallons shipped in for his inauguration.

Aquarena Center (1 Aquarena Springs Dr., San Marcos, tel. 512/245–7575 or 800/999–9767). Famous for its glass-bottom boats that tour the crystal-clear waters of Spring Lake, the Aquarena Springs Resort is built around the natural springs that have risen for millions of years from the limestone strata of the Balcones Fault. The focus here is on educational fun; exhibits cover subjects such as endangered species, archaeology, and the history of the region.

Bandera County. This Hill Country county, once a staging ground for the thrilling cattle drives of yesteryear, has earned its reputation as the "Cowboy Capital of the World" in more recent times by cornering the Texas dude-ranch market: When ranching fell on hard times in the 1930s, an enterprising rancher began charging city slickers to show them the ropes. Today, dude ranches dot the county, and rodeos, trick-roping exhibitions, and country-and-western dances are the county's bread and butter. The *Lost Maples State Natural Area* (Vanderpool, tel. 830/966–3413), which preserves the rare and majestic Big Tooth Maple; the *Hill Country State Natural Area* (10 mi southwest of Bandera, tel. 830/796–4413), the largest state park in Texas open to equestrians; and the canoe-friendly Medina River round out the county's attractions. Kayaks, canoes, and tubes can be rented at *Fred Collins Workshop* (Hwy. 16, ½ mi north of Bandera, tel. 830/796–3553).

Barton Springs. Austin's natural, rock-bottom swimming hole is on Barton Creek about half a mile from its junction with the Colorado River; like Spring Lake in San Marcos, its waters rise from the ancient Balcones Fault. Located amid the picnic areas, soccer fields, and other recreation options of 400-acre *Zilker Park* (2201 Barton Springs Rd., tel. 512/476–9044), the 68°F springs bubble to the surface at a rate of 32 million gallons daily and attract about 200,000 visitors a year.

Fredericksburg. This little town (population 7,000) swells with visitors who have discovered its quaint German ancestry and picturesque setting atop Edwards Plateau in the heart of Hill Country. Founded in 1846 by German immigrants and now the seat of Gillespie County, the town has a mile-long Main Street populated by a mix of century-old limestone houses and storefronts and newer structures born of the tourist trade. These include a number of lively restaurants, most notably the *Altdorf Biergarten* (301 W. Main St., tel. 830/997–7865). The *Admiral Nimitz Museum and Historical Center* (340 E. Main St., tel. 830/997–4379), in the restored steamboat-shaped Nimitz Hotel and extending into the outdoor Japanese Garden of Peace, chronicles the Pacific War and the life of Fleet Admiral Chester Nimitz, commander in chief of the United States' Pacific troops during World War II. The *Pioneer Museum* (309 W. Main St., tel. 830/997–2835), a converted home and general store built in 1846, houses items of all kinds from the city's earliest German settlers.

Georgetown. This 18,000 resident town is county seat for the second-fastest growing county in the nation. It has, however, continued to hang onto its cozy charm. In 1997, Georgetown was one of five national winners of the

Great American Main Street Award, cosponsored by the National Trust for Historic Preservation's Natural Main Street Center, recognizing the extensive renovation in its downtown historic district. The *Georgetown History and Visitor Information Center* (101 W. Seventh St., tel. 512/863–5598), can provide a Georgetown map, brochures on area attractions, and walking-tour booklets and cassettes. Family travelers enjoy *Inner Space Cavern* (tel. 512/863–5545), west of I-35 at exit 259. This cave, discovered during construction of the interstate, is a cool getaway for summer travelers and was once a hideaway for animals as well. Just across I-35, you can see numerous types of candles being dipped at the *Georgetown Candle Factory* (tel. 512/863–6025).

King William Historic Area. San Antonio's leading German merchants built their Victorian mansions here in the late 19th century, and it's still a quiet, leafy neighborhood. Madison and Guenther streets are particularly pretty for a stroll or drive. A few houses, like the *1876 Steves Homestead* (509 King William St., tel. 210/225–5924), offer daily tours; you can pick up a brochure there for a self-guided walking tour of the neighborhood.

River Walk. Several miles of scenic stone pathways on both banks of the San Antonio River downtown are built a full story below street level, accessible by stairway. In some places the River Walk, or Paseo del Rio, is peaceful and quiet; in others, you'll find a mad conglomeration of restaurants, bars, hotels, and strolling mariachi bands, all of which can be seen from river taxis. In January, when parts of the river are drained to clean the bottom of debris, locals revel in the River Bottom Festival and Mud Parade. San Antonio's most beautiful attraction at all times, the River Walk is best at night.

Wimberley. This community of 7,200, north of San Antonio between Blanco and San Marcos, swells on weekends as folks come to enjoy dozens of specialty stores, art galleries, and studios. Try to visit on Market Day, held the first Saturday of every month from April through December, when over 400 vendors come to Wimberley to sell antiques, collectibles, and arts and crafts.

Restaurants

In Fredericksburg, the Teutonic soul of the Hill Country, you can feast on eight types of schnitzel and gravy-soaked potato dumplings at **Friedhelm's Bavarian Inn** (tel. 830/997–6300), moderately priced and low-key. About 9 miles north of Fredericksburg on U.S. 87, the **Hill Top Cafe** (tel. 830/997–8922) is one of the region's most famous and reasonably priced restaurants. The owner, a former member of the country-and-western band Asleep at the Wheel, often entertains guests at the piano while his cooks serve up top-quality Cajun and Greek fare.

Threadgill's (tel. 512/459–3855) home-cookin' restaurant dishes up the best chicken-fried steak in Austin—and, arguably, all of Texas—but also offers creative vegetable dishes, including a mean vegetable jambalaya. A more expensive Austin favorite, but not as stuffy as it sounds, **Jean-Pierre's Upstairs** (tel. 512/454–4811) eschews the expected haute French cuisine in favor of creations with a Texas twist: grilled quail with pecan honey sauce, say, or salmon poached in corn husks.

Decorated with photographs of the Alamo City, San Antonio's **Alamo Cafe** (tel. 210/341–4526) offers an authentic Tex-Mex dining experience, with moderately priced specialties such as tortilla soup and chicken fajitas. Just one flight up from the River Walk, the upscale **Stetson Restaurant** (tel. 210/222–1400) in the Hilton Palacio del Rio Hotel combines a fabulous view of the river with a fine American menu that includes good steak and fresh seafood with a southwestern flair. **Zuni Grill** (tel. 210/227–0864), also on the River Walk, serves hip and delicious southwestern food and potent Cactus Margaritas.

Tourist Information

Austin Convention and Visitors Bureau (201 E. 2nd St., Austin 78701, tel. 512/474–5171 or 800/926–2282). **Bandera Convention and Visitors Bureau** (1808 Hwy. 16 S, Bandera 78003, tel. 830/796–3045 or 800/364–3833). **Fredericksburg Convention and Visitors Bureau** (106 N. Adams Rd., Fredericksburg 78624, tel. 830/997–6523). **Georgetown Convention and Visitors Bureau** (Box 409, Georgetown 78627, tel. 512/930–3545 or 800/GEO-TOWN). **Salado Chamber of Commerce** (Box 81, Salado 76571, tel. 254/947–5040). **San Antonio Convention and Visitors Bureau** (Box 2277, 121 Alamo Plaza, San Antonio 78298, tel. 210/270–8700 or 800/447–3372). **San Marcos Convention and Visitors Bureau** (Box 2310, San Marcos 78667, tel. 512/393–5900 or 800/782–7653, ext. 177). **Wimberley Chamber of Commerce** (Box 12, Wimberley 78676, tel. 512/847–2201).

Reservation Services

Bed and Breakfast Hosts of San Antonio (Box 831203, San Antonio 78283, tel. 210/824–8036). **Be My Guest Travel Services** (110 N. Milam, Fredericksburg 78624, tel. 830/997–7227). **Gastehaus Schmidt Reservation Service** (231 W. Main St., Fredericksburg 78624, tel. 830/997–5612).

Austin Street Retreat

231 W. Main St., Fredericksburg 78624, tel. 830/997–5612, fax 830/997–8282

Only a block from Main Street and minutes from Fredericksburg's shopping district, this B&B is actually a compound of five historic homes. Owned by a Chicago couple and managed by a local reservation service, these stylish retreats have created a new standard for area properties. The luxurious whirlpool bath for two found in each structure is your tip-off that hedonistic luxuries are emphasized here.

From the outside, you might wonder how Annie's Cabin could be one of the top guest rooms in Fredericksburg, requiring reservations months in advance. The answer comes as soon as you walk in the room: over-the-top decadence, handcrafted for honeymooners. With smoky-rose-colored walls in the bedroom, the cabin is dominated by a king-size bed made from a fence reconfigured by a craftsman Cupid to resemble hearts and arrows; it's covered with a thick layer of linens, a tapestry duvet, and a sumptuous pile of pillows.

In Kristen's Cabin, a king-size iron bed overlooks a fireplace in the front bedroom. An Italian tapestry sofa and chair complete the look, and a painting of the owner's grandmother in her wedding dress lends a romantic air. Connected to the bedroom by a Saltillo-tile hallway is the bath, its focal point a whirlpool bath on a limestone pedestal. The bars on the windows are there because the room served as a cell in 1885 when the town jail burned. Outside, a private flagstone courtyard with a three-tiered fountain provides a quiet, private retreat.

Eli's Cabin is less frilly, starting with the cast-iron mantel saved from a Philadelphia mansion. A pencil-post bed, Mexican tin mirror, and a staghorn chandelier add a southwestern touch. This cabin also has a private courtyard with a double hammock.

The oldest structure of the five is Maria's Cabin, a log cabin built in 1867. Its two bedrooms preserve its historic flavor with plank floors, twig furniture, chinked log walls, and historic paintings, but pamper visitors with extras the pioneers never enjoyed: two queen-size beds with down comforters and a whirlpool bath.

But none of the other getaways shares the aged elegance of El Jefe (The Boss). Decorated in 1900s southwestern style, this two-story cottage has beamed ceilings and appointments that range from frayed sombreros to well-worn leather chairs to antique suitcases. Upstairs, the whirlpool bath overlooks the complex through French doors.

🏠 *4 1-bedroom cabins, 1 2-bedroom cabin. Air-conditioning, phones, whirlpool baths, cable TV in 2 cabins, CD players in 2 cabins, fireplaces in 4 cabins, coffee bar with microwave,. $125, Continental breakfast. AE, D, MC, V. No smoking, no pets.*

The Beckmann Inn and Carriage House

222 E. Guenther St., San Antonio 78204, tel. 210/229–1449 or 800/945–1449, fax 210/229–1061

Betty Jo and Don Schwartz, Illinois natives, fell in love with San Antonio as a result of many trips to visit their children in college. During those excursions, the couple liked to drive through the King William District to a home they dreamed of owning. Built for a daughter of the Guenther flour mill family and later owned by noted architect O'Neil Ford, the 1886 Greek Revival–style home features an original cypress picket fence and a wraparound porch.

Five years after first admiring the historic structure, they found it was for sale. They bought it and turned it into an elegant B&B. Today guest rooms are filled with Victorian furnishings, public areas have such touches as a wood mosaic floor imported from Paris and arched pocket doors, and there are wide porches to sit on and enjoy the quiet neighborhood. The most private rooms are in the adjacent Carriage House, and they have more modern decor, carpeting, and a shady brick courtyard.

All guests enjoy a full breakfast that might include cinnamon-stuffed French toast with apricot glaze or Canadian bacon, and, in keeping with the area's German heritage, a breakfast dessert.

🏠 *5 double rooms with baths. Air-conditioning, cable TV, turndown service, mini-refrigerators, trolley stop. $90–$130, full breakfast. AE, D, DC, MC, V. No smoking indoors, no pets, no children, 2-night minimum on weekends.*

The Bonner Garden

145 E. Agarita St., San Antonio 78212, tel. 210/733-4222 or 800/396-4222, fax 210/733-6129

The Bonner Garden was built in 1910 in what is now San Antonio's historic Monte Vista area. Louisiana aristocrat Mary Bonner's four previous residences all burned to the ground, so she wanted a structure guaranteed to be fireproof. Atlee Ayers, the architect commissioned for the project, responded with a concrete house, reinforced with steel, cast in iron, and coated with stucco.

Bonner, who spent much of the time in Paris, became known for her etchings and prints. Current owners, the Stenoien family, decorated the interior of the 4,000-square-foot Palladian-style villa in keeping with the house's artistic heritage. Bonner's work is displayed throughout. Detached from the main residence, the artist's former studio is now a guest cottage. With a Saltillo-tile floor, stone walls, and Santa Fe furniture, it is the most private room on the property. The villa's architectural embellishments, including hand-painted porcelain fireplaces and tile floors original to the house, are splendid, and Bat-

tenburg lace and antique armoires fill the bedrooms. A rooftop garden affords a 360-degree view of the city.

🏠 *5 double rooms with baths. Air-conditioning, TV, VCR, and phone in all rooms, CD player in sitting room, videotape library, outdoor pool. $85–$115, full breakfast. AE, D, DC, MC, V. No smoking, no pets, 2-night minimum on weekends.*

The Bullis House Inn

621 Pierce St., Box 8059, San Antonio 78208, tel. 210/223-9426, fax 210/299-1479

The Bullis House was built in 1906 for John Lapham Bullis, the commander of the Seminole Indian scouts used by the U.S. cavalry in the late 1800s to track the enemy Comanches and Apaches during the Indian wars. The neoclassic-style main house offers bed-and-breakfast facilities to visitors, and the former carriage house serves as an international youth hostel.

Bed-and-breakfast guests are treated to large rooms, most equipped with TVs; however, only two have private baths. One is the Harvey Page Room, featuring a king-size four-poster bed, a sitting area with a large round oak table, and a fireplace. In the morning, guests can enjoy a Continental breakfast while innkeeper Mike Tease cranks up classical music on a state-of-the-art player piano. Three nights a week, the Bullis House shows movies (with popcorn) in the main house, bringing hostelers from Germany, England, Australia, and other nations into contact with the B&Bers.

🏠 *2 double rooms with baths, 5 doubles share 4 baths. Air-conditioning in all rooms, cable TV in some rooms, outdoor pool, picnic grounds. $59–$89, Continental breakfast. AE, D, MC, V. Smoking in guest rooms only, no pets, 2-night minimum on weekends.*

Carrington's Bluff

1900 David St., Austin 78705, tel. 512/479-0638 or 800/871-8908, fax 512/476-4769

Look out from the 35-foot front porch of Carrington's Bluff, where the woodsy yard takes a sharp drop to meet rippling Shoal Creek, and it's not difficult to imagine what it was like to live on this estate 115 years ago. Then, this Texas farmhouse was on the edge of no-man's-land—the line between the settlement of Austin and Indian country. There's still the hint of wilderness about this place, though it is only seven blocks from the University of Texas and nine from the state capitol.

The decor here is country English, complete with Laura Ashley prints in the guest rooms. Innkeeper Lisa and Ed Mugford carry out the English atmosphere with tea and coffee service, including the inn's own grind.

Many guests spend the afternoons relaxing on the large porch that overlooks a 500-year-old oak tree. Guests can arrange in-room massages, bicycle rentals, or golf or tennis nearby. Downtown Austin, with attractions ranging from the State Capitol to the Sixth Street entertainment district, is just a few minutes from the country atmosphere of Carrington's Bluff.

▥ *8 double rooms with baths. Air-conditioning, cable TV and phones in all rooms, Caswell-Massey toiletries. $80–$110, full breakfast, tea. AE, D, DC, MC, V. No smoking indoors.*

The Comfort Common

717 High St., Box 539, Comfort 78013, tel. 830/995-3030, fax 830/995-3455

They don't tear down many buildings in Comfort. Since the late-19th century, when the business district was erected, only the livery stable has been razed, making the downtown area of this Hill Country city the best preserved in the state. At the heart of the business district is the Comfort Common, called the Ingenhuett-Faust Hotel when it was built in 1880.

The two-story limestone structure, its wide porch and balcony stretching across the building and fronted by wood posts, was designed as an eight-room facility; eight more rooms were added before the turn of the century. The hotel had been in decline for several decades when it was purchased in 1985 by Bob and Diane Potter, who used the property as an antiques shop. Current owners and hosts, Jim Lord and Bobby Dent, converted the complex to a B&B and oversee the 13 antiques dealers on the premises, maintaining the place with enthusiasm. Each of the guest rooms, along with the small cottages behind the hotel, is decorated with authentic antiques, in themes ranging from handcrafted Early American to lacy Victorian to cowboy kitsch.

▥ *5 double rooms with baths, 2 suites, 2 cottages. Air-conditioning, TVs and fireplaces in some rooms. $65–$110, full breakfast. AE, D, MC, V. No smoking, no pets, no children, 2-night minimum on holiday and special-event weekends.*

Crystal River Inn

326 W. Hopkins St., San Marcos 78666, tel. 512/396-3739, fax 512/353-3248

Crystal River Inn hosts Mike and Cathy Dillon might have been content to rely on their proximity to the rivers San Marcos, Blanco, and Guadalupe to attract visitors to San Marcos, a small city 51 miles north of San Antonio. But the Dillons are more creative than that: They offer guests murder mystery weekends, "ladies' escape" weekends, gourmet picnics, river excursions, and other diversions to make a visit to their inn a special experience.

Mike, a manager of high-rise office buildings in Houston, and Cathy, a nurse, were shopping for a peaceful place to live when they fell in love with this 1883 mansion. It was built by Judge William Wood, a rancher, banker, and cofounder of San Marcos's Southwest Texas State University, and mixes Greek columns with Victorian gables and a double-decker porch. In order to justify its purchase and costly renovation, they decided to turn it into a B&B. That was in 1984; more than a decade later, the Dillons' business includes two other buildings: the Young House, a restored 1885 Victorian home across the street, and the Rock Cottage, also a former residence.

The houses are decorated, as the Dillons put it, "with furniture we like"; the emphasis is not on antiques but on casual elegance. The guest rooms—each named for a Texas river—have themes that range from Victorian to Southwestern. The four suites are luxurious: The Blanco, which overlooks the main house's second-floor veranda, has 12-foot ceilings and unusual fabric-upholstered walls; the San Marcos, in the Rock Cottage, features a marble garden tub with 24-carat gold fixtures, fireplace, and skylight.

As part of the popular murder mystery weekend, where the foul deed that costumed guests work to unearth is based on people and events in San Marcos history, guests enjoy a welcoming party and dessert buffet on Friday and a sunset cruise at Aquarena Springs and a multi-course dinner on Saturday. During the summer, a tubing trip down the San Marcos River is also included. Year-round, the owners put together packages including treats as diverse as massages, European facials, and carriage rides.

7 double rooms with baths, 4 2-bedroom suites. Air-conditioning in all rooms, TV in most rooms, mini-refrigerator and microwave in cottage. $70–$140, full breakfast. AE, D, DC, MC, V. No smoking, no pets, 2-day minimum most weekends.

Das Kleine Nest

231 W. Main St., Fredericksburg 78624, tel. 830/997–5612, fax 830/997–8282

In a fitting testament to this "Little Nest's" charm as a honeymoon retreat, owners Pat and Toni Keating constructed a chapel on the premises. But there's a certain irony to this act: The limestone cottage was built in 1875 by a bachelor for his betrothed—just before their nuptials were called off.

As the German name suggests, Das Kleine Nest is a tiny place, a two-room cabin with a spiral staircase that leads to a bedroom loft. The loft has barely enough room for the queen-size bed it supports; below, the doll-house-size kitchen spills into the living room. But for those who don't mind their surroundings cozy—or who prefer them that way—this snugly fits the bill. The house mixes antiques and contemporary furnishings, including colorful Mexican-tile floors and hand-loomed rugs. An enclosed patio at the back door and a larger patio area in the yard are fine for lounging with a good book.

1 double room with bath. Air-conditioning, cable TV, phone, ceiling fans, coffeemaker, small refrigerator, stove, microwave. $68, breakfast not included. AE, D, MC, V. No pets.

Delforge Place

710 Ettie St., Fredericksburg 78624, tel. 830/997–6212 or 800/997–0462, fax 830/990–8320

One of the few traditional host homes remaining in Fredericksburg, where self-contained guest houses are the norm, Delforge Place is the lair of Betsy Delforge, the great-granddaughter of a sea captain. With help from her husband, George, and son Peter, Betsy has turned her 1898 Victorian house into a veritable walking tour of American history, with an emphasis on things nautical.

The Map Room features an original oil painting of her ancestor Captain B. Jones, sailing into the port of Hong Kong in 1860. The room's other heirlooms include a trunk that Jones took to sea and an 1854 atlas presented to him aboard his ship in Singapore. The Quebec and American rooms each have their own sitting area and are furnished with antiques from the American Revolution and Civil War eras. An exterior staircase leads to a wooden platform shaped like a ship's bow, where the Upper Deck room, with porthole windows, resembles a captain's quarters. Betsy, a retired home economist, serves a breakfast that usually includes her famous sour cream twists, along with homemade crepes and a cold fruit soup.

🏠 *3 double rooms with baths, 1 suite. Air-conditioning, cable TV and refrigerator in each room. $65–$95, full breakfast. AE, D, MC, V. No smoking, no pets.*

Fredericksburg Bed and Brew

245 E. Main St., Fredericksburg 78624, tel. 830/997–1646, fax 830/997–8026

The sign says ROOMS FOR RENT UPSTAIRS, and downstairs are a restaurant, beer garden, and meeting hall. The second "B" of this B&B stands for beer, not breakfast: Included in the room rate is a sampler of the Fredericksburg Brewing Co.'s four current beers. The food there is also quite good.

A stay here fits in well with a weekend shopping trip—why not try out the furniture you're considering buying? Each room is done by a different store, with themes ranging from kinky (Red Stallion) to Mexican (El Nicho) to rustic (Happy Trails), and everything is for sale. Some guests switch rooms nightly. Because the B&B is right on Main Street, it's convenient for shopping and local sightseeing.

🏠 *12 rooms with baths. Air-conditioning in all rooms. $79–$89, beer sampler.*

MC, V. *No smoking, no pets, no children.*

The Herb Haus

Drawer 927, 402 Whitney St., Fredericksburg 78624, tel. 830/997–8615 or 800/259–4372, fax 830/997–5069

For lovers of herbs, gardening, or just originality, the Herb Haus is one of the more unusual B&B experiences in Texas. The 1940s frame guest house is on the Fredericksburg Herb Farm, a 4-acre plot of organic herb and flower gardens just six blocks off Main Street. Guests can sample the farm's homemade herb teas and breads in the tearoom. In the chemist's shop, owners William and Sylvia Varney sell items from their national mail-order business, including oils, potpourris, and fragrances.

A botanical theme fittingly dominates the two-bedroom guest house, once the home of the town's midwife. Dried flowers and herbs hang from the ceiling; one of the bed frames is fashioned out of grapevines. Herbal toiletries are provided in the bath, and the breakfast of choice is "Continental herbal cuisine," including herb breads, spiced butter, fresh fruit, and even juice garnished with edible flowers. The gardens that surround the guest house are creatively landscaped, and the Varneys' faith is echoed in flowers arranged to resemble various Christian symbols.

🏠 *1 2-bedroom guest house. Air-conditioning, cable TV, phone, ceiling fans, kitchen. $105, Continental breakfast. AE, D, DC, MC, V. No smoking, no pets, no children.*

Inn on the Creek

Box 858, Salado 76571, tel. 254/947–5554, fax 254/947–9198

Suzi Epps is a picky one. Ask her about most any bed-and-breakfast in Texas and she's been there—and found it lacking. That kind of perfectionism, along with Epps's experience as a professional architect, has helped turn the Inn on the Creek into a reason to stop in Salado, a little town 45 miles north of Austin known mostly for its well-preserved 19th-century Main Street.

Inn on the Creek is a collection of five houses, three of which were salvaged from condemnation and brought to a shady spot on Salado Creek from elsewhere in Texas; all were painstakingly restored by Suzi, along with her parents, Bob and Sue Whistler, and her husband, Lynn. The oldest of the houses, an 1892 woodframe Victorian imported from Cameron, is connected to another house by a covered wooden walkway to form the inn's main complex. The second building, a two-story, wood frame, includes a large dining room that on weekends opens for dinner as a full-service restaurant. The breakfasts served here tend toward the exotic, ranging from German puff pancakes to Italian frittatas.

The furnishings throughout the main complex are anything but exotic; they run toward the simpler, more understated pieces of the Victorian age. The rooms exude a quiet elegance, each furnished with Victorian antiques, family photographs, and antique dresser sets. White wrought iron and wicker fill the Tyler Room. In the Rose Room, a Victorian walnut bed is covered with a collection of antique pillowcases. The most impressive is the spacious, third-floor McKie Room, which has a king-size bed as well as a library nook with a daybed that overlooks the creek—the perfect spot for a lazy weekend afternoon.

Directly across the street is the Holland House, built circa 1880, and up the block the Reue House, a Civil War–era farmhouse with four guest rooms. Its highlight is the Kiowa Room, which has a bed made from a 300-year-old loom. Sally's Cottage, a tiny one-bedroom hideaway with an adjoining living room, rounds out the inn's facilities.

All the guest rooms at Inn on the Creek have private baths—some with a pair of vintage bloomers hanging from the wall. Evenings at the inn, and throughout Salado, are quiet. Most guests just sit on the back porch and listen to the cicadas sing on a warm summer evening.

🛏 *18 double rooms with baths, 2 cottage suites. Limited restaurant, air-conditioning, cable TV, phone, small refrigerators in some rooms, golf privileges. $70–$125, full breakfast. MC, V. No smoking, no pets.*

The Nagel House

231 W. Main St., Fredericksburg 78624, tel. 830/997–5612, fax 830/997–8282

In 1907 this two-story house was built by 14 men in 11 days. When its current owners, retired minister Charlie Tatum and his wife, Joan, restored the deteriorating homestead in 1986, the process was considerably more time-consuming. The effort paid off, however; the Nagel House is one of the prettier Victorian guest homes in Fredericksburg.

Smooth pastels and lace curtains lend a soft touch to the period light fixtures and antiques in each room. The downstairs guest room is formal and elegant; its bathroom includes an etched-glass window, claw-foot tub, and pedestal sink. The two upstairs bedrooms have an English country flavor.

The kitchen is stocked with food for guests to prepare, including sausage rolls, ham, and muffins. Depending on your mood, breakfast can be a dressy affair in the dining room, complete with fine china and crystal, or a casual nosh in the breakfast area, with its country decor and brightly colored stoneware.

🛏 *1 3-bedroom cottage. Air-conditioning, cable TV, phone, microwave, refrigerator, and stove. $85, Continental breakfast. AE, D, MC, V. No smoking, no pets.*

The Ogé House on the Riverwalk

209 Washington St., San Antonio 78204, tel. 210/223-2353 or 800/242-2770, fax 210/226-5812

A classic plantation house built during the Greek Revival craze that spread across the South in the years before the Civil War, the Ogé (pronounced OH-jhay) House is the crowning glory of San Antonio's historic King William neighborhood. Owners Patrick and Sharrie Magatagan have created an understated tribute to the antebellum South, complete with a veranda from which one can look out over the pecan-shaded estate. But it has all the modern amenities: From the registration desk to the in-room premium cable TV and the state-of-the art telephone system, their inn has the ambience of a luxury hotel.

Built in 1857 by pioneer Texas ranger and cattle rancher Louis Ogé, the three-story manse sits on 1.5 acres of landscaped lawns and gardens overlooking the Paseo del Rio. It had been a boardinghouse before the Magatagans purchased it in 1991 and set out to transform it into San Antonio's brightest B&B. Kitchenettes were turned into lovely vanities; walls were painted in creamy whites; bathrooms were overhauled; and pine floors were polished and draped with fine Oriental rugs.

Patrick, who had lived with San Antonio native Sharrie in Connecticut for eight years before returning to the Alamo City, fell in love with antiques while living in the northeast, and—ironically, in this antebellum Southern mansion—purchased many of the furnishings for the inn there. Even one of the home's tributes to things Texan—a bullhorn sofa in an upstairs lounging area—was purchased "up nawth." Texas-theme furnishings are also found in the Bluebonnet Room, complete with a rolling-pin bed and a West Texas judge's desk. Otherwise, early-American Victorian furniture dominates the guest rooms and suites.

The house's second floor is the main floor, with an entryway, sitting room, library, kitchen, dining room, and two guest rooms. The first floor is an English basement, which houses a guest room and suite as well as the Magatagans' living quarters. The three third-floor suites are the most impressive: Each has access to the wide veranda or, in one case, a small private balcony.

Sharrie prepares the Continental breakfast, which may consist of scones, croissants, sweet rolls, popovers, and hot and cold cereals. It's served in the formal dining room or on the front veranda.

🏠 *5 double rooms with baths, 4 suites. Air-conditioning, cable TV, telephone, refrigerators, fireplace in 2 rooms and in all suites. $135, suites $165-$195, full breakfast. AE, D, DC, MC, V. No smoking indoors, no pets, no children, 2-night minimum on weekends, 3-night minimum on holidays.*

Page House

1000 Leander Rd., Georgetown 78628, tel. 512/863-8979 or 800/828-7700

The largest bed-and-breakfast in Georgetown is the Page House, conveniently located on Interstate 35. This grand Queen Anne style home dates back to 1903 when it was owned by J. M. Page, a former gold prospector, rancher, and postmaster.

Eventually the grand three-story structure became the property of the Horace M. Weir family. Under their ownership, the house and grounds had their most unique role: home of "Cowboy Polo." Stables became a training center for the cutting horses used as polo ponies in a game identical to the original—but with the addition of cowboy regalia.

Today the training barn has been converted to a meeting center, and the former carriage house now contains guest accommodations. Two rooms offer visitors privacy and can be joined for family groups. The largest room includes a king and a twin bed, television, antique dining table, and antique treadle sewing machine, with some feminine touches in an otherwise rustic, wood paneled room. For more traditional accommodations, four rooms on the second floor of the Page House are for those looking for antique furnishings and historic elegance.

🏠 *6 doubles with baths. Air-conditioning, TV in some rooms. $75–$95, full breakfast weekends, Continental breakfast weekdays. AE, D, DC, MC, V. No smoking, no pets, 2-night minimum on holidays.*

Riverwalk Inn

329 Old Guilbeau, San Antonio 78204, tel. 210/212–8300 or 800/254–4440, fax 210/229–9422

For many travelers, mention of the Paseo del Rio or River Walk brings to mind images of shops, festive sidewalk cafés, and high-rise hotels. Just minutes from this bustling stretch of tourist activity, however, a quieter part of the River Walk winds through the King William Historic District and past the Riverwalk Inn. Composed of five log cabins brought in from Tennessee, these lodgings recall the atmosphere of San Antonio's earliest days when Tennessee volunteers Davy Crockett and Jim Bowie fought at the nearby Alamo.

Each of the guest rooms is decorated with country antique furnishings, from woven rugs to patchwork quilts. The rustic spirit continues with a fireplace in every room that casts long shadows across the square hewn beams. For many guests, however, the country mood is best enjoyed out on the long porch that connects these log buildings. Lined with rocking chairs, the porch offers a view of one of the quieter sections of the River Walk and in the evenings visitors often stroll up to enjoy a few hours of festive dining and evening entertainment before returning to this country getaway.

🏠 *11 doubles. Air-conditioning, cable TV and phones. $99–$155, full breakfast. AE, D, MC, V. Smoking outdoors only, no pets.*

Schmidt Barn

231 W. Main St., Fredericksburg 78624, tel. 830/997–5612, fax 830/997–8282

Charles and Loretta Schmidt, both German speakers who trace their families to Fredericksburg's founders, can claim much of the credit for the transformation of their sleepy town into Texas's B&B capital. After they restored an 1860s farmhouse as their own residence, they turned their attention to the roofless remains of a century-old barn in the backyard. By 1983, the Schmidts had transformed it into one of the city's first guest houses and launched the Gastehaus Schmidt Reservation Service, which now books the great majority of the city's more than 90 such establishments.

The downstairs living area of the tastefully furnished barn features a comfortable sleeper sofa and a rustic kitchen and bath, both accented with blue-and-white terrazzo tile; a sunken tile tub is the bathroom's highlight. The bedroom is in an upstairs loft. The Schmidts are happy to furnish firewood for the antique wood-burning stove; they also stock the house's refrigerator with a German-style breakfast of meats, cheese, and pastries.

🏠 *1 1-bedroom guest house (sleeps 4). Air-conditioning, phone, ceiling fan, CD and tape player, microwave, coffeemaker. $85, Continental breakfast. AE, D, MC, V.*

Settlers Crossing

Settlers Crossing Rd., Rte. 1, Box 315, Fredericksburg 78624, tel. 830/997–2722 or 800/874–1020, fax 830/997–3372

Ever wondered what it was like for German settlers on the American frontier in the 19th century? You and your clan can spend the weekend in your own "Little Haus on the Prairie" at Settlers Crossing, a 35-acre tract located in the rolling countryside between Luckenbach and Fredericksburg. Dotted by log cabins, mesquite trees, and friendly farm animals, this is easily the best family-oriented B&B in the Hill Country.

Of course, the German settlers didn't have access to a whirlpool bath—a feature of the luxurious Von Heinrich Home, one of four guest houses on the estate of hosts David and Judy Bland. The structures are close enough to one another to be convenient for groups or family reunions, but far enough apart to allow for private getaways.

The Pioneer Homestead, a stone-and-log cabin original to the property, was constructed in the 1850s by the Kusenberger family, German immigrants who were among Fredericksburg's first settlers. The modern appliances in the full kitchen of the two-bedroom house are skillfully tucked away to preserve a feeling of authenticity. The most striking feature is a robin's-egg-blue stenciled ceiling, painted when the house was built. Also original to the grounds, the Baag Farm House was built in the 1920s as a wedding gift for a Kusenberger descendant. The simple, blue wood-frame house has a wood-burning stove and antique dining room table that seats eight.

Outside the Indiana House, you may well encounter bleating sheep, grazing goats, and braying donkeys, who like to approach the split-rail fence surrounding the house. The log cabin was built in the Hoosier state in 1849 and transported to Settlers Common by the Blands. The mood of the living room is set by an antique camelback sofa; the high-ceiling master bedroom features a queen-size, four-poster bed with acorn finials. The hosts live in a nearby three-story house imported from Kentucky.

But the most remarkable guest home on the property is the Von Heinrich Home, a two-story German fachwerk cottage built in Pennsylvania in 1787. Inside is an outstanding collection of 19th-century folk art, including an antique horse sculpture and an old hooked rug over the fireplace.

🏠 *5 2-bedroom guest houses, 1 3-bedroom guest house, 1 1-bedroom guest house. Air-conditioning, TV, VCR, phones, fireplaces or wood-burning stoves in all houses, full kitchen in 5 homes, whirlpool baths in 4 homes. $95–$135, Continental breakfast. AE, D, MC, V. No smoking.*

Stage Stop Ranch

Stage Stop Ranch, 100 Old Mail Route Road, Fischer 78623, tel. 830/935-4455 or 800/782-4378, fax 830/935-4445

From Wimberley to Blanco stretches a ridge of hills called the Devil's Backbone—an area often thought of as one of the most scenic in Texas. Right in the heart of this region is the Stage Stop Ranch, a combination B&B inn and guest ranch that's right on a former stagecoach trail.

"People get here and are uptight and by the next day they're relaxed and smiling and really seem to find themselves," explains Lee Caffey. Lee and husband Troy own and operate the Stage Stop Ranch together, coming to the B&B business after living all around the world as a navy family.

Many guests here relax with horseback rides on trails that follow parts of the old stage route, winding among tall oaks and alongside rock walls that predate the Civil War. Riding uses nearly every muscle in the body," says Lee, who also recognizes the sport's psychological benefits. "Someone once said there's something about the outside of a horse that's good for the inside of man. It's very true." For after those long rides—or those not interested in riding—there are hot tubs for relaxing.

Days at Stage Stop begin with a full breakfast prepared by Lee in the country kitchen. A favorite dish is Pecan Praline French Toast. Morning and afternoon activities are as active or leisurely as guests choose, ranging from quiet strolls along the country road to horseshoe pitching to horseback riding. Wranglers are available to teach novices the basics so that anyone can participate in a ride along the trails that snake along the expansive property. For other visitors, a day's fun might include fishing for rainbow trout below the dam of nearby Canyon Lake or shopping for antiques in the community of Wimberley.

After a day of ranch fun, evenings at Stage Stop often feature a Western theme as well. Live music, chuck-wagon suppers, campfire dinners and sing-alongs, hay rides, and other activities recall the cowboy heritage of this western ranch.

🏠 *3 double rooms with bath, 13 cabins, 1 cottage. Air-conditioning in all rooms, mini-refrigerators in some rooms, 10 private hot tubs, bicycles for guest use, horseback riding, Western outdoor activities. $85–$225, full breakfast. AE, D, MC, V. Smoking outdoors only, no pets, minimum 2-night stay during holidays.*

Woodburn House

4401 Ave. D, Austin 78751, tel. 512/458–4335, fax 512/458–4339

Herb and Sandra Dickson run the only B&B in Hyde Park, Austin's oldest residential suburb. About a mile north of downtown, the turn-of-the-century neighborhood hosts a collection of Victorian homes, Texas frame farmhouses, and Craftsman-style bungalows. Sandra can provide a brochure detailing a walking tour of this historic area, pointing out the Elisabet Ney Museum and moonlight towers that once illuminated the neighborhood.

Built in 1909, the Woodburn House is named for former owner Bettie Hamilton Woodburn, the daughter of a provisional governor of Texas. Its rooms are simply and functionally decorated, with rocking chairs and firm mattresses. The two rooms upstairs have access to a wide balcony, from which you can watch squirrels darting up the pecan and elm trees. This is the kind of place where you can feel comfortable lounging on the living room couch, shoes off, watching a ball game on TV. Breakfast may include eggs, waffles, or any number of treats; Herb boasts that a guest can stay 10 days and never be served the same thing twice.

🏠 *4 double rooms with baths. Desks, phones in all rooms, TV and VCR in living room, exchange library. $68–$95, full breakfast. AE, MC, V. Smoking on porches only, no pets, no children under 10.*

A Yellow Rose

229 Madison St., San Antonio 78204, tel. 210/229–9903 or 800/950–9903

Nestled in the King William Historic District, A Yellow Rose is an 1878 Texas Victorian structure. After a major renovation in 1982, A Yellow Rose is a home that's dressy but not stuffy, filled with Victorian antiques.

Days begin at the bed-and-breakfast with a full breakfast served at 9 AM in the elegant dining room. The five guest rooms welcome guests with period furnishings accompanied by modern amenities. The Magnolia Room, highlighted by a four-poster bed, has a separate entrance and a porch overlooking the garden, a good choice for those looking for privacy. The Bluebonnet Room, with its cheery blue and white decor and turn-of-the-century antiques, also offers a porch for afternoon relaxation. The Green Sage Room and Victorian Rose Room each have private baths, but these are located a few steps away from the guest room (terry robes are provided).

Guests have use of a parlor, living room, and dining room furnished with period antiques and also wide porches where they can spend the evenings unwinding after a day downtown.

▦ *5 double rooms with baths. Cable TV in all rooms, Caswell-Massey products in baths, trolley stop 1 block away. $75–$110, full breakfast. AE, D, MC, V. Smoking on porches only, no pets, no children under 9, 2-night minimum on weekends.*

Ziller House

800 Edgecliff Terr., Austin 78704, tel. 512/462–0100 or 800/949–5446, fax 512/462–9166

The premier host home in Texas's capital city is the perfect antidote for those weary of formal, frilly Victorian B&Bs. Ziller House offers a unique brand of contemporary sophistication that has drawn such famed visitors as Dennis Quaid, Meg Ryan, and Linda Ellerbee. In February 1997 the Ziller House underwent a renovation with the purchase of the property by Royce Wilson—the carriage house was completely redone and a pool and hot tub were added in addition to numerous other changes. A gated, secluded estate on the cliff above the south bank of Town Lake, the 1938 Italian-style mansion is at the very center of Austin, a stone's skip from the Texas capitol.

The four guest rooms, three of which are upstairs, have their own personalities. The Library Room, for example, is lined with bookshelves and offers a pretty view of the lake. The balcony that gives the Balcony Room its name is surrounded on all sides by live oaks; the room's bathroom, with its dynamic black-and-saffron-yellow color scheme, is also striking. The Sun Suite has a queen-size bed and a separate sitting area with TV and carved pine daybed. Fifty feet from the main house, a guest cottage includes a private patio and porch.

There are plenty of places to relax on the grounds, from the stone patio, to the cliffside gazebo, to the spa and the swimming pool. The self-contained qualities of the guest rooms, which feature a small refrigerator tucked in the service cabinet, a microwave oven, and a cordless cellular phone especially appeals to business travelers.

▦ *3 double rooms with baths, 1 suite, 1 cottage. Air-conditioning, cable TV in each room, CD player in living room, hot tub, swimming pool. $120–$200, full breakfast. AE, MC, V. No smoking indoors, no pets, no children.*

West Texas

When Francisco Coronado and his explorers arrived in West Texas more than 400 years ago, they found the grass high and the terrain devoid of landmarks. Resembling Hansel and Gretel on horseback, the Spaniards drove stakes in the soil to blaze a path across the region they called Llano Estacado, or staked plain.

Today, interstates carve the vast, high plains of West Texas into manageable chunks and connect the widely scattered cities. This is the Texas that many picture with a mention of "the Lone Star State," a land of leathery-faced cowboys, rolling tumbleweeds, lonesome windmills, and pumping oil derricks. Roads stretch straight to the horizon, and distances are measured not in miles but in hours. Locals consider an 80-mile haul "right around the corner."

Country singer Mac Davis once sang "happiness is Lubbock, Texas, in my rearview mirror," but for many this plains community is an oasis. With more than 20,000 students at Texas Tech University, the city has many cultural events. Lubbock is also the heart of Texas's burgeoning wine business, and its award-winning operations recall the tradition of the staked plain, albeit for grapevines these days.

About 120 miles north, Amarillo is the cultural and commercial capital of the Texas Panhandle. From a humble beginning as a staging area for the Fort Worth and Denver City Railroad in the 1880s, the city became a center for cattle ranching, wheat and cotton farming, and oil production. Today, Amarillo is a city of 170,000, home of Amarillo College, Amarillo Symphony Orchestra, and the Lone Star Ballet.

Amarillo is also the gateway to the nation's second-largest canyon: Palo Duro. Here, majestic cliffs create a backdrop for the Lone Star State's most popular outdoor drama, the summer production of TEXAS

The few B&B establishments in West Texas operate as pioneers, functioning without centralized reservation services. Most do not share the opulent atmosphere found in the long-running B&B capitals of East and Central Texas, but they do provide plenty of West Texas hospitality and a chance to look at the most rugged portion of the Lone Star State.

Places to Go, Sights to See

Antiques. Route 66, one of the nation's most famous highways, slices through downtown Amarillo as Sixth Street. This historic strip is lined with more than 200 antiques and specialty shops. South of Lubbock, Post is home to Old Mill Trade Days, an antiques show and flea market, on the Friday, Saturday, and Sunday before the first Monday of each month. The sale draws as many as 500 vendors.

Cadillac Ranch. What do you get when you cross 10 old Cadillacs, one eccentric Texan, and a large pasture? The Cadillac Ranch—a collection of junkers representing the golden age of Route 66—west of Amarillo. Buried nose down at the same angle as Cheops's pyramid, the cars are dotted with graffiti and are likely to be surrounded by grazing cattle.

Palo Duro Canyon State Park. Truly a Texas-size attraction, this natural wonder stretches 120 miles and drops 1,200 feet, making it the nation's second-largest canyon. Visitors to *Palo Duro State Park* (tel. 806/488–2227) can tackle the park on foot along miles of hiking trails or on horseback. Summer guests can enjoy *TEXAS* (tel. 806/655–2181), an outdoor production that brings to life the struggles of the area's pioneers and native residents. The drama, featuring everything from blizzards to sandstorms, resonates within the canyon walls.

Wineries. The rich soil and temperate weather of this region has drawn wineries and international acclaim to Lubbock. *Llano Estacado* (tel. 806/745–2258) is probably the most celebrated. *CapRock Winery* (tel. 806/863–2704), housed in a European-style chalet, is the state's second largest. Both offer tours and tastings.

Restaurants

In Lubbock, the Warehouse District is home to many of the city's best eateries and nightspots. **Stubb's Bar-B-Q** (tel. 806/747–4777) serves up brisket and ribs with live music on the side. Nearby, the **Depot Bar** (tel. 806/747–1646) has a diverse menu ranging from chicken-fried steak to chili relleno to fillet of sole béarnaise.

The **Big Texan Steak House** (tel. 806/372–6000) is Amarillo's most famous restaurant and also a tourist attraction—there's a free 72-ounce steak for anyone who can eat it in one hour. Along with good ol' Texas beef, there are more exotic dishes such as rattlesnake and buffalo.

Tourist Information

Amarillo Convention and Visitors Council (1000 Polk St., Amarillo 79101, tel. 806/374–1497 or 800/692–1338). **Lubbock Convention and Visitors Bureau** (Box 561, Lubbock 79408, tel. 806/747–5232 or 800/692–4035). **Post Chamber of Commerce** (104 S. Broadway, Post 79356, tel. 806/495–3461).

Broadway Manor

*1811 Broadway, Lubbock 79401, tel. 806/
749–4707 or 888/749–4707*

Just down the street from Texas Tech
University, the Broadway Manor exudes
the style of an aged professor—dignified, traditional, and a wee bit world-
weary.

Built in 1923 by a prominent Lubbock
banker, this home was once a fraternity
house. With a complete restoration, it
was converted to a B&B and is also a
popular site for social functions and business meetings because of a large game
room and its proximity to campus. There
are several common areas: a formal living room with a gas fireplace and Oriental rug; a large room with TV and VCR;
and a burgundy-wall dining room sprinkled with tables where the resident manager serves full breakfast and fresh juice.

Each guest room features antique furnishings, such as the Country Charm
Room, filled with patchwork quilts that
carry out the country theme. Most
unique is the Mountain Lodge, the base-
ment-turned-guest quarters, which has
a separate outdoor entrance. Caramel-
colored pine walls, antlers above a rock
fireplace, antique sewing tables, and a
buffalo-plaid comforter give the room a
woodsy feel.

▦ *2 double rooms with baths, 3 doubles
share bath. Air-conditioning, phone
hookups in rooms, cable TV with VCR
in public room. $65–$95, full breakfast.
AE, MC, V. No smoking, no pets.*

Harrison House

*1710 S. Harrison St., Amarillo 79102,
tel. 806/374–1710*

Two of Amarillo's homes share more
than just their roles as bed-and-breakfasts: They were built at the same address. In the 1920s, Parkview House (*see
below*) was located on South Harrison
Street. After it was hauled to Jefferson
Street, today's Harrison House rose on
the lot.

Now owned by David and Michele Hors-
ley, a writer and attorney, respectively,
this classical-revival home has one guest
room downstairs. The Horsleys had enjoyed B&Bs on their travels, and in 1994
their home became Amarillo's newest
accommodation.

Visitors enjoy a sunny bedroom with antique furnishings and a large bathroom.
Guests also have full use of the downstairs—they can converse with David
while he prepares his special whole-
wheat pancakes in the country kitchen,
watch a movie with the family's two children in the TV room, or play the piano
in one of two living areas.

David has a special interest in old
homes, and he's happy to point out the
features of his, from its coved ceilings to
the montage of items he recovered from
the home's duct work. Mounted and displayed in the kitchen, the collection includes everything from Victrola needles
to hair pins to a brass cartridge found in
the attic, which the original owners used
as a shooting gallery on rainy days.

▦ *1 double room with bath. Air-
conditioning, TV with VCR in TV room,
use of full kitchen. $65, full breakfast.
MC, V. Smoking on porches only; pets
outside, in garage, or in yard only.*

Hotel Garza Historic Inn and Conference Center

*302 E. Main St., Post 79356, tel. 806/495–
3962*

Innkeepers Janice and Jim Plummer are
a busy pair. They left their respective
jobs as legal secretary and radio executive in Lubbock to be self employed and
work together. The result is a completely
restored historic property that is the
only B&B in town.

Located 45 miles southwest of Lubbock,
Post was founded as a utopian commu-

nity by Charles Post, of Post Toasties fame. The cereal king had visions of a city where saloons were prohibited and residents were required to have three references before moving to town. The Hotel Garza, built in 1915 (after Post's death), had lesser ambitions. Post's version of a red-light district, the hotel was the kind of place that locals crossed the street to avoid.

But in 1992 the Plummers saw that the hotel, vacant beneath a heavy coat of West Texas dust, had potential. Post had recently undergone transformation as a federally designated "Main Street City," and the Plummers began their own renovation. Room by room, they refinished floors, repainted, and added baths to produce a two-story inn with still more rooms planned. Today's B&B combines elegant dining with clean, simple accommodations that reflect the mood of an earlier time.

The expansive lobby, with over a dozen antique tables and a corner sitting area, greets guests. Its wood floors were protected through the years by layers of linoleum and now gleam with a new finish. Above, the original pressed-tin ceiling has fresh white paint. Ceiling fans hum on warm afternoons, and chandeliers illuminate the room.

Like a Western hotel in the area's earliest days, its guest rooms are off long hallways, now lined with antique benches. In the small, spartan rooms, many of the furnishings are original to the hotel. Most have an iron bed, antique dressers, and area rugs. Guests are free to enjoy the mezzanine-level library filled with a collection of first editions, along with popular titles, games, and a TV. Wainscoting and a stained-glass window recall the hotel's early days.

Early risers can head to the kitchen to brew a pot of coffee or wait for a plate of Janice's egg casserole, sausage, and homemade breads. On Friday and Saturday, the Plummers serve lunch to the public. On evenings when the neighboring Garza Theater hosts a production, the Hotel Garza also serves dinner.

▦ *7 double rooms with baths, 4 doubles share 2 baths, 2 suites. Limited restaurant, air-conditioning, TV in library, theater packages. $45–$95 for doubles, $35–$80 for singles, full breakfast on weekends, Continental breakfast on weekdays. AE, MC, V. No smoking, no pets.*

Parkview House

1311 S. Jefferson St., Amarillo 79101, tel. 806/373-9464

A collector's dream, or a minimalist's nightmare, the Parkview House is packed to the rafters with items Carol and Nabil Dia have gathered from antiques shops and garage sales. Filling display cases, covering kitchen walls, and spilling into the guest rooms, Carol's collectibles are conversation starters for visitors, many of whom come to shop in Amarillo's famed antiques shopping area.

But more than the colonial hats or cutwork glass, it's the personalities of the owners that bring guests to this B&B. Carol, from upstate New York, and Nabil, from Jordan, bring to their establishment a love of after-dinner conversation. Together, they personify "Texas-friendly." Their home, too, has a history of welcoming guests: In the 1920s it operated as Amarillo's Waldorf Hotel, and in the next decade it served as a railroad hotel.

Room styles vary from colonial to country, but romantics should request the Victorian Rose Suite, with its own sitting area and reading niche with a fur rug. The Kindernook has a sleigh bed tucked beneath the eaves and is filled with memories of childhood: toys, books, and some child-size furniture.

▦ *3 double rooms with baths, 2 doubles share bath, 1 cottage with bath. Air-conditioning, cable TV in living room and kitchen, phone hookups in rooms, bicycles, hot tub. $65–$105, Continental breakfast. AE, MC, V. No smoking, no pets.*

Utah

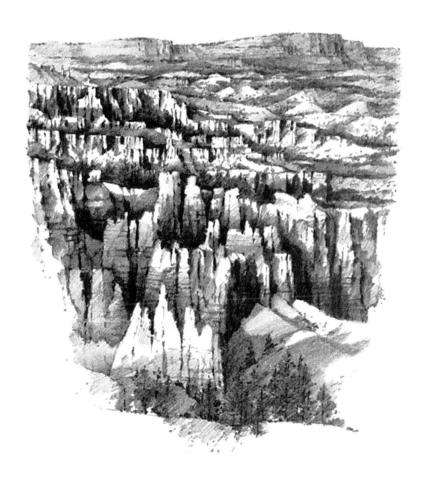

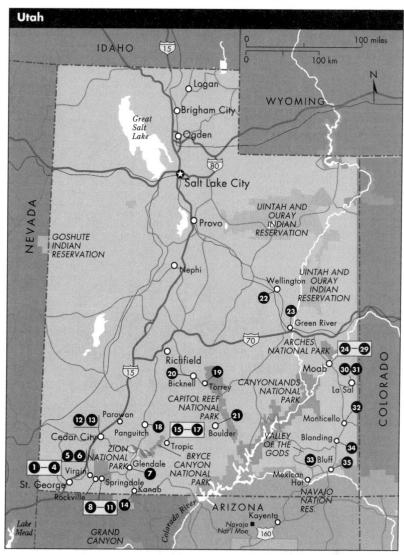

Utah

An Olde Penny Farthing Inn, **2**

Bankurz Hatt, **23**

The Bard's Inn, **13**

Blue Heron Bed and Breakfast, **29**

Boulder Mountain Lodge, **21**

Bryce Point Bed and Breakfast, **15**

Castle Valley Inn, **24**

Desert Rose Inn, **35**

Dream Keeper Bed and Breakfast, **25**

Eagle's Nest Bed & Breakfast, **7**

Entrada Ranch, **26**

Fox's Bryce Trails Bed and Breakfast, **16**

Francisco's, **17**

Grayson Country Inn, **34**

Greene Gate Village, **1**

Grist Mill Inn, **32**

Harvest House, **8**

La Sal Mountain Guest Ranch, **30**

Lodge at Red River Ranch, **20**

Mt. Peale Bed-and-Breakfast, **31**

Nine Gables Inn, **14**

Nine Mile Ranch Bunk and Breakfast, **22**

Novel House Inn, **9**

O'Toole's Under the Eaves Bed & Breakfast, **10**

Pack Creek Ranch, **28**

Paxman's Summer House, **12**

Quicksand and Cactus Bed & Breakfast, **3**

Red Rock Inn, **11**

Rogers House B&B, **5**

Seven Wives Inn, **4**

SkyRidge Bed and Breakfast, **19**

Snow Family Guest Ranch, **6**

Sunflower Hill, **27**

Valley of the Gods Bed and Breakfast, **33**

William Prince Inn, **18**

Southwestern Utah

Seven Wives Inn

Dubbed "Color Country" by Utah boosters, the southwestern part of the state is a region of exceptional beauty, encompassing both alpine and desert climate zones at vastly differing elevations. The area has forests, lakes, and farmlands, but punctuating it all is ancient red rock that has been buffeted by wind and sand, carved by rivers, and thrust up and apart by geologic forces deep within the earth.

These days millions of travelers arrive each year from all over the world to marvel at the scenery of Zion and Bryce Canyon national parks, but the area's early Anglo settlers did not come for the views. They were Mormon pioneers in the mid-1800s who, after enduring arduous journeys across the United States, were asked by their church leaders to leave the growing towns of northern Utah and colonize the southern reaches of the territory.

All across southwestern Utah, the homes that these Mormon pioneers built, whether simple or elegant, have been preserved with an uncommon devotion. Most of the area's towns have historic districts where yards bright with carefully tended flower beds hearken back to the days when the pioneers were striving to meet the challenge issued by their leader, Brigham Young, to "make the desert blossom as a rose."

Southwestern Utah thrives for most of the year on a healthy tourist trade. Although summer remains the busiest time, each season brings a different face to the land. Spring dots the meadows and river sides with wild flowers and provides excellent hiking, biking, and golf weather before the hotter days of summer. Savvy travelers plan to visit the region before Memorial Day or in the fall when autumn leaves add extra fire to the ruddy sandstone found everywhere.

In winter, the climate of southwestern Utah remains more moderate than that of the state's northern half. However, because of the area's vast differences in elevation, snow ranges from a dusting at Zion National Park to more than 400 inches a season at Brian Head Ski Resort. There's almost always enough to ensure satisfying cross-country skiing around the rim of Bryce Canyon. The contrast of dazzling white snow set on warm-toned red rock is a sight not soon forgotten by winter visitors.

Throughout the region, bed-and-breakfast establishments range from simple homestays to elegant inns in grand pioneer homes to newer houses decorated with flair. In some small towns, where proximity to a national park or other major attraction is the area's claim to fame, homestays may be the only kind of B&B experience available. Generally speaking, B&Bs in southwestern Utah are better established and more sophisticated than those in the southeastern part of the state. Accordingly, prices are slightly higher, but often B&B room rates here are equivalent to those of area motels.

Places to Go, Sights to See

Boulder. Until the 1940s, residents of the remote town of Boulder received their mail by mule. Although Boulder remains small and quiet, its location on Scenic Route 12—which is on the edge of the new Grand Staircase–Escalante National Monument (*see below*)—has brought an end to its relative anonymity. *Anasazi*

State Park (tel. 435/335–7308) marks the site of an Anasazi village that predates AD 1200.

Bryce Canyon National Park (Rte. 12, Bryce Canyon 84717, tel. 435/834–5322). A Paiute legend has it that the formations of Bryce Canyon National Park were once exotic animals and birds who were turned to stone for angering the god Coyote. Today you can hike and horseback ride through thousands of delicate spires and pillars and mazes walled with quilted drapes of stone in variegated tones of orange, pink, and cream. A 37-mile round-trip drive takes you to several viewpoints overlooking these huge natural amphitheaters.

Capitol Reef National Park (Rte. 24, Torrey 84775, tel. 435/425–3791). Named for a formation resembling the U.S. Capitol, Capitol Reef is an inviting mixture of wild desert and stone canyons and domes carved out of the Waterpocket Fold, a 100-mile bulge and uplift of the earth's crust. The Fremont River, which flows through the park, has encouraged settlement of the area—from the ancient Fremont Native American culture to hardy Mormon pioneers. Here you can view 1,000-year-old petroglyph panels, hike through canyons and gorges, or explore the backcountry in four-wheel-drive vehicles. Verdant orchards planted in the 1800s border the campground at the settlement of Fruita, inviting grazing deer on summer evenings. A 25-mile scenic drive is also popular.

Cedar Breaks National Monument (82 N. 100 East, Cedar City 84720, tel. 435/ 586–0787) is similar to Bryce in that it, too, is a natural amphitheater filled with jutting columns of multicolored sandstone. However, Cedar Breaks is much smaller than Bryce, and its west slope location and 10,000-foot elevation have encouraged the growth of forests and grassy meadows around its rim. Hiking trails pass through ancient bristlecone pines to a variety of scenic overlooks.

Cedar City. When Mormon settlers arrived in late 1851, they named the town for its abundance of cedar trees; it turned out they were junipers, but the name stuck. Cedar City is a quiet place with wide, tree-lined streets and well-maintained homes, but from June to September, the *Utah Shakespearean Festival* (tel. 435/586–7878 or 800/752–9849) transforms this university town into an Elizabethan village; featured plays rotate nightly in two indoor theaters and an outdoor replica of Shakespeare's Globe Theater. A free Greenshow, with musicians, puppeteers, jugglers, and vendors is offered nightly as is a Renaissance Feast. About 12 miles from Cedar City on Route 14, the *Zion Overlook* has a sweeping vista and an interpretive chart detailing the formations of distant Zion National Park.

Coral Pink Sand Dunes State Park (12 mi off Hwy. 89, near Kanab, tel. 435/ 874–2408) has undulating piles of coral-color sand. Although it's popular with off-highway vehicle users, it can also be a very introspective spot with the sunshine playing up the vibrancy of the sand.

Grand Staircase–Escalante National Monument (Accessed by Hwy. 89 from Kanab and by Rte. 12 from Boulder, Escalante, and Tropic; tel. 435/826–4219) was created in September of 1996, and covers 1.7 million acres. The name was inspired by a series of geologic steps that create a staircase effect throughout the area, and also for the scenic canyons carved by the Escalante River. Most of the monument area is considered backcountry and services and facilities are scarce. However, there are several moderate hikes and many scenic vistas along the paved routes through the monument (*see* Scenic Route 12, *below*).

St. George. Named for George Albert Smith, a beloved counselor to Brigham Young, St. George was the site of the *first Mormon temple in Utah* (200 E. 400 South), built in the late 1800s; although the stately white structure is not open to visitors, the grounds and visitor center are open daily. A self-guided walking tour of the many homes and buildings of the town's *historic district* is available from the Washington County Travel and Convention Bureau (*see* Tourist Information, *below*). At the bureau you can also pick up a listing of the 14 golf courses in and around St. George, which attract enthusiasts year-round.

Scenic Route 9. Picturesque and quiet *Virgin and Rockville* lie along Rte. 9 between I-15, north of St. George, and Zion National Park. Just off Rte. 9, across an old bridge, a dirt road leads to the ghost town of *Grafton*—the setting for the famous bicycle scene in the film *Butch Cassidy and the Sundance Kid*—and its mournful desert cemetery. Rte. 9 continues east through Zion National Park, including a mile-long tunnel engineered and cut through solid rock during the 1920s.

Scenic Route 12 is known for some of southern Utah's most beautiful and varied scenery. Along its 122 miles, the road passes through the northern portions of *Bryce Canyon National Park*, across the heart of the *Grand Staircase–Escalante National Monument*, then over the mountains of the *Dixie National Forest* to the town of Torrey, near *Capitol Reef National Park*.

Shopping. The *Company Store at Ruby's Inn* (tel. 435/834–5341), a motel complex adjacent to Bryce Canyon National Park, carries a large selection of Native American pottery and jewelry in various price ranges. Across the street, a row of tiny stores with rustic facades sell a variety of souvenirs. Inside Capitol Reef National Park, the *Gifford Homestead* (tel. 435/425–3791) is a historic farmhouse and gift shop with handcrafted reproductions of utensils and other household items from the late 1800s, including everything from nutmeg graters and bootjacks, to quilts, rag dolls, and handsome wooden spoons. In Hurricane, between St. George and Zion National Park, the *Chums Store* (tel. 435/635–9836 or 800/323–3707) is the factory outlet for Hello Wear—a line of sturdy outdoor clothing designed and manufactured on site. Just outside St. George, *Zion Factory Stores* (tel. 435/674–9800 or 800/269–8687) is southern Utah's only factory outlet mall with 39 manufacturer outlets including J. Crew, Corning, and Coach Leather Goods. Springdale, the access to Zion National Park, seems to have kitsch purveyors without end. Luckily, it also has some standout shops: *Art In Nature Emporium* (tel. 435/772–3877) carries local art, jewelry, casual clothing, and a thoughtfully selected collection of books. *Zion Rock & Gem* (tel. 435/772–3436) has open-air displays of common and exotic minerals, crystals, fossils, and petrified wood. At *Red Rock Jewelry* (tel. 435/772–3836), goldsmith Karla Player creates gold and silver baubles set with a rainbow of precious and semiprecious stones. The *Worthington Gallery*, (tel. 435/772–3446) in a pioneer home built in

1871, features pottery, sculpture, and watercolor art created by more than 20 Utah and western states artists.

Skiing. *Brian Head Ski Resort* (Rte. 143, Brian Head 84719, tel. 435/677–2035), 12 miles southeast of tiny Parowan, gets at least as much snow as the more famous resorts in northern Utah. In summer, the seven chairlifts become high-speed transportation for mountain bikers, ascending to a height of 10,850 feet for the ultimate downhill ride. Low-key *Elk Meadows Resort* (Box 511, Beaver 84713, tel. 435/438–5433), 17 miles east of Beaver on Route 153, has an excellent children's ski school, making it a particular favorite with families. Cross-country enthusiasts enjoy the miles and miles of trails, both groomed and pristine, in *Cedar Canyon*, about 10 miles east of Cedar City on Route 14. *Ruby's Inn* (Box 1, Rte. 63, Bryce Canyon 84764, tel. 435/834–5341), near Bryce Canyon National Park, grooms canyon-rim trails and provides ski rentals; many ungroomed trails within Bryce Canyon are also popular.

Snow Canyon State Park (11 mi northwest of St. George, tel. 435/628–2255) is one of the most photogenic spots in southwestern Utah, its red Navajo sandstone contrasted by an overlay of harder black lava rock and soft beige sandstone layers. Several trails lead to hidden formations and secluded spots. A paved road, particularly popular with bicyclists, runs through the wide canyon to the town of Santa Clara.

Tuacahn (tel. 435/674–0012 or 800/746–9882) is a heritage arts complex near St. George and Snow Canyon State Park. Its main draw is *Utah!*, an outdoor musical drama based on the history of Utah's early explorers and residents; it's staged nightly.

Zion National Park (Rte. 9, Springdale 84767, tel. 435/772–3256). Towering monuments with awestruck names such as the Great White Throne and Angel's Landing dominate the views at Zion, where the Virgin River has carved a deep canyon whose ruddy walls are stained with carbon residue (a.k.a. "desert varnish"). This is Utah's most popular national park; each summer the 6-mile scenic drive from the mouth of Zion Canyon to the Zion Narrows Trail begins to resemble a parking lot. After exploring Zion Canyon, continue east on Route 9, which climbs high above the canyon floor and passes through a tunnel carved out of solid rock. Overlooks and trails on this side of the park are generally less crowded. The surprisingly easy Canyon Overlook Trail, just east of the tunnel, is a 1-mile round-trip route that leads to unmatched views of the Zion Canyon formations. *Zion: Treasure of the Gods*, is a 37-minute film shown hourly on a six-story high, 80-foot wide screen at the Zion Canyon Cinemax Theater at the south entrance to the park (tel. 435/772–2400).

Restaurants

Although 3.2% beer and wine coolers are widely available in grocery and convenience stores throughout southern Utah, restaurants in some smaller towns may not have liquor licenses. When in doubt, call ahead or ask your server, who is frequently able to serve (but not offer) alcohol to customers.

Dinner at **Hell's Backbone Grill** (tel. 435/335–7460) in Boulder (*see* Boulder Mountain Lodge, *below*) could start with a bed of fresh greens topped with smoked trout and one of several homemade dressings. From there, it's on to entrées like Boulderian Chicken, a boneless breast served with a chili-lime sauce, rice, and fresh vegetables. Add a slice of fresh berry pie and you have a most memorable meal. **Bryce Lodge** (tel. 435/834–5361), restored to its original 1920s rustic charm with exposed beams and massive native stone fireplaces, serves Continental cuisine. In Cedar Canyon, east of Cedar City, **Milt's Stage Stop** (tel. 435/586–9344) is *the* place for tender steaks and all the trimmings, served in a rustic Western environment. Hurricane's New Agey **New Garden Cafe** (tel. 435/635–9825) is decidedly casual; here you'll find vegetarian and ethnic specialties and the only espresso machine for miles. In St. George, **Basila's Cafe** (tel. 435/673–7671) serves both Greek and Italian entrées in a small cobalt-blue-and-white room; salads here are delicious and have lovely embellishments. **Andelin's Gable House** (tel. 435/673–6796) has a varied menu upstairs in the Garden Room, and five-course dinners downstairs in the Captain's Room. Entrées cover such fare as fish, ribs, stir-fries, brisket, and homemade chicken pot pie. Also in St. George, the **Pizza Factory** (tel. 435/628–1234) in Ancestor Square serves up pizzas and standard pastas; dessert means scoops of chocolate chip cookie dough (served baked as well).

The **Bit and Spur Saloon** (tel. 435/772–3498) in Springdale has out-of-the-ordinary Southwestern-style Mexican food in a dining room lined with the works of local artists. In good weather, tables on the wraparound patio are scented by the flower and herb gardens on the grounds. **Zion Pizza and Noodle Company** (tel. 435/772–3815) sits on Springdale's busy main street in an old church. You'll find more than cheese pizza here; try the burrito pizza with jalapeños or the Thai chicken pizza with peanuts and carrots. Six different pasta dishes are offered with fresh vegetables and several cheeses. Ruddy tile floors and crisp white walls make **Café Diablo** (tel. 435/425–3070) in Torrey a pleasant setting for upscale Southwestern cuisine. Offerings range from hearty chipotle fried ribs, or trout crusted with pumpkin seeds, to jicama salad with eggplant sopapillas. The **Capitol Reef Cafe**, also in Torrey (tel. 435/425–3271), serves everything from peanut butter, honey, and banana sandwiches to shrimp-stuffed mushrooms and flaky, smoked rainbow trout caught locally.

Tourist Information

Capitol Reef Country/Wayne County Travel Council (Box 7, Teasdale 84773, tel. 800/858–7951). **Color Country Travel Region** (906 N. 1400 West, Box 1550, St. George, 84771, tel. 435/628–4171 or 800/233–8824). **Iron County Tourism and Convention Bureau** (Box 220, Cedar City 84720, tel. 435/586–5124). **Kane County Travel Council** (Box 728, Kanab 84741, tel. 435/644–5033). **Washington County Travel and Convention Bureau** (425 S. 700 East, St. George 84770, tel. 435/634–5747 or 800/869–6635).

Reservation Services

There are no bed-and-breakfast reservation services in southwestern Utah. **Bed and Breakfast Inns of Utah, Inc.** (Box 3066, Park City 84060) and the **Utah Travel Council** (Council Hall/Capitol Hill, Salt Lake City 84114, tel. 801/538–1030 or 800/200–1160) both publish free directories.

An Olde Penny Farthing Inn

278 N. 100 West, St. George 84770, tel. 435/673-7755

One of several inns and homestays in St. George's Historic District, An Olde Penny Farthing Inn was built in the 1880s by a Mormon settler named Erastus Whitehead to house his large family. It was constructed with adobe walls 18 inches thick, which have helped the house survive over a century of desert heat. A stucco exterior and "painted lady" accent colors were added by Alan and Jacquie Capon, the current owners and innkeepers.

Inside Penny Farthing are several guest rooms where original, reconstructed, and totally revamped elements of design blend nicely—pine floors twined with hand-painted ivy, antique beds perching on Saltillo tile floors, and quilts the colors of a desert sunset stitched with pioneer patterns.

The inn is large enough to ensure privacy when it's wanted, but not so big that guests have a hard time finding their hosts for conversation. Don't miss a leisurely after-breakfast stroll beneath the huge pecan trees planted by Erastus Whitehead and his neighbors more than a century ago.

▦ *5 double rooms with baths, 1 with a large jetted tub. Cable TV in common room. $80–$120, full breakfast. D, MC. V. No smoking, pets and children by prior arrangement.*

The Bard's Inn

150 S. 100 West, Cedar City 84720, tel. 435/586-6612

Now pillars of the Utah Shakespearean Festival Guild in Cedar City, Jack and Audrey Whipple got hooked on the bard during their first visit to town. Their 1900s-era golden shingle-and-brick bungalow reflects their passion for the playwright, from dolls in Elizabethan costumes to guest rooms named after the characters in Shakespeare's plays.

The well-traveled Whipples have acquired scores of unique antiques and decorations for their inn. Audrey designed and created the stained-glass panels—some reassembled from discarded church windows—seen throughout the house. A salvaged oak banister follows the slow curl of the stairway from an enclosed porch to the three upstairs guest rooms.

It is the unexpected touches—creamy crocheted gloves lying across a drop-leaf desk in the upstairs sitting room, a Chinese checkerboard in a bathroom—that make this such a fascinating place to stay. Everything in the house seems to have a story; ask Audrey to tell you how she rescued the claw-foot stool from a sheep pasture in northern Idaho.

The Katharina Room has a turn-of-the-century high-back walnut bed with spring-colored linens, and a big braided runner on the floor; its small alcove has a twin walnut sleigh bed. Across the hall, the Olivia Room features cranberry carpeting, antique oak furnishings, and a collection of ceramic figures on an intricately carved wall shelf. A strawberry border trails around the ceiling of the Titania Room, and stained-glass circles are suspended in two windows. On the main floor is the sophisticated Mistress Ford suite, with a sunny private library. The Beatrice Suite, in the basement, is fitted with matching twin oak beds and a double bed. Thoughtful items in all the rooms include night-lights and plump pincushions bristling with needles and thread.

The inn has a refrigerator and sink for guest use and a small dining area with a festive collection of marbles centered on the table. Audrey's healthful but delicious breakfasts might include her home-baked Boston raisin bread, poppy-seed rolls, almond cherry zucchini bread, and

Jack's personal favorite, made from an old recipe passed down verbally—dainty, frosted *colachis*, a Czech-Slovakian pastry filled with apricots.

🏨 *3 double rooms with baths, 2 suites, 1 duplex cottage. Kitchen in cottage and 1 suite, off-street parking. $85–$100, full breakfast. MC, V. No smoking indoors, no pets. Closed Nov.–Mar.*

Boulder Mountain Lodge

Hwy. 12, Box 1397, Boulder 84716, tel. 435/335–7460 or 800/556–3446, fax 435/ 335–7461

The town of Boulder is populated mostly by ranch families who have lived on their "spreads" for generations. And though it's situated at a crossroad for travelers in southern Utah, until recently, Boulder has never been considered much of a destination. In the early 1990s, Mark Austin, a builder and craftsman with a passion for the outdoors, took a hard look at the possibilities offered by Boulder's incredible mix of mountains and desert, and began making plans—Boulder Mountain Lodge is the result.

The rustically chic Lodge is a complex of buildings that are stuccoed sandstone red with rough wooden columns and artistically rusting roofs. The setting is a combination of meadow and wetlands, bordered by odd hummocks of rocky ground rolling away to sandstone cliffs. Three buildings have guest rooms. The small restaurant, Hell's Backbone Grill, is adjacent (*see above*). Each structure is angled for privacy and the best views of the surrounding landscape.

The motel-style guest rooms and suites are individually decorated with colorful upholstered furniture scattered with wild horses, or other Western-style themes. The beds and other furniture are a mix of Mission style and sturdy, handcrafted peeled-log designs. In most rooms, handmade quilts brighten one wall. Each room has a private patio or porch area.

In the main building, the Great Room functions as a gathering place. During the cooler months, the distinctive smell of wood smoke lingers from nightly fires in the native stone fireplace. Sofas and chairs are upholstered in a Southwestern pattern. There are books to read, and huge fabric art pieces to admire. Both areas have views of Schoolhouse Lake, the Lodge's own private bird sanctuary.

Mark Austin, his wife Katie, and their easygoing staff are happy to arrange guided hikes, jeep tours, fly-fishing outings, horseback rides, and cross-country skiing.

🏨 *18 double rooms with baths, 2 suites. Restaurant, air-conditioning, TV, and phones in all rooms, mini-refrigerators in some rooms, library. $75–$150, Continental breakfast. MC, V. No smoking indoors.*

Bryce Point Bed and Breakfast

61 N. 400 West, Box 96, Tropic 84776, tel. 435/679–8629

The ruddy tan exterior of this B&B echoes the cliffs of Bryce Canyon National Park, only minutes away. Guests are welcome in the remodeled, Depression-era cottage of Lamar and Ethel LeFevre, the friendly owners, but most prefer to sit on the wraparound porch or redwood deck of the guest annex and enjoy the fabulous views of Bryce Canyon.

Each of the guest rooms, named for members of the LeFevre family, has a 7 × 5-foot picture window facing the canyon. The peachy rose Clark and Stacey Room has pretty teal-blue bedspreads, while the walls of the Lynn and Karen Room are a gallery for memorabilia from the former's aeronautics career. The Les and Dela Room has a fire-fighting theme, complete with bright-red linens.

Ethel's special breakfast is 7UP pancakes with apple cider syrup, but she also makes delicious oat bran muffins to accompany bacon and eggs.

The LeFevres grew up in this area and have entertaining stories and dependable recreation suggestions.

🏠 *2 double rooms and 3 triples, all with baths. Ceiling fans and TV/VCRs in all rooms, outdoor hot tub, guest barbecue, off-street parking. $65–$80, full breakfast. MC, V. No smoking, no pets.*

Eagle's Nest Bed & Breakfast

500 W. Lydia's Canyon Rd., Box 160, Glendale 84729, tel. 435/648–2200 or 800/293–6378, fax 435/648–2221

Though they had traveled the world, when Dearborn and Shanoan Clark passed through southwestern Utah on a bicycling tour, they fell in love with the landscape, and when they discovered the angular, modern house that was to become Eagle's Nest B&B, they decided to stay.

Eagle's Nest is in a small canyon midway between Zion and Bryce Canyon National Parks—its high-desert setting seems like it's a million miles from the hustle usually associated with major tourist attractions. A stay here is a bit enigmatic; a mingling of rustic elements—like a graded dirt access road—contrasted by the pure luxury of eating sumptuous breakfasts of omelettes stuffed with crisp vegetables and oozing cheeses, served on fine china and silver. Guest rooms are equally luxurious with art from Tibet decorating the walls, dangling crystal orbs in sunlit windows, piles of velvet and silk pillows, and swaths of rich tapestry draping the beds.

Granted, with its somewhat new age leanings, this may not be the right choice for traditional B&B afficionados, but the quiet setting makes this an intriguing option for those craving introspection.

🏠 *4 double rooms with baths. Ceiling fans in some rooms, fireplaces in 2 rooms, woodstove in common area, mini-refrigerator and microwave for guest use, outdoor hot tub, pond, waterfall, guided hiking and biking by arrangement. $70–$120, full breakfast, evening snacks, other meals by arrangement. MC, V. No smoking, no pets, no children.*

Fox's Bryce Trails Bed and Breakfast

1001 W. Bryce Way, Box 87, Tropic 84776, tel. 435/679–8700, fax 435/679–8727

This property is in a residential area of Tropic and it really looks like someone's well-tended home—although it was actually built to accommodate visitors to Bryce Canyon National Park. And though it may seem odd, this homestay-type B&B is one of the town's better accommodations.

From spring to fall, Fox's Bryce Trails has decks and porches festooned with terra-cotta pots of foxtails, pansies, petunias, and marigolds, which provide guests with casual places to gather. In winter, when temperatures drive guests indoors, the B&B's open room design provides lots of space for hanging out.

The guest rooms are named after trails that traverse the depths of Bryce's stone amphitheaters: Queen's Garden, Mossy Cave, and the like.

Breakfasts including pancakes, an egg casserole, or fresh blueberry bran muffins are prepared and served by hostess Elaine Haas, who visited family members living in the vicinity of Bryce regularly from her childhood until she moved here to manage the B&B in 1994.

🏠 *6 double rooms with baths. TV in rooms. $70–$80, full breakfast. MC, V. No smoking, no pets, no children.*

Francisco's

51 Francisco La., Box 3, Tropic 84776, tel. 435/679–8721 or 800/642–4136

You never know what will happen at Francisco's. Take the night that a guitar-playing guest teamed up with the neighbor from across the street for a little night music. Before long, there were 30 cars, a band on the porch, and a yard filled with people singing and dancing.

This modern log cabin on 10 acres isn't luxurious, but it appeals to those who enjoy sitting in an old church pew on a flower-filled front porch, and who appreciate such sights as the sun setting over Bryce Canyon or the mid-morning antics of wild turkeys strutting through freshly plowed fields. The large, plain guest rooms all have impressive views and a peek under the bedspread may reveal an intricately patterned handmade quilt.

Host Charlie Francisco is retired from his job as a horse wrangler in Bryce Canyon National Park; his wife, Eva Dean, is the architect of huge breakfasts of pancakes, eggs, sausage or bacon, fresh or home-preserved fruit, and delicious sourdough or sweet breads.

🏠 *3 double rooms with baths. TV in guest rooms, hot tub, farm animals, off-street parking. $55–$75, full breakfast. AE, D, DC, MC, V. No smoking, no pets indoors.*

Greene Gate Village

62–78 W. Tabernacle St., St. George 84770, tel. 435/628–6999 or 800/350–6999

Diagonally across from the historic adobe Mormon Tabernacle, Greene Gate Village looks like a tiny pioneer settlement, and, in a way, it is. This unusual complex brings together seven pioneer-era structures—among them adobe homes, a rock granary, and spruced-up wooden cabins—moved from sites scattered across the St. George Valley. In most cases, an entire house can be rented, making this an excellent place to stay with family or a group of friends. The spacious interior yard is a perfect group common area, with its flower beds, tidy lawns, and postcard-pretty swimming pool.

Built in the mid-1800s and the only village structure original to this site, the tan stucco Orson Pratt House has a gingerbread-trimmed porch. The first-floor Shanna suite of rooms has brass and oak furniture and hand-quilted floral bedspreads. Next door, in the Lindsay Room, the paper-white cutwork shams and bedspread stand in crisp contrast to the royal blue carpet; photographs of Orson Pratt, a counselor to Brigham Young, hang over the fireplace. The bathroom is tiny, but there's a large whirlpool tub in a separate room.

Creaking wicker chairs sit on the rustic porch of the weathered two-room Tolley cabin, which looks out toward the swimming pool. Inside, where a family of 13 once lived, are two simply decorated rooms, each with a fireplace.

Village founders Mark and Barbara Greene had to reconstruct the two-bedroom Morris House, originally located several blocks away: On moving day, the axle on the house trailer broke, and the two-story home suddenly became a pile of shattered glass, adobe brick, and broken door- and window frames.

Breakfast, served in the garden room of the Bentley House, usually includes omelets, bacon, sausage, juices, and either pecan waffles, homemade bread, or croissants.

🏠 *Village: 3 double rooms; 2 triples, and 5 quads, all with baths. Off-site: 4 doubles and 1 quad room with baths; Greene House complex (house and carriage house), which can sleep 22. Telephone and TV in all rooms, kitchens in 2 rooms, fireplaces in 6 rooms, whirlpool tub in 4 rooms, pool, walking tour, off-street parking, 5-course dinners served Thurs.–Sat. by reservation. $75–*

$175, full breakfast, afternoon refreshments. AE, MC, V. No smoking, no pets, 2-night minimum for Greene House complex.

Harvest House

29 Canyon View Dr., Box 125, Springdale 84767, tel. 435/772–3880

Just off Springdale's main drag, Harvest House is a two-story ranch-style structure built of mottled tan-and-brown brick and buttery stucco; the inn opened about a decade ago. In 1997 it was purchased by current owners Roger and Leslie Coleman and Roger Coleman Sr.

One room has pink-and-black wicker furniture, including a chaise longue for reading or dreaming. Another bedroom has a wide window facing a neighboring apple orchard where deer congregate in the evenings. On warm summer nights, the sound of the Virgin River is a soft counterpoint to conversation on two private decks.

Breakfast at Harvest House is an elegant spread—items such as poached eggs and basil hollandaise or cheese blintzes with fresh fruit topping are served as are fresh bread or pastries and stout coffee.

🏠 *3 double rooms with baths, 1 triple with bath, 1 suite. Air-conditioning, TV, VCR, video library, wet bar in living room, outdoor hot tub, fishpond, off-street parking. $85–$110, full breakfast, afternoon refreshments. D, MC, V. No smoking, no pets, children by prior arrangement.*

Lodge at Red River Ranch

Hwy. 24, Box 280, Bicknell 84715, tel. 435/425–3322 or 800/205–6343, fax 435/425–3329

Though this property was built in the early 1990s, stepping into the Great Room of The Lodge at Red River Ranch is like being whisked back in time to an era when the rich and famous went rusticating in grand lodges (although they were never really too primitive to offer the very best). Massive oxen yoke and wagon-wheel chandeliers hang from a soaring, beamed ceiling accented by high windows. There are moose, elk, deer, and buffalo mounted on the log walls and Oriental rugs cover the floors. A large ceremonial sand painting rug, woven in 1929, hangs above a monument-size Frederic Remington sculpture near a huge stone fireplace.

The three-story lodge, constructed of peeled pine, is equally impressive from the outside. Ringed by ancient cottonwood trees and flanked by sandstone-slab walkways, the structure, which sits where an old stagecoach rest stop once stood, has jutting dormers and a lava stone foundation. The expansive grounds include a network of trails; a 2-acre, spring-fed reservoir stocked with rainbow trout; and over 5 miles of the Fremont River bottoms, popular for fly-fishing.

The lodge is owned and managed by the John Alexander family, originally from California. In the late 1970s, the Alexander's bought nearly 2,000 acres of property in the verdant Fremont River Valley, which they dubbed Red River Ranch. For almost 20 years, John Alexander sketched design elements and dreamed of building a grand lodge on the ranch. Meanwhile, his wife Linda began purchasing pieces of antique furniture, which today fills the lodge. Their efforts came to fruition in 1994 when the Lodge at Red River Ranch opened for business.

Guest rooms, each with a fireplace and a balcony or patio, are on three levels. The Rodeo Room is a salute to cowboy culture; the Saratoga Room is bedecked with horse-racing paraphernalia; the Safari Room sports exotic taxidermy mounts—a wildebeest, a kudu, and an impala. The Vintage Room is a little more sedate—the walls are papered in a rich, leafy pattern and a handmade quilt covers the bed.

Home-style breakfasts and dinners of simple fare are served in the dining room, which has a tin ceiling and cast-iron chandeliers. A miniature train circles the room on a track just below the ceiling.

▥ *7 double and 8 triple rooms with baths. Restaurant, ceiling fans in all rooms, projection TV in recreation room, outdoor hot tub, guided fly-fishing and game-bird hunting packages, guided hiking in Capitol Reef National Park by prior arrangement. $90–$140, meals extra. AE, D, MC, V. No smoking, no pets.*

Nine Gables Inn

106 W. 100 North, Kanab 84741, tel. 435/644-5079

White stucco now covers this 1890s two-story ranch house originally built of sun-baked adobe brick, and a picket fence encloses a tidy vegetable garden—and if you're lucky, blooming perennials. Inside, many of this inn's furnishings are treasured antiques.

One guest room has a first-edition Zane Grey novel on the nightstand; a reminder that the author was once a frequent guest in this home. In a room down the hall are a honey-color oak bedstead, and the most comfortable chair in the inn: a reupholstered horsehair rocker, retrieved from an old milk house. The bedroom in the back of the house features a curly maple rolltop desk that invites letter writing and a trunk that held the belongings of innkeeper Jeanne's grandfather when he emigrated from Norway.

Each morning, Jeanne and her husband, Frank, provide excellent conversation to accompany light breakfasts of hot or cold cereal, pastries, juices, and fresh fruit. A summer treat to hope for is a bowl of huge raspberries from the backyard berry patch.

▥ *4 double rooms with baths. Air-conditioning and ceiling fans in all rooms, TV in common area, off-street parking. $70–$85, Continental breakfast. MC, V. No smoking, no pets. Closed Nov.–mid-May.*

Novel House Inn

73 Paradise Rd., Box 188, Springdale 84767, tel. 435/772-3650 or 800/711-8400, fax 435/772-3651

You certainly don't have to be a bibliophile to appreciate the decor of this modern, two-story, ranch-style house, but if you are, it's just that much more enjoyable. The guest rooms are all tributes to owners Ross and Norma Clay's favorite authors, furnished with a sense of the imagination and genre of each writer. The stunning backdrop for this booklovers' fantasy is nearby Zion National Park. (Each room has an excellent guest packet with information on what to see and do in the park; it also includes Ross's version of the obligatory B&B "rules" rendered with dry humor.)

The Western Room, from the earthy linens and plaid duvet to the horseshoe nailed over the door, might have been dreamed up by Louis L'Amour or Zane Grey. There's also an antique wardrobe with powder-horn handles. Mosquito netting billows around the head of the bed in the Rudyard Kipling Room. The Brontë Room breathes romance with lace curtains topped with delicate floral swags and a bedspread like a field of flowers. In the Robert Louis Stevenson Room, a massive sleigh bed is piled high with pillows of various tartans, and an N. C. Wyeth illustration from *Treasure Island* hangs on one wall.

There are also bears and bells of some sort in each room—Norma's touch—and creamy stationery for guests to pen their own memoirs or correspondence.

On the main floor, you'll find a library stocked with games, cards, puzzles and, of course, books—an eclectic assembly where texts on photojournalism share shelves with Dr. Seuss, Shakespeare, and Carl Sagan. Book stands hold volumes open to favorite passages, and guests wander in and out to borrow a book or to sit down and talk about authors and other topics.

Across the foyer, a simple afternoon tea is a good way to meet fellow guests, which makes breakfast time a bit of a reunion. Novel House's breakfasts are buffets of fruit, cranberry nut or apple strudel muffins, and hot dishes like asparagus egg strata or vegetarian quiche served with souffle potatoes.

🏠 *10 double rooms with private baths. Air-conditioning and phones in all rooms, TV or TV/VCR in some rooms, fireplace in the library, off-street parking. $95–$115, full breakfast. AE, MC, V. No smoking, no pets, no children.*

O'Toole's Under the Eaves Bed & Breakfast

980 Zion Park Blvd., Box 29, Springdale 84767, tel. 435/772–3457, fax 435/772–3324

A guest once dubbed the front porch of O'Toole's B&B "the best in southern Utah." Furnished with Adirondack-style chairs and tables, and festooned most of the year with flower-filled pots, the porch is truly lovely, and a pleasantly incongruous sight on Springdale's motel-lined main street.

Owners Rick and Michelle O'Toole bought this mock-Tudor property (an already-established B&B) in the spring of 1993 and have made the B&B thoroughly their own. Rick is a former restaurateur from Salt Lake City, and Michelle has a background in marketing, so they were well prepared for innkeeping.

Just inside the front door is the sunny dining room, made more cheerful by light yellow walls. Breakfast highlights include breads, muffins, and casseroles, quiches, or a Southwestern souffle with green chilies and Monterey Jack and cheddar cheeses.

Near the dining room are two small guest rooms that share a bath. Both are furnished simply with antique beds and colorful Polo linens (found on all the beds here). Each room is illuminated by an antique light fixture taken from an old saloon in Pioche, Nevada. Upstairs, a suite encompasses the entire second floor. Its kitchen and sitting area overlook the backyard gardens, and additional windows face Zion Canyon; the tiny bathroom has a claw-foot tub.

Behind the main house, a cottage has three small rooms, each with a private entrance. One has a high brass bed and a shelf of tiny ceramic knickknacks. In another room with soft green walls, a print from Andrew Wyeth's "Helga pictures" hangs above an oak bed. Each of these rooms has a stained-glass window in its compact bathroom. In the basement, which is kept cool by the cottage's sandstone foundation, a handsome sleigh bed dominates the third room, and the bathroom has a jetted tub with shower.

🏠 *3 double rooms with baths, 2 doubles share one bath, 1 suite. Air-conditioning and kitchenette in suite, garden gazebo, off-street parking. $75–$85, suite $135, full breakfast. D, DC, MC, V. No smoking, no pets, 2-night minimum some weekends.*

Paxman's Summer House

170 N. 400 West, Cedar City 84720, tel. 435/586–3755

Popular with longtime attendees of the Utah Shakespearean Festival, just a short stroll away, this tan-and-rose brick Victorian farmhouse is large enough to provide privacy, but cozy enough that guests feel comfortable striking up a conversation. Three porches afford views of the quiet neighborhood and colorful flower beds shaded by mature ash and fruit trees. Karlene Paxman, a former home-economics teacher, has owned the home since 1963.

The front parlor has tall lace-curtained windows and a dignified upright piano. An upstairs sitting area with a blue velvet settee is surrounded by three guest rooms with sturdy antique beds and furnishings. In the Pine Room, a high, pioneer-era bed has the requisite bedside stool. A main-floor master bedroom with its own secluded side porch is popular in the summer.

In the dining room, a pump organ occupies a bay window nook. The breakfast menu varies daily, with treats like nutball coffee cake or homemade cinnamon rolls. Fresh peaches and cherries come virtually straight from the tree to the table.

▦ *3 double rooms, 1 triple, all with baths. TV in rooms, off-street parking. $75–$90, full breakfast. MC, V. Smoking on porches only, no pets.*

Quicksand and Cactus Bed & Breakfast

346 N. Main St., St. George 84770, tel. and fax 435/674-1739 or tel. 800/381-1654

Juanita Brooks was a respected author and Mormon historian whose areas of expertise were the people and events that shaped the history of southern Utah. Quicksand and Cactus B&B (named after Brooks' autobiography) is in an original rock home built in 1878 by Juanita's grandfather from chips and odd-shape rocks discarded at the construction sites of the St. George Mormon Temple and Tabernacle, where he was employed as a stonemason.

This small property is unique not only for its historic aspect, but also because of innkeeper Carla Fox's passion for Juanita Brooks' life and work. Quicksand

and Cactus, with its shady porches, vivid floral-papered walls, and simple but elegant furnishings, can easily provide a fine night's rest and an excellent morning meal. A more leisurely stay promises time to relax in the sitting room and listen to Carla Fox speak eloquently about an exceptional woman of the American west.

▦ *3 double rooms with baths. Air-conditioning and TV/VCR in rooms. $65–$95, full breakfast. D, MC, V. No smoking, no pets.*

Red Rock Inn

998 Zion Park Blvd., Box 273, Springdale 84767, tel. 435/772-3139

When goldsmith Karla Player (*see* Shopping, *above*) and Eileen Crookes, a self-proclaimed "corporate dropout" from Salt Lake City, decided to open a bed-and-breakfast in Springdale, they knew that in order to succeed they needed to set their property apart from the motel jungle stretching toward Zion National Park. Red Rock Inn, a cluster of five cottage-style rooms, was their solution.

Each room inside the stucco and sandstone exterior is architecturally designed to provide a unique view of the sculptured cliffs of Zion, and to ensure privacy for every guest. The guest rooms, which have vaulted ceilings, are individually decorated.

In the evenings, Eileen and Karla hustle from cottage to cottage, chatting and asking guests about breakfast time and beverage preferences. Morning finds them delivering baskets of yogurt, fruit, one of several egg specialties, and hot, Glorious Morning muffins filled with raisins, shredded apples and carrots, and pecans off the old-growth trees that shade Red Rock Inn's central lawn.

▦ *4 double rooms with baths and jetted tubs, 1 suite with outdoor hot tub. Cable TV, phones, ceiling fans in rooms. $80–*

$130, full breakfast. AE, D, MC, V. No smoking, no pets, children by prior arrangement.

Seven Wives Inn

217 N. 100 West, St. George 84770, tel. 435/628-3737 or 800/600-3737

In the heart of St. George's Historic District, two neighboring houses compose Seven Wives Inn, named for an ancestor of one of the owners, who indeed had seven wives. The larger two-story house, built in 1873, has a double-tier veranda and a wood-shingled roof projecting gables in three directions; its attic was the occasional hiding place of die-hard polygamists fleeing federal marshals after multiple marriages were outlawed in 1882. The adjacent President's House, a modified two-story Renaissance Revival cube built in 1883, often provided lodging for visiting presidents of the Mormon Church.

Innkeepers Jay and Donna Curtis are always keeping their eyes open for antiques to add to those collected in the parlors of both houses and throughout the guest rooms.

In the main house, the Lucinda Room is a study in pastels, with an elaborate antique brass bed; soft, gray hooked rugs; a rose-colored velvet sofa and chair; and a green French ceramic stove. Small children can be accommodated in a Murphy bed that descends from an antique armoire. The romantic, high-ceiling Melissa Room on the second floor has a lace minicanopy over the bed and a private balcony. The notorious Attic Room is brightened by a skylight and an Art Deco pewter chandelier; a high, floral-painted bed sits against a wall of exposed adobe brick.

The four rooms in the President's House are accessed by a steep, narrow staircase. The Caroline Room has dark green walls lightened by large windows, and a kaleidoscopic "Nine Patch" quilt on the bed. Spring is eternal in the small Rachel Room, where the walls are papered with pastel tulips. The furnishings are white wicker, and floral swags arch over white wooden blinds.

The high-ceiling dining room in the main house has tables set for two or four. In addition to homemade granola, breakfast choices might include German apple or apple pecan pancakes, bread pudding, sausage *en croûte*, or bacon, eggs, and cheese in a nest of hash browns.

🏠 *10 double rooms, 2 triples, 1 single, all with baths (4 rooms can be combined as suites). TV and phone in all rooms, fireplaces or stoves in 4 rooms, private balconies in 4 rooms, outdoor pool, off-street parking. $70-$150, full breakfast. AE, D, DC, MC, V. No smoking, no pets.*

SkyRidge Bed & Breakfast

Hwy 24, Box 750220, Torrey 84775, tel. and fax 435/425-3222

A returning guest once told the proprietors of this inn near the western boundary of Capitol Reef National Park, "I dream about SkyRidge." It's not difficult to imagine why: Simply put, owners Sally Elliot and Karen Kesler have made SkyRidge a beautiful, serene destination.

The three-story structure, which was built in the early 1990s, is painted the same soft green color as the blooming rice grass that surrounds the inn. You can catch great desert and mountain views from many of the inn's seventy-five windows.

Inside, art furnishings created by Karen (who is a nationally exhibited artist), blend with a collection of contemporary art, photographs, antiques, and ethnic and folk sculpture displayed in the guest rooms and common areas. If you look closely in the Gallery Living Room, you'll notice discreet prices for many of the decorations, and returning guests often find their favorite mirror, painting, or piece of Navajo folk art has been sold. Luckily, something equally interesting usually takes its place.

All of SkyRidge's guest rooms are equally intriguing. Walls throughout have been layered with a palette of hues to create distinctive visual textures. On the second floor, the Sagebrush Room's private deck and hot tub face aspen-covered slopes, and the headboard Karen made for the room's king-size bed reflects the folk art elements found in the hand-stitched coverlet. From the high-back bed in the Juniper Room, a bay of six windows provides a vista of Capitol Reef's domes and cliffs silhouetted against the sunrise. The Pinyon Room has a cathedral ceiling and an elegant plaid spread on its four-poster bed. The very private Chamisa Room has stunning views from its dormered windows; it's the only room on the third floor.

Breakfast is served in the main floor dining room, where finches, piñon jays, and other colorful birds are attracted to feeders outside seven tall windows. Sturdy wicker chairs provide comfortable seating for Sally's culinary specialties—croissant French toast, Mexican frittata with fresh tomatillo salsa, smoked trout omelet, or apple spice pecan waffles—all accompanied by yogurt, granola, and seasonal fruit harvested from the pioneer orchards of Capitol Reef National Park.

🏨 *4 double rooms with baths (2 with private, outdoor hot tubs), 2 suites. Air-conditioning and individual heat controls, TV/VCR, phones in all rooms, fax, fireplace in living room, outdoor hot tub, video library, horseshoe pits, picnic area, barbecue, off-street parking, activity planning. $85–$125, full breakfast, afternoon snacks. MC, V. No smoking indoors, no pets, children by prior arrangement, 2-night minimum on holiday weekends.*

Snow Family Guest Ranch

633 E. Hwy. 9, Box 790190, Virgin 84779, tel. 435/635–2500 or 800/308–7669

Travelers to Zion National Park are often distracted by Snow Family Guest Ranch. In fact, people regularly pull off the road to photograph the sleek horses grazing in the irrigated pasture behind the crisp white rail fences of the ranch. Some passersby even venture up to the door of the modern, redbrick ranch house to ask if they can ride the horses. That's when hosts Steve and Shelley Penrose politely explain that the horses are just for ranch guests to ride, adding, "We'd love to have you stay with us." At that point, after a quick look around, many visitors borrow the phone to cancel any prior motel reservations.

The Penrose's purchased this 12-acre horse ranch less than a decade ago, naming it for Shelley's grandfather, Leo Snow, who was instrumental in the 1909 designation of Zion Canyon as a national monument. Together, Shelley and her husband have fashioned a destination that has the relaxed attitude of a dude ranch, with frills and comforts that no real cowboy would ever dream of.

Each guest room is bright and spacious with tongue-in-cheek Western decor: peeled pine log beds and nightstands; denim and bandanna prints; and lots of Western paraphernalia—boots, lariats, branding irons, cowboy hats. Several rooms have window seats beneath wide, scrupulously clean windows. Here you can sit and watch the horses frolic, or check on the resident family of ducks swimming in the backyard pond.

Breakfast is served in the great room, not far from where John Wayne's "quick draw" is displayed by a larger-than-life cardboard cutout of the man himself. A big-screen TV stands in an adjacent nook, beside a chunky wood-burning stove. The morning meal is served family-style and could be pancakes with homemade peach syrup and bacon, an omelet, link sausages, and a pile of ranch-style hash browns, or perhaps, cream gravy ladled over biscuits accompanied by locally grown fruit. For those who prefer to get an early start, a Continental breakfast of cereal, muffins, and rolls is available by request.

🏠 *9 double rooms with baths. Air-conditioning in rooms, ceiling fans in some rooms, big-screen TV, outdoor swimming pool, hot tub, gazebo, garden pond, guided horseback rides for guests (additional charge). $85–$135, full breakfast, afternoon refreshments. MC, V. No smoking, no pets, older children by prior arrangement.*

William Prince Inn

185 S. 300 East, Panguitch 84759, tel. 435/676-2525

The tiny William Prince Inn was the first brick home built in the Panguitch valley. Its rosy exterior is accented by symmetrical, rectangular windows and white-washed porches. Leo and Claudia Crump moved from Salt Lake City to restore this historic home and its backyard granary, naming the property after its original owner, a mover and shaker from the valley's settlement era in the mid-1800s.

A steep, narrow stairway leads to the guest rooms. In Grandpa Billy's Room, the green-painted pine floors match a rose-and-green wall-hanging Claudia quilted in a star pattern. A skirted basin and claw-foot tub with handheld shower sit opposite an antique bed; there is a private toilet alcove.

For Louisa's Garden, Claudia made a quilt that echoes the border of sunflow-

ers she stenciled near the ceiling. Next door, Anna Caroline's Room has blue-gray walls, a Rail Fence-patterned quilt on the bed, and a window draped with a delicate, cutwork tablecloth threaded on a slender, tree-branch rod. These rooms share a small bathroom with a short but deep—4 feet—bathtub.

In the Granary Cottage, a black-and-white tiled floor accents white wicker furniture and a collection of teacups fills a glass-front cabinet. In the bathroom, a surprisingly accurate scale from the 1920s confronts weight-conscious guests.

The main house has a tiny parlor with a woodstove and a petite pump organ, but most guests prefer to congregate on the porches or on the willow furniture scattered around the wildflower-filled yard. Guests are also welcome in the kitchen anytime, and have been known to play cards at the round oak table, scavenge for midnight snacks, and mix up a batch of cookies—just for the novelty of baking them in the 1940s-era oven.

Each morning, with sun streaming through windows curtained in geranium-strewn fabric, the kitchen becomes the setting for Leo's breakfasts of sourdough waffles or pancakes with ham and sausage. The smell of breakfast usually brings a few whines from "Coca-Cola," the Crump's Old English sheepdog. For guests in a hurry to get on their way, Leo sets out fresh coffee cakes and fruit. For those anxious to see more examples of Claudia's exquisite quilting, her shop, "Snowed-In Quilts" is just three blocks east on Main Street.

🏠 *1 double room with bath, 2 doubles share 1 bath, 1 cottage. $50–$70, full breakfast. MC, V. No smoking, no pets, children by prior arrangement.*

Southeastern Utah

Castle Valley Inn

Early explorers who charted the rivers and canyons of southeastern Utah filled their journals with superlatives and the margins of their maps with exclamations of awe. Modern writers such as Edward Abbey and Terry Tempest Williams built careers trying to find words to describe their responses to these landscapes. In many ways, this cataclysmic region—a vast, open area filled with solitary places—is still a wilderness waiting to be discovered.

The area wasn't without early settlers. The Anasazi people hunted and farmed here from roughly AD 400 to AD 1500, leaving evidence of their civilization in stone granaries and dwellings perched under cliff overhangs and in intriguing panels of rock art on canyon walls. Mormon pioneers and other hardy settlers who came in the mid- to late 1800s left marks of their society beside the remnants of the early Native American culture.

Explorations of the rapids and placid stretches of the Green and Colorado rivers have changed a great deal since Civil War hero John Wesley Powell made the first recorded venture into the canyons in a wooden boat in 1869. These days, both

Canyonlands and Arches national parks, and the national monuments and other scenic attractions scattered across the region, have paved roads and maintained day hikes; dozens of outfitters offer river or bicycle adventures; and four-wheel-drive tours complete with gourmet meals.

This region's agelessness is evident not only in its rivers and canyons, but also in the rock itself. Sandstone, eroded by wind and water is transformed into the 1,000-foot cliffs, bizarre needles, and serpentine mazes of Canyonlands National Park, and the arcing stone ribbons at Arches National Park. These parks have long been the showcase for the region, but, more and more, the acres of rolling dunes surrounding their boundaries are coming to be seen as a mountain-biking mecca, the slickrock—sandstone eroded by wind and slick with tiny grains—providing a particular challenge for bikers.

Moviemakers have appreciated southeastern Utah since John Ford's Westerns immortalized it in the late 1940s. It was near Canyonlands' Island in the Sky District—not the Grand Canyon, as most people assume—that Thelma and Louise took their final leap, and it was in Arches National Park that a young Indiana Jones discovered the cross of Cortez in Indiana Jones and the Last Crusade. Local artists have taken advantage of the stunning scenery as well: Each summer, ballet and opera performances are mounted along the Colorado River with sandstone boulders and towering cliffs as their backdrops.

In some of the better known destinations, like Moab, there has been a rush to accommodate the influx of visitors and new residents, with towns sprouting subdivisions, motels, gift shops, and fast-food outlets right and left. Other places are proceeding with caution and waiting for visitors to discover them rather than clamoring to be found. Often, repeat visitors opt to base their explorations in locales south of the Moab hub, and steady development attests to these areas' ability to accommodate these canny travelers.

The B&B business, which began in the mid-1980s with residents informally taking visitors into their homes during the busy spring and fall seasons, has evolved to include much more upscale and elaborate properties. Motels or apartment complexes calling themselves "inns" are still a part of the mix, but there are an increasing number of true bed-and-breakfast experiences to be found. In some southeastern Utah destinations, the best B&B option is simply a homestay in a spectacular setting, or a small property that serves excellent food or has intriguing hosts. The fact that the B&B here is still much more casual than in many parts of the country is simply in keeping with the nature of a region whose stunning backyard vistas can't be rivaled by even the finest amenities elsewhere.

Places to Go, Sights to See

Arches National Park (Box 907, Moab 84532, tel. 435/259–8161). A 41-mile round-trip scenic drive leads to many of the huge stone monoliths that were eroded from an ancient seabed, but Arches National Park is best experienced on foot. The park has a well-developed series of hiking trails, ranging from effortless walks to all-day explorations of canyons sheltering pristine arches and other formations. The park's most famous formation, Delicate Arch, rising 45 feet above a smooth sandstone basin, is reached via a moderate 1.5-mile march over buff-and-orange sandstone. A ranger-guided trip into the Fiery Furnace is offered daily spring through fall. The Arches Visitor Center is 3 miles north of downtown Moab, off U.S. 191.

Blanding. On an enormous white sandstone mesa between the city of Monticello and tiny Bluff, Blanding mixes cowboy culture with Native American and prehistoric heritage. Its *Edge of the Cedars State Park* (660 W. 400 North, tel. 435/678–2238) is an Anasazi ruin adjoined by a museum housing Anasazi artifacts. The *Dinosaur Museum* (754 S. 200 West, tel. 435/678–3454) is an accredited federal fossil repository. Its collection includes life-size dinosaur models, skeletons, fossilized dinosaur skin, and a huge petrified tree over 250 million years old.

Bluff. On U.S. 163 across the San Juan River from the vast Navajo Reservation, Bluff was established in 1880 by an expedition of about 200 Mormon pioneers. At one desperate point during their trek, the determined settlers lowered their wagons through a cliff fissure to reach the Colorado River more than 1,000 feet below. The adobe brick homes built by members of this so-called "Hole in the Rock Expedition" still dot this little town. The adjacent *San Juan River,* one of the fastest-flowing rivers in the United States, is a particular favorite with river runners. A petroglyph panel depicting five images of Kokopelli (the mischievous humpbacked flute player from Pueblo Indian culture) is found at *Sand Island Campground*, 3 miles southwest of town.

Canyonlands National Park (2282 S. West Resource Blvd., Moab 84532, tel. 435/259–7164) is a series of rugged landscapes in three distinct districts—Island in the Sky, Maze, and Needles—divided by the Green and Colorado rivers. Easily Utah's least developed national park, Canyonlands is best known for its solitude; four-wheel-drive trails, popular with bikers as well, lead to the most rugged landscapes. In the Island in the Sky district, hikes are punctuated by panoramic vistas from atop a towering peninsula; the visitor center here has information on activities and attractions throughout the park. Treks through color-banded spires and pinnacles in the Needles section, accessible near Monticello, lead to overlooks, arches, and the ruins of ancient civilizations. The Maze portion of the park is serious backcountry, not to be explored without maps.

Green River. Settled in 1878 on the site of a centuries-old river crossing, this town is best known as a launch point for *rafting trips* on the Green River (*see* River Rafting, *below*). At the *John Wesley Powell River History Museum* (885 E. Main St., tel. 435/564–3427), a multi-image slide presentation matches the explorer's journal entries with the sights of a modern-day river expedition. Also known for the variety of melons it grows, the town holds a *Melon Days* celebration each September.

Moab. A Mormon settlement started near the banks of the Colorado River in 1855, Moab prospered from uranium mining in the 1950s and '60s. Now, the surrounding petrified dunes—especially popular with mountain bikers—are the town's major draw, challenged only by Moab's proximity to Canyonlands and Arches National Parks. On the south end of Moab, *Arches Vineyard* (420 Kane Creek Blvd, tel. 435/259–5397), Utah's only commercial winery, has a tasting room that allows visitors to savor the award-winning wines produced here. *Dead Horse Point State Park* (34 mi northwest of Moab, tel. 435/259–2624) is an isolated island mesa with views of the La Sal, Abajo, and Henry mountain ranges; Canyonlands' Island in the Sky District; and the lazy Colorado River, 2,000 feet below.

Monticello. Fifty-three miles south of Moab, the town of Monticello sits beneath the Abajo Mountains, which appear a somber blue when viewed from a distance (hence their local nickname, "The Blues"). Monticello is lush compared to many of the desert towns nearby, which is why a member of one of the founding Mormon families, a native Virginian, named the town after Thomas Jefferson's home. *Abajo Scenic Drive*, a U.S. Forest Service road, winds through 40 forested miles from Monticello to Blanding; check with the Manti-La Sal National Forest (tel. 435/587–2041) for road conditions.

Monument Valley Navajo Tribal Park. Because of its striking red rock spires, buttes, and mesas, this valley south of Bluff via Highway 163 is known worldwide as the setting for dozens of movies and television commercials. But beyond the scenery, the park offers a taste of Navajo Culture at the historic Goulding's Trading Post (*see* Shopping, *below*), and Navajo-guided explorations can be arranged at the Tribal Park headquarters (tel. 435/727–3287) on the Utah-Arizona border.

Mountain Biking. About a decade ago, southeastern Utah became a magnet for "fat-tire" enthusiasts who wanted to test their mettle on the area's seemingly endless supply of undulating rock; enthusiasts continue to claim the area as the "mountain-biking capital of the world." *Bicycle Utah* (Box 738, Park City 84060, tel. 435/649–5806) publishes a free directory of area trails. Among them are the extremely popular *Moab Slickrock Bike Trail*, a 10.3-mile roller coaster loop 4 miles east of Moab, marked only by paint slashes on the rock. Less intense choices near Moab are *Hurrah Pass* in Kane Creek Canyon and the *Gemini Bridges Trail* outside town. One of the ultimate mountain-biking treks is the 96-mile *White Rim Trail* in the Island in the Sky district of Canyonlands National Park. Off-road opportunities are not as plentiful in Arches National Park, but the paved 41-mile road through the park makes a scenic full-day ride. Road cycling is also popular on the *Colorado River Scenic Byway* (SR 128), part of Utah's multiagency-sponsored scenic roads program. West of Monticello, the *Abajo Mountains* offer heat-beating Alpine rides. Blanding is a convenient starting point for exploring the *Trail of the Ancients*, famous for rock art. Two good choices for bike rentals, tours, and solid advice in Moab are *Rim Cyclery* (1233 S. U.S. 191, tel. 435/259–5333) and *Poison Spider Bicycles* (497 N. Main St., tel. 435/259–7882 or 800/635–1792).

Nine Mile Canyon. Off Highway 6/191 north of I-70 is a 40-mile-long gallery with hundreds of petroglyphs and pictographs marking its boulders and cliffs. The rock art and the remnants of dozens of habitation sites are the work of the Fremont Indians, who lived in the area from AD 300 to 1250. The canyon also has the remains of several homesteads, stage stops, and ranches. The best way to experience Nine Mile Canyon is to go with a guide. *Reflections on the Ancients* (tel. 435/637–5801 or 800/468–4060) has archaeologist-led tours that explain Nine Mile's oddities, including why a canyon 40 miles long came to be named Nine Mile.

River Rafting. The San Juan, Green, and Colorado rivers, which traverse this area, offer myriad opportunities for both white-water and float trips, including stunning excursions through Canyonlands National Park. *Raft Utah* (153 E. 7200 South, Salt Lake City 84047, tel. 801/566–2662) publishes a complete list of outfitters that serve the region; additional information is available at the park visitor centers and at visitor centers in Moab and Monticello.

Shopping. Of the six trading posts in Blanding, *The Purple Sage* (tel. 435/678–3620) has some of the best deals on Native American rugs and weavings. Several *pottery plants* clustered along Blanding's main street (U.S. 191) give demonstrations of pottery crafting, decorating, and firing. The *Cedar Mesa Pottery Store* (tel. 435/678–2241) sells ceramics seconds at half price. In Bluff, the *Cow Canyon Trading Post* (tel. 435/672–2208) carries Zuni, Hopi, and Navajo jewelry. An adjoining room is filled with books on everything from Japanese art to scholarly works on Native American religions, art, and culture. Named for the formation above them, the *Twin Rocks Trading Post and Gift Shop* (tel. 435/672–2341) sit side by side. The Trading Post stocks collectable-quality jewelry, rugs, and pottery, while the Gift Shop stock leans toward postcards, T-shirts, and local arts and crafts. Moab's Main Street has plenty of shops and galleries, but the cozy *Western Plaza* just south of Center Street is a good bet for finding something unique. The several small stores sell things like Mexican folk art, handmade clothing, fresh-baked treats, and the work of local photographers. *Soapy's Gallery and Gifts* (tel. 435/587–3021) in Monticello, is a community arts-and-crafts co-op. With a reputation extending back to 1923, *Goulding's Trading Post* (tel. 435/727–3231) in Monument Valley has a wide selection of authentic Navajo jewelry, rugs, pottery, and such, as well as rows of arts-and-crafts booths.

Valley of the Gods. An 18-mile graded dirt road, accessible from Highways 163 and 261, winds through this dramatic expanse filled with oddly eroded rock formations and towers. Though this location is remote, the road is well maintained and safe in dry weather.

Restaurants

Although 3.2% beer and wine coolers are widely available in grocery and convenience stores throughout southern Utah, restaurants in some smaller towns may not have liquor licenses. When in doubt, call ahead or ask your server, who is frequently able to serve (but not offer) alcohol to customers.

In Bluff, the **Cow Canyon Trading Post** (tel. 435/672–2208) serves three dinner entrées daily. Offerings may include chicken and vegetable shish kebabs on a bed of wild rice, a phyllo pie stuffed with spinach and ham, or cold carrot soup and a salad of spring greens drizzled with a fresh herb vinaigrette. Popular with the river-running crowd, **Ray's Tavern** (tel. 435/564–3511) in Green River has the best (and biggest) burgers in town; service may be slow but the food is worth the wait, and there are billiard tables in the back. Some standouts among Moab's many restaurants are the spare and modern **Center Café** (tel. 435/259–4295) for nouvelle pasta, chicken, and fish dishes; **Eddie McStiff's** (tel. 435/259–2337), which offers good pizza and freshly brewed beer in a family dining area or a more rowdy lounge; and **Honest Ozzie's Cafe** (tel. 435/259–8442) serving breakfasts, lunches, and dinners of what they bill as "natural and unnatural foods." Specialties include potato madness hash browns, veggie burgers with sweet potato chips, and a Cajun catfish wrap. The **Poplar Place** (tel. 435/259–6018) is a Moab landmark known for its appetizers, pizzas, and sandwiches, and famous for its hot wings. In Monticello, the **MD Ranch Cookhouse** (tel. 435/587–3299) specializes in buffalo stew (yes, it's made with buffalo meat), stuffed pork chops, and Utah red trout. A more formal option is **The Lamplighter** (tel. 435/587–2170), where steaks, chicken, and seafood are served in a Victorian atmosphere. The dining room at the **Grist Mill Inn** (tel. 435/587–2597) serves gourmet dinners and desserts that look as luscious as they taste (*see below*).

Tourist Information

Moab and Green River Visitor Information (805 N. Main St., Moab 84532, tel. 435/259–8825 or 800/635–6622). **San Juan County Multi-Agency Visitor Center** (117 S. Main St., Box 490, Monticello 84535, tel. 435/587–3235 or 800/574–4386).

Reservation Services

There are no bed-and-breakfast reservation services in the area; write the statewide **Bed and Breakfast Inns of Utah, Inc.** (Box 3066, Park City 84060) or contact the **Utah Travel Council** (Council Hall/Capitol Hill, Salt Lake City 84114, tel. 801/538–1030 or 800/200–1160) for a free brochure.

Bankurz Hatt

214 Farrer St., Green River 84525, tel.
435/564-3382

Lana Coomer and her husband, Ben, stumbled into the B&B business when they decided to restore her grandparents' 1897 wooden clapboard four-square, set in a sleepy neighborhood near the banks of the Green River. The result, Bankurz Hatt, is an incongruously sumptuous lodging in a river-rat town. Guests like to lounge on the tree-shaded front porch—perhaps because the elegant Victorian parlor and dining room seem to require them to be on good behavior.

Directly off the dining room, through discreetly curtained glass doors, a sage-carpeted master bedroom holds an 1850s-era mahogany bedroom set with intricately carved head and footboards, chairs, and a gentleman's chiffonnier. The three sunny rooms upstairs are decorated with rose and green florals, antique beds, and elaborate window treatments; their shared bath has a massive shower.

Ben prepares huge breakfasts, say, lamb chops and eggs, quiche, or eggs Benedict, with fresh fruit from a neighboring orchard. Equally delicious dinners are served by reservation.

▥ *1 double room with bath, 3 doubles share bath. Ceiling fans in rooms, outdoor hot tub, guest bicycles, off-street parking. $80–$160, full breakfast. AE. No smoking, no pets. Closed Jan.–Mar.*

Blue Heron
Bed and Breakfast

214 Farrer St., Green River 84525, tel.
435/564-3382

This bed-and-breakfast is a multicolored brick and wood house on 4 acres of property adjacent to an 875-acre wetlands preserve owned by the Nature Conservancy. Because of the Blue Heron's prox-

imity to the wetland—home to many species of wildlife not found elsewhere—the wildlife-watching opportunities here are unique.

Owners Wylie and Terri Gerrard named the B&B for blue herons they found nesting within walking distance of the house. As you might expect, the Gerrard's are very knowledgeable about the flora and fauna of the Colorado River corridor.

Each of the Blue Heron's guest rooms is named after a species of bird seen regularly on the property: the nuthatch, Canyon Wren, Gold Finch, and Marsh Hawk. Breakfast here is generous to fuel the hungriest outdoor adventurer, and in summer, is served on the backyard patio, near a small pond.

▥ *2 doubles with baths, 2 doubles share a bath. Bicycle storage. $75–$95, full breakfast. MC, V. No smoking, no pets, children by prior arrangement.*

Castle Valley Inn

CVSR Box 2602, Moab 84532, tel. 435/259-6012

When guests arrive at Castle Valley Inn, they're surrounded by ragged-topped cliffs—and a lot of silence. There is a tendency to want to linger outside in the 11 acres of yard and orchards, and it's easy to do so. A large patio adjacent to the inn's main wood and stone house and the balconies on the three private bungalows, each face a different aspect of Castle Valley's wildly eroded backdrop. There are also lighted paths, hammocks on wheeled stands, and benches scattered about to take advantage of the vistas.

Innkeepers Robert Ryan and Hertha Wakefield bought Castle Valley Inn from its former owners in early 1996. They had been watching for an opportunity to purchase a bed-and-breakfast, but had been unable to find the perfect project. When they saw an advertisement offering this inn for sale, they answered it on the first day it ran, and had signed a contract before the end of that weekend!

Their ongoing process of adding personal touches to the inn intrigues repeat guests. Some of the changes are subtle, like the addition of several small, black-and-white photographs of young and old Navajos to the entry of the main house. Other changes are tactile; higher thread-count sheets on all of the beds for example, and some—like new outdoor walkways, skylights in previously darkened rooms, and rosy Saltillo tile replacing old carpets—are dramatic.

Robert and Hertha have concentrated on refining the main-house guest rooms with new color combinations, curtains, lamps, and a blend of tile and sisal flooring. They're now doing the same in the bungalows. The skylight they've installed in the Fremont Bungalow is perfectly positioned for stargazing in bed.

When it comes to food, Hertha says that regardless of what changes she makes in menus, a few Castle Valley Inn traditions remain: breakfast always includes lots of fresh fruit harvested from the inn's orchards, with plenty of fresh-ground coffee, and it's served on the patio whenever possible.

🏠 *5 double rooms with baths, 3 double bungalows. Air-conditioning, kitchens in bungalows, VCR and video library in common room, outdoor hot tub. $95–$130, bungalows $150, full breakfast, afternoon refreshments. D, MC, V. No smoking indoors, no pets, no children, 2-night minimum stay on weekends. Closed mid Dec.–mid Feb.*

Desert Rose Inn

600 East and Black Locust Ave., Box 148, Bluff 84512, tel. 435/672-2239

Desert Rose Inn is one of the oldest houses in Bluff. It was built in the 1890s by Jens Nielson, a Danish convert to the Mormon church who became the leader of the church's first organized congregation in Bluff. After several decades of vacancy, the building had a brief incarnation as a Thai restaurant in the mid 1990s. In the summer of 1996, Amer and Cindy Tumeh opened the house as the Desert Rose Inn.

Each of the guest accommodations has been named for a member of Jens Nielson's family. His namesake suite has a simple fireplace and a narrow, screened porch with two rocking chairs, just like the half dozen that sit on the inn's front porch. The Maggie Room has a mix of colors and visual textures: The bedspread is appliqued with several shades of blue, a woven rug has a Navajo design, and an elegant, but sturdy, chair is upholstered in needlepoint. In the Isabelle Room, a star-patterned quilt covers a bed with plump pillows. A small rocking horse stands beside a washstand, complete with basin and pitcher.

The last four steps on the way upstairs are narrow and steep, representing the original staircase. The Elizabeth Room is a wash of soft pastels and has an elegant antique wardrobe instead of a closet. Across the landing, the Samuel Room has a wonderful view of rolling sandstone cliffs beyond the Bluff Town boundaries.

In the small parlor on Desert Rose's main floor, guests enjoy perusing an album filled with photos taken during a Navajo wedding celebration that Cindy and Amer coordinated at the request of two guests from the Netherlands, complete with costumed jingle dancers, a traditional meal of frybread and stew, and a marriage ceremony conducted by a Navajo Holy Man.

🏠 *4 double rooms with baths, 1 suite. Ceiling fans in rooms, fireplaces in parlor and suite. $70–$90, breakfast voucher for café on the historic loop. MC, V. No smoking, no pets, no children.*

Dream Keeper Bed and Breakfast

200 S. 200 East, Moab 84532, tel. 435/ 259-5998

The oversized front door on Dream Catcher Bed and Breakfast was a whim. Not something owners Michael and Mary Wilson wanted, but a detail dreamt up by the teenage uranium millionaire who built this house in the mid-1950s. The enormous lot on which it sits was another of his eccentricities. It is easily three times the size of any other in the neighborhood.

The Wilsons relocated from the northern Utah ski resort town of Park City to Moab after purchasing this house in 1997. They quickly added their own separate quarters, converting the good-size bedrooms of the main house to accommodate bed-and-breakfast guests. All the guest rooms are decorated with an abundance of color, mixing antiques with folk art, and other fun bric-a-brac. Each has access to the outside swimming pool and patio.

The Wilsons serve breakfast of what Mary terms healthful, hearty food: waffles, French toast, or pancakes accompanied by apricots, peaches, and grapes that come from the backyard.

▦ *5 double rooms with baths. Air-conditioning, TV and fireplace in living room, swimming pool, bicycle storage. $70–$95, full breakfast. MC, V. No smoking, no pets, no children.*

Entrada Ranch

Entrada Ridge Rd., Box 567, Moab 84532, tel. and fax 435/259-5796

Entrada Ranch in its entirety spreads 400 acres along the Dolores River between Moab and Grand Junction. In the 1860s the ranch was homesteaded by a German family. These days, Rusty Wheaton and her husband Bruce operate Entrada as a no-frills guest ranch,

and for those willing to trade indoor amenities for solitude, stars, and scenery, it's the perfect place to be.

Entrada Ranch has lodgings ranging from rustic to really rustic (some options require the use of an outhouse). On any given day, the houses, cabins, and outdoor shelters, screened from each other by sandstone boulders and piñon trees, may be populated by people traveling solo, groups of river runners, or cyclists taking a break from the Kokopelli Trail, which winds between Grand Junction, Colorado and Moab. The ranch also gets a steady stream of people who have heard about it from friends, and come to explore the side canyons on the ranch and adjacent areas administered by the Bureau of Land Management.

For meals, guests can choose to fend for themselves or order breakfasts and dinners from a small menu and have them delivered to their room.

▦ *3 4-person houses with electricity, baths, and kitchens; 2 2-person cabins with electricity, outdoor hot shower, and shared outhouse, 2 outdoor shelters with no facilities. Air-conditioning in houses, wood-burning stoves in 2 houses, horseback riding, bicycling, river running, hiking, rock climbing, swimming hole. $65 to $135 (outdoor shelters may be used at no charge when houses are rented). MC, V. No smoking, pets welcome by prior arrangement.*

Grayson Country Inn

118 E. 200 South, Blanding 84511, tel. 435/678-2388

Grayson Country Inn, a 1908 Victorian-style ranch house known formerly as the Old Hotel B&B, is a soothing place that guests revisit year after year.

Innkeepers Dennis and Lurlene Gutke bought the B&B in 1994 and promptly set about making it their own. A bay window with sheer lace curtains brightens the small living room where guests can try out a restored 1894 pump organ. An eye-catching selection of family antiques fills a nook above the stairway. Glider rocking chairs sit in several of the guest rooms, which are all individually decorated with brass beds topped by crocheted spreads, and accents like kerosene lamps, cowboy pistols, Native American pottery, and wreaths made of dried desert plants. Three rooms have stained-glass windows.

Breakfast, served in what was once the screened porch, generally includes homemade bread, a fruit cup, and granola.

🏨 *7 double rooms with baths. TV and air-conditioning in rooms. $45–$65, light breakfast. AE, MC, V. No smoking, no pets.*

Grist Mill Inn

64 S. 300 East, Monticello 84535, tel. 435/ 587–2597 or 800/645–3762, fax 435/587–2580

When Charles O'Berry wanted to abandon northern Utah's urban rush and open a dude ranch, his wife, Brenda, was more than willing to join. In 1996, while searching for a ranch to buy, they were presented with the opportunity to purchase the Grist Mill Inn from the local family who had painstakingly restored the community landmark, and built its excellent reputation as a country inn. How could they resist?

The three-story flour mill was constructed in 1933 of wooden clapboard. The exterior is now sheathed in light gray siding, with a bright blue metal roof. Flower beds follow steps made of railroad ties to the inn's front door.

Inside, the lobby is a small conversation nook with a multicolored firebrick hearth, plush purple wing chairs, and soft lamplight. If you look up you'll see the driveshaft for a grain sacker that sits a few feet away—one of the many original pieces of mill equipment left throughout the inn. There are several other common areas, including the second-floor Blue Goose TV room, named after an old saloon in town, and a library on the third floor where a bank of high, square windows bathes the room in evening light.

Guest rooms here were named after the previous owners' family members, and characters from local lore. The O'Berrys retained many of the inn's antique furnishings and have added an engaging variety of Victorian and Western touches. Many of the inn's rooms are the size of what other properties call suites. Some sleeping areas are in elevated or sunken nooks.

Breakfast offerings might include oatmeal walnut pancakes, French toast stuffed with peaches and cream cheese, or a fluffy egg strata served with a fancy edible garnish.

The O'Berrys' most impressive change in the inn's operations is the addition of gourmet dinners, served to guests and by reservation to the public several nights a week. The chef is their son, Tobias, who trained in Germany. Typically, an elegantly arranged salad accompanies a choice of two or three entrées served with fresh vegetables followed by a single dessert option, all exquisitely presented.

🏨 *5 double rooms, 2 triples, all with baths, 3 doubles with baths in neighboring granary. TV in some rooms, gift shop, outdoor hot tub. $85–$105, full country breakfast, gourmet dinners. AE, D, DC, MC, V. No smoking indoors, no pets.*

La Sal Mountain Guest Ranch

Hwy. 46, Box 247, La Sal 84530, tel. 435/ 686–2223

La Sal (not to be confused with Old La Sal, *see* Mt. Peale B&B, *below*) is a company town. All of its buildings are owned by La Sal Livestock, an operation which has been running cattle on nearly a million acres of southeastern Utah since about 1915.

La Sal Mountain Guest Ranch is run by Sunny Redd and her family. It's part of a working cattle ranch division of La Sal Livestock, and rents out small houses that once lodged ranch hands and their families. Although there are no opportunities here to join a "cattle drive" or "ride the range," this property offers an intriguing look into the ranching industry, past and present.

The best accommodations to request are the Log Cabin, or one of two suites in the Kiva House. Other lodgings are more spartan, but do fill up in spring and fall, the most popular times to visit this area of the state. Breakfast is served in the main ranch house. If it's pancakes, request Sunny's buttermilk vanilla syrup.

🏨 *Log cabin sleeps 4 with 1 bath, 1 Kiva House Suite sleeps 10 with 2 baths, the other sleeps 6 with 1 bath. Ranch can accommodate up to 80 people. $60–$90, full breakfast. D, MC, V. No smoking, no pets.*

Mt. Peale Bed-and-Breakfast

Rte. 46, Box 366, Old La Sal 84530, tel. 888/687–3253, 435/260–1305 mobile

Although it has straight-shot access to national parks and monuments, resort towns, and more, Mt. Peale Bed-and-Breakfast maintains a pretty low profile.

Surrounded by a low rail fence—which twinkles with hundreds of tiny lights after dark—Mt. Peale is a square, two-story cabin-style building with a steep green roof and a chimney built of lava rock and sandstone. Behind the inn, Mt. Peale rises to 12,721 feet. A little to the left is Mt. Tukuhnikivatz, an Indian name meaning "first light, last light."

Lisa Ballantyne and Teague Eskelsen opened Mt. Peale in 1995. Although both women participate in running the inn, Teague says when it's time to cook, she mostly does the chopping and other prep work and lets Lisa mastermind the meals. For breakfast, Lisa might make Southwestern potatoes with cheese, black beans, green chilies, and crunchy salsa, served with fresh berry muffins or currant scones served warm with cream cheese. Guests particularly enjoy her unique pancakes and waffles, both made from a blend of cornmeal, oatmeal, wheat flour, and almonds.

On weekends, Lisa prepares two dinner entrées from either chicken, steak, fish, or a vegetarian specialty. She'll prepare an evening meal for guests on weekdays, generally, pizza, pasta, or chicken; they need only let her know by breakfast time that they'll be dining in that night. During summer, there are often dinner concerts of local and nationally known musicians staged in the meadow behind the inn.

Each guest room has knotty-pine paneling or beams produced by the local sawmill, and a cedar-lined closet. The simple beds and other furnishings were handmade by a cabinetmaker from Olympia, Washington. All the rooms in the house, including the common areas, portray a distinct sense of fun. Plants and mobiles hang here and there, food is served on bright pottery, and the dining room tables have bouquets of wild flowers gathered from the mountainside.

🏨 *1 double with bath, 2 doubles share a bath. Restaurant, fireplace and TV in living room, terry-cloth robes, outdoor hot tub, hiking, cross-country skiing, cycling, guided tours arranged. $70–$90, full breakfast and afternoon snacks, lunch and dinner at an additional charge. No smoking, no pets, 2-night minimum on holiday weekends.*

Nine Mile Ranch Bunk and Breakfast

In Nine Mile Canyon, Box 212, Wellington 84542, tel. 435/637–2572

This is the only guest accommodation in Nine Mile Canyon, a historic corridor with remnants of the ancient Fremont culture (*see above*). As such, this "bunk and breakfast" provides a unique opportunity to explore the remote canyon thoroughly, taking more than one day to cover its 40 miles by horseback, on a bike, or in a car. Be aware, however, that this property is fairly primitive, and there are only a couple of indoor rooms available to be rented.

A recommended option is to reserve one of the tall, white "tepees" that owners Ben and Myrna Mead erect each summer. You must provide your own sleeping bags, just as you would in any other tent, but for the rental price, you'll get shelter, a huge country breakfast, and the right to watch the sheep, turkeys, chickens, and llama that roam the ranch, and to wade in the Mead's stretch of Nine Mile Creek. For an additional $10 per person, you can enjoy one of Ben and Myrna's excellent Dutch-oven dinners.

🏨 *2 double rooms share a bath, tepees and a small rustic cabin share chemical toilets. Guided canyon tours and horseback riding available at an additional cost. $35–$50, full breakfast.*

Pack Creek Ranch

La Sal Mountain Loop Rd., Box 1270, Moab 84532, tel. 435/259–5505, fax 435/259–8879

From Moab, it takes about a half hour to get to Pack Creek Ranch. You can do it faster, but you'll miss the chance to savor the subtle changes in the landscape: red sand and barren rock transition to piñon pine and juniper. Roll down the windows—the air is pungent with sagebrush.

Pack Creek Ranch is a 300-acre spread set in the foothills of the La Sal Mountains. It was once a working cattle operation, but these days, it's more of a cross between a dude ranch and a resort. There are horses to ride, mountain and desert trails to explore, but also excellent meals to savor and a sauna, spa, swimming pool, and masseuse to enjoy.

Housing between two and five guests, Pack Creek's rustic wood cabins have red roofs and stone porches. Inside are fully equipped kitchens, rock fireplaces, and bent-willow furnishings. Colorful linens and rugs accent log beds. Multi-paned windows are curtained in lengths of bright calico, but keep them open: it would be a shame to block the mountain view beyond. Cabin assignments are made according to availability and the size of groups traveling together. However, this arrangement seldom proves to be a problem, and requests for specific cabins can often be accommodated.

Pack Creek is a year-round destination. During its main season, the ranch's rates include three meals a day. In the winter, guests prepare their own meals, with the rates reduced accordingly. Meals are served in a cozy dining hall replete with wagon-wheel chandeliers and a massive bull elk mounted above the stone fireplace. Breakfast is usually a hot meal of the eggs-and-bacon variety, with juices and cereal available for those on the run. Lunch is a buffet of the necessary fixings for assembling a hearty picnic. Dinner (also served to the public) includes ranch specialties like barbecued chicken and potatoes cooked in a Dutch oven, but also more sophisticated entrées such as Cajun cream shrimp or French pepper steak.

🏨 *12 cabins, each with 1 to 4 double rooms with private and shared baths, common kitchen-living room area in each cabin. Restaurant, fireplaces in some cabins, kitchens in all cabins, pool, gift shop, masseuse, outdoor hot tub, sauna, trail rides (additional charge), horse packing, 4-wheel-drive tours, guided biking or hiking, river trips by* *arrangement. $140 per person, includes all meals; November–March $55 per person, without meals. AE, D, MC, V. No smoking, no pets.*

Rogers House B&B

412 S. Main St., Blanding 84511, tel. 435/ 678–3932 or 800/355–3932, fax 435/678– 3276

This two-story bungalow was built in 1915 by David and Elizabeth May Rogers, who were some of the earliest residents of Blanding. They raised a family of 12 children here. Pete Black's forebears were another of Blanding's early families. Pete and his wife, Charlotte, bought this historic home in 1993, and renovated it in hopes of again "filling the house," but this time with appreciative bed-and-breakfast guests.

Charlotte decorated the inn with an unerring eye for mixing color and texture. The thing that seems most appreciated by guests is her practicality—she chooses sturdy furniture and firm mattresses. Bedside baskets are filled with current magazines. There are plenty of towels—and then there's the matter of the bathtubs. Before installing jetted tubs in most of the bathrooms, Charlotte special-ordered extra-long tubs to ensure that she (and other tall people) would be able to lie back and enjoy them.

In one romantic guest room, a swag of dried flowers arches above the windows, and a sleigh bed, dressed in white eyelet ruffles, is pretty against the pale rose walls. In another room, an antique Navajo rug, a Ute flute, and a cradle board hang on the walls. The black, pencil-post bed has a striped black, red, and white spread with matching shams and teal-and red paisley accent pillows. In a Western-style room, a brass bed has a maroon-and-teal paisley comforter. A pair of chaps, a hat shaped for some absent cowboy's head, and boots with spurs sprawl at the end of the bed.

In fair weather, guests can sit on the porch in the evening or before breakfast

and enjoy the sight and scent of old-fashioned flower beds in the front and side yards. Cooler evenings mean a fire in the living room's marble fireplace and a chance to play the old mahogany upright piano.

Breakfast begins with juice, and a seasonal fruit cup followed by orange pecan French toast, or perhaps, a crustless quiche served with muffins or hot croissants.

🏨 *4 double rooms with baths. Ceiling fans, TVs, and phones in rooms, fireplace in living room. $55–$80, full breakfast. MC, V. No smoking indoors, no pets. Open only by arrangement Dec.– Feb.*

Sunflower Hill

185 N. 300 East, Moab 84532, tel. 435/ 259–2974, fax 435/259–3065

Behind a hedge of white roses lining a split-log fence, Sunflower Hill, owned and managed by the amiable Stucki family, has two lodgings. The Garden Cottage is an elegant, two-story cedar shingled structure with a wraparound porch painted creamy white. Across a shady yard defined by low, stacked rock walls and beds of day lilies with small clusters of ferns and perennials, is the Farm House, built in the late 19th century by a farmer who did some cattle rustling on the side.

Sunflower Hill's guest rooms are varied in size, but each has a distinctive character. In truth, there's not a bad choice among them. However, the rooms in the Garden Cottage are the most elegantly appointed. The French Bedroom, which serves as the inn's bridal suite, is decorated in gradations from cream to sand. It has billowing lace curtains, and an exquisite French antique bedroom set. The Loft is a cheerful room with cozy, green-checked chairs, and a tiny deck overlooking the gardens. Accessed from the Farmhouse's enclosed porch, the Sun Porch Room has been fitted with floor-to-ceiling windows covered in vertical miniblinds for privacy. A woven sunflower throw draped on a quilt stand echoes the ceiling border blooming with golden sunflowers.

The Great Room in the Garden Cottage serves as the indoor gathering place for both buildings. Late afternoon refreshments, from hot apple pie with cheddar cheese to slabs of locally grown watermelon, are served.

Breakfast is served in the Farm House dining room, where mismatched antique chairs are pulled up to several small tables covered with blue-and-white checked cloths; a century-old Austrian sideboard with dishes peeking through its heavy glass-pane doors sits between windows curtained in crisp white ruffles. Sunflower Hill's breakfasts are a variety of sturdy homemade breads, fruity muffins, yogurt, honey granola, and lots of fresh fruit, or hot entrées like Southwestern eggs, or whole-wheat waffles with tangy berry patch syrup. If they choose, guests can eat on the adjacent terrace which is edged with beds of vibrant gloriosa daisies.

🏠 *11 double rooms with baths, some with jetted tubs. Air-conditioning, TVs, and phones in all rooms, Room Bar baskets, gift shop, outdoor hot tub, bicycle storage. $75–$145, full breakfast, gourmet picnic lunches, dinner offered on a limited basis by advanced reservation only. MC, V. No smoking, no pets, children by prior arrangement.*

Valley of the Gods Bed and Breakfast

Lee Ranch, Box 310-307, Mexican Hat 84531, tel. 970/749–1164 cellular, fax 435/683–2292

Just a half mile off Route 261, between the tiny towns of Bluff and Mexican Hat, Valley of the Gods Bed and Breakfast is in the proverbial middle of nowhere. Located on what longtime residents of this corner of the state still call the Lee Ranch, this is the only habitable building within the Bureau of Land Management's Cedar Mesa Cultural and Recreational Management Area; it's bordered on all sides by state and federal land. From the porch, it is possible to see landscapes associated with four states.

The inn's name comes from the surrounding valley, which is filled with red rock spires and bizarre pinnacles. Castle Valley Inn has a photovoltaic electrical system and a cellular phone link. Still, guests here find themselves falling into an easy sort of peace and quiet which seems to belong to another century.

Innkeepers Gary and Claire Dorgan are from Flagstaff, Arizona, where Claire was manager of another inn, and Gary worked for the National Park Service. They developed an affinity for this property as frequent guests, eventually purchasing the inn from the owners who had served as their hosts.

The inn is decorated in a frontier–meets–Santa Fe–chic fashion. The rugged stone walls of the ranch house, and massive ceiling beams salvaged long ago from an abandoned oil derrick, blend easily with the Dorgan's antiques and handsome Southwestern-style furniture. Guest rooms are small and simply furnished, but this just seems to be in keeping with the relaxed attitude the inn inspires.

Claire prepares breakfasts of freshly baked baguettes and croissants and vegetarian quiches, or ranch standards like eggs with bacon and toast. She and Gary work together to prepare a healthy Sunset Dinner Buffet of salads, fresh bread, marinated chicken skewers, or grilled beef dusted with herbs, and plenty of fresh vegetables. The dining room of choice is generally the porch, which wraps around two sides of the house.

🏠 *5 double rooms with baths. Raft trips, pack horse or llama trips, and archaeological tours available by arrangement. $75–$90, full breakfast; dinners by advance reservation only. MC, V. No smoking indoors, pets and children by prior arrangement.*

Directory 1
Alphabetical

Directory 2
Geographical

Notes

Notes

WHEREVER YOU TRAVEL, *H*ELP IS NEVER FAR AWAY.

From planning your trip to

providing travel assistance along

the way, American Express®

Travel Service Offices are

always there to help

you do more.

American Express Travel Service
Offices are found in central locations
throughout the United States.

For the office nearest you, please call
1-800-AXP-3429.

do more AMERICAN EXPRESS

Travel

http://www.americanexpress.com/travel